THE RULES OF PLAY

A VOLUME IN THE SERIES

Cornell Studies in Political Economy

edited by Peter J. Katzenstein

A full list of titles in the series appears at the end of the book.

The Rules of Play

National Identity and the
Shaping of Japanese Leisure

DAVID LEHENY

Cornell University Press

ITHACA AND LONDON

Copyright © 2003 by Cornell University

cau

All rights reserved. Except for brief quotations in a review, this
book, or parts thereof, must not be reproduced in any form without
permission in writing from the publisher. For information, address
Cornell University Press, Sage House, 512 East State Street,
Ithaca, New York 14850.

First published 2003 by Cornell University Press

Printed in the United States of America

Library of Congress Cataloging-in-Publication Data
Leheny, David Richard, 1967–
   The rules of play : national identity and the shaping of Japanese
leisure / David Leheny.
      p. cm. — (Cornell studies in political economy)
Includes bibliographical references and index.
   ISBN 0-8014-4091-2 (cloth : alk. paper)
   1. Leisure—Government policy—Japan.   2. Leisure—Economic
aspects—Japan.   I. Title.   II. Series.
   GV125 .L43 2003
   306.4'8'0952—dc21   2002151027

Cornell University Press strives to use environmentally responsible
suppliers and materials to the fullest extent possible in the publishing
of its books. Such materials include vegetable-based, low-VOC inks
and acid-free papers that are recycled, totally chlorine-free, or partly
composed of nonwood fibers. For further information, visit our
website at www.cornellpress.cornell.edu.

Cloth printing   10 9 8 7 6 5 4 3 2 1

For Kato Kozo and in memory of Viola Vilardi

Someone should do a book. Japanese all over the world, in front of the world's greatest monuments, taking pictures of each other. That's what somebody should do.

—Jimmy Dell (Steve Martin) in David Mamet's
The Spanish Prisoner (1997)

CONTENTS

PREFACE

As the crow flies, it is only about four hundred miles between Ithaca, New York, where I started working on this project, and Newbury, Massachusetts, where I am finishing revisions. The distance from beginning to end feels far greater, however, primarily because of the number of times I have stopped along the way and received help, advice, and support. Among the many people I need to thank, the first and most important is Peter Katzenstein. The idea for the project originated in his office, and Peter has continued to be a crucial guide. Peter is almost certainly the most thanked scholar in the field of international relations, and I would add only that he is the best adviser I can imagine. The book, quite literally, would never have been begun or finished without him, and I am extremely grateful for all of his help.

At Cornell, I owe special thanks as well to Benedict Anderson not only because of his speedy and perceptive comments on various drafts but also because his own research and ideas have been crucial touchstones for the book. Mary Brinton and Valerie Bunce stepped in to read an earlier version of the manuscript, and both offered superb advice that affected the final shape of the book. My friends Eugene Cobble, Alex Moon, Nilanjana Bhattarachya, Loren Gatch, Steve Casper, and

Lisa Sansoucy all discussed the elements of the book with me at great length. Two other friends in the United States, Jo Miller and Katherine Bliss, made perceptive suggestions, and I hope they recognize that the book is a better one for their efforts.

In Japan, I am grateful to three scholars who not only were generous with intellectual guidance but also provided me with the institutional support necessary for my work. Tsujinaka Yutaka of the University of Tsukuba gave me the opportunity to study in Japan from 1994 to 1996 and was an especially kind host during my time at Tsukuba. Jonathan Lewis persuaded me to apply for a position at the Institute of Social Science at the University of Tokyo and has been one of my best friends and critics since then. And Hiroshi Ishida took a great amount of time from his busy schedule to serve as a sounding board for my forays into sociology as well as to organize opportunities for me to present my work.

My time in Japan was made much easier because of the friendship and intellectual companionship of Obi Michiyo, Barbara Weiss, Wellington de Amorim, Kudo Akira, Banno Junji, Nitta Michio, Masahiro Kawai, Fujiwara Kiichi, Hiwatari Nobuhiro, Sandra Wilson, Andrew DeWit, Mark Tilton, Stephen Frank, Annamari Konttinen, Tiana Norgren, Paul Talcott, and Miura Mari. I especially thank Katherine Tegtmeyer Pak, Verena Blechinger, Beth Katzoff, Masuyama Mikitaka, and Alexis Eastwood, helpful critics and sources of good humor in addition to being remarkably good guides to Japanese politics. Some visitors to the Institute of Social Science probably have no idea how much their guidance meant to me, but I thank especially J. A. A. Stockwin, Carol Gluck, John Campbell, and Len Schoppa for their advice and help. T. J. Pempel, whom I first met at Shaken, has been unfailingly supportive throughout the course of this project.

My colleagues at the University of Wisconsin deserve more thanks, largely because they were willing to give me a chance in spite of the weirdness of my research topic. I am especially grateful to Michael Barnett, Bruce Cronin, Charo D'Etchevarry, Paul Hutchcroft, Gina Sapiro, Leigh Payne, Julia Thomas, Hawley Fogg-Davis, and Kathryn Hendley, all of whom read drafts. Revisions would have been far more difficult without my opportunity to spend a year at Harvard's Program on U.S.–Japan Relations, where Susan Pharr, Ezra Vogel, Kawashima Yutaka, Frank Schwartz, Christina Davis, Izutsu Shunji, Ethan Scheiner, and Kim Reimann were excellent colleagues.

My work would have been impossible without the help of Japanese organizations that deal with tourism development. The staff of the International Tourism Development Institute of Japan (ITDIJ) provided me with useful documents, advice, and insight. I am particularly grateful to Arai Koichi, Kamio Kiyotaka, Uno Shiro, Kumagai Akira, Sampei Fumihiro, and Shimada Kaori. I also benefited tremendously from my association with the ASEAN Centre, and especially with Investment Bureau Director Atienza and Minami Kaori of the general staff. Finally, Yamamoto Masanori of the Leisure Development Center provided me with access to much-needed documents, and went far beyond the call of duty in sharing his thoughts with me and making an office available during my research trips.

Additionally, I thank officials at the Australian Tourist Commission, the Tourism Authority of Thailand, and the Czech Tourist Authority, who took the time to meet with me and also provided me with information. In addition, the tourism administrators I met at the JICA Comprehensive Tourism Seminar in 1995 (from countries as disparate as Jamaica, Brunei, Cameroon, and Mongolia) helped to instill in me respect for their profession and a renewed commitment to my topic.

Obviously, a research project of this duration relied on crucial financial support. I am grateful to the Mellon Foundation, the Foreign Language and Area Studies Program, and the Japanese Ministry of Education. The East Japan Railroad Culture Foundation also supported my trips to speak with tourism bureaucrats in other countries, and this research has been so useful that I must thank them especially for their faith in my work.

I also thank Oxford University Press and the Institute of Social Science at the University of Tokyo. Portions of chapter 3 were previously published as "'By Other Means': Tourism and Leisure as Politics in Pre-war Japan," in *Social Science Japan Journal* 3, 2 (2000): 171–86. I appreciate their permission to reprint some of the material here.

I am indebted to audiences at the University of Tokyo, the University of Wisconsin–Madison, Cornell University, Columbia University, Connecticut College, the International Center for Research on Japan, the German Institute of Japanese Studies, and the International House of Japan, the International Convention of Asia Scholars, the American Political Science Association, and the Western Political Science Association. Each round of questions and comments helped to steer me away from looming disasters and to refocus my efforts.

Roger Haydon's reputation as an editor is deservedly sterling. Whatever the book's flaws, the version the reader is holding is far better than the initial draft, and the credit for this goes entirely to him. Two anonymous reviewers for Cornell University Press made helpful and encouraging suggestions. Manuscript editor Karen Hwa and copy editor Dawn Hall both deserve thanks for having fixed numerous problems with the manuscript in preparing it for publication. And I need also to thank Nishiyama Yasuko, who helped me decipher some of the trickier financial data in chapter 3, and Amy Demarest, who proofread the manuscript.

Finding appropriate illustrations at the last minute posed an especially daunting challenge, though I received terrific help. Two research assistants—Takakazu Kimura and Hayakawa Miyako—were intrepid in their search for images, and I am especially grateful to Hayakawa-san. Inoguchi Kuniko, one of Japan's best and busiest political scientists, helped the students gain access to important pictures, for which I am thankful. Special gratitude goes to Merry White of Boston University, who allowed me to use photographs that she took for her own research, and to Kuniko Yamada McVey of Harvard's Yenching Library, who went out of her way to find some beautiful prewar illustrations for me.

Last but not least, I have been exceptionally fortunate in my friends and family outside the academy. I could not hope for more supportive or loving parents, and I am lucky too to have my hilarious sisters Vivienne and Cara. Two couples—Joshua Winchell and Karin Perkins in the United States, and Hiroshi and Mihoko Yamanouchi in Tokyo—have been extremely generous friends since before I began this project. Without them, I would never have finished.

It would take too long to explain why I am dedicating this book to my friend and colleague Kato Kozo and to my dearly missed grandmother, Viola Vilardi. Suffice it to say that I consider myself privileged to have known both.

CONVENTIONS AND ABBREVIATIONS

Throughout the text, Japanese names are written in Japanese order (family name—given name) except for those cases when Japanese authors of English- or French-language reports have themselves listed their given names first. Macrons have been omitted in commonly known words and names (e.g., Tokyo).

In citations to Japanese-language reports produced by organizations, I give the Japanese name of the organization unless the English-language name is widely used.

All translations are by the author unless otherwise noted.

ANA   All Nippon Airways
ASEAN   Association of Southeast Asian Nations (as in ASEAN Centre)
CDC   Commonwealth Development Corporation
CLAIR   Council of Local Authorities for International Relations
EPA   Economic Planning Agency
IBRD   International Bank for Reconstruction and Development
IFC   International Finance Corporation
ILO   International Labour Office
ITDIJ   International Tourism Development Institute of Japan
JAL   Japan Air Lines
JATA   Japan Association of Travel Agents
JET   Japan Exchange & Teaching Program

JICA	Japan International Cooperation Agency
JNTO	Japan National Tourist Organization
JR	Japan Railways
JTB	Japan Tourist Bureau (prewar); Japan Travel Bureau (postwar)
LDP	Liberal Democratic Party
METI	Ministry of Economy, Trade, and Industry
MHA	Ministry of Home Affairs (prewar)
MITI	Ministry of International Trade and Industry
MLIT	Ministry of Land, Infrastructure, and Transport
MOC	Ministry of Construction
MOE	Ministry of Education
MOF	Ministry of Finance
MOFA	Ministry of Foreign Affairs
MOHA	Ministry of Home Affairs (postwar)
MOT	Ministry of Transport
ODA	Official Development Assistance
OECF	Overseas Economic Cooperation Fund
TAT	Tourism Authority of Thailand
YKC	Leisure Development Center (Yoka Kaihatsu Sentā)

THE RULES OF PLAY

A Japanese tourist guidebook for Manchuria and Korea, early twentieth century. Photo by permission of the Harvard-Yenching Library.

Guns, Butter, or Paragliding?

Why would a government be interested in paragliding?

In 1992, a Japanese government thinktank, the Leisure Development Center (Yoka Kaihatsu Sentā, YKC), produced a report designed to encourage people to consider skiing and paragliding more.[1] For those observers who generally consider the basic options of government spending as "guns or butter," defense and security versus welfare, government encouragement of paragliding seems about as likely as a decision to outlaw chocolate milk.

Political scientists have done reasonably well by focusing on more explicitly "political" topics such as elections, trade rules, and decision-making procedures. Do we really need to address why a government would take a courageous stand on paragliding, skiing, international travel, or amusement parks? When one looks at Japan, one finds a government that has been involved for much of the century, and especially since 1970, in trying to affect how its citizens enjoy themselves. Is this because the Japanese need political guidance in how to take it easy? Or because of international criticism of the Japanese as worka-

1. YKC, *Kokusaika Katachi Yoka Katsutō no Fukyū ni Kan Suru Chōsa Kenkyū* (Research on the Spread of Internationalization-Style Leisure Activities) (Tokyo: YKC, 1992).

holics? Or does it simply mean that the Japanese government is involved in people's private lives in ways that Americans, to name an obvious example, would find stifling? Maybe leisure lies somewhere beyond "butter" on a continuum of government activities: after a state provides security and welfare for all, will it inevitably turn to doing more for its people in order to organize society more effectively?[2]

If we want to know why the Japanese government has become involved in the leisure lives of citizens, we need to think about what social changes these policymakers have been trying to accomplish. Equally important, we must explore where they got the idea that certain types of leisure activities, such as traveling abroad, are desirable and that others do not merit political action. The Japanese government determined, for example, that golf course development merited state support but has not made the same determination about video game arcades.[3] Like international tourism, another activity that would attract official support, golf has been seen as something that "normal" people do. The Japanese government believes that the Japanese should be more normal.

This is more than a mere theoretical issue, and leisure has become an increasingly attractive topic for English-language scholarship on Japan.[4] Leisure industries have grown to be among the world's largest, and investment in the hotel and resort sector turned out to be far more important in 1990s Japan than anyone could have predicted. When the overvalued real estate markets in Japan and in Southeast Asia (which

2. I sidestep the terminological debate over what leisure is, not so much because it is a pointless debate (which it often is), but rather because it is not particularly relevant. Stanley Parker argues leisure refers to the time in a day not used for formal employment or for basic human necessities. See *The Sociology of Leisure* (London: George Allen & Unwin, 1976), 17–20. Sebastian de Grazia argues that it should instead be seen more metaphysically, as "a state of being in which activity is performed for its own sake or as its own end." See *Of Time, Work, and Leisure* (New York: Vintage, 1990), 15. Because I focus here on leisure policy, this book allows the policies to define leisure, at least insofar as it is accepted that the Japanese government has as much right as anyone else to define what leisure is.

3. This is not simply because golf is bigger business than video games, which have been exceptionally successful in and for Japan. Nor is it because golf is objectively better than video games. I, for one, play video games more than I golf (unless one counts golf video games), and I have many Japanese friends who do the same.

4. Two recent edited volumes on Japanese leisure include essays primarily from sociologists, anthropologists, and cultural historians. See Sepp Linhart and Sabine Frühstück, eds., *The Culture of Japan as Seen through its Leisure* (Albany: State University of New York Press, 1998); and Joy Hendry and Massimo Raveri, eds., *Japan at Play: The Ludic and the Logic of Power* (London: Routledge, 2002).

were largely pumped up by resort and tourism investment encouraged by the Japanese government) popped with the Japanese financial bubble in 1990, the nation's current economic tailspin became evident to nearly all observers. Partly because Japanese officials were trying to figure out how to make a better life for Japanese citizens, and because they hoped to create lifestyle changes that would serve broad economic goals, they inadvertently contributed to a chain of events that culminated in financial meltdown.

I believe that the explanation for these leisure initiatives lies not just in national economic interests or in quotidian bureaucratic quests for budgets and turf. It exists at least in part in long-standing debates over who the Japanese are: whether they are a "unique" nation unlike any other or an "advanced industrial nation" of people who socially resemble Americans, western Europeans, Australians, and the like. Although Japanese policymakers have generally had specific goals in mind, such as fostering local economic development through resort development, their programs have almost invariably drawn on and emulated examples from the West. In encouraging Japanese to adopt these recreational habits, however, they have generally tried to tweak them, to make them somehow more authentically "Japanese." The Japanese, in this logic, should behave—should *want to* behave—like Americans and Europeans, but they need also to remain uniquely Japanese. And it is the government's job to ensure that they do both.

How To Create a "Lifestyle Superpower"

The use of models from the West has long been explicit in Japanese leisure policies, especially after those policies were formalized in the early 1970s. When the YKC opened its doors in 1972 as a special foundation of the Ministry of International Trade and Industry (MITI), it immediately began to conduct research aimed at its central purpose: promoting the development of leisure and leisure-related industries in Japan. It produced fifteen documents in its first year, ranging from research reports on leisure for the elderly and for housewives to the development of computer information systems for nationwide leisure. Among these reports was the first of many international comparative studies that it would complete over its first quarter century. In part because of the budgetary and time constraints facing the organization, *Yoka Oyobi Yoka Katsudō ni Kan Suru Imēji ni Tsuite no Kokusaiteki Hikaku Chōsa Hōkokusho* (Report on the International Comparative

Study of Images of Leisure and Leisure Activities) lacked some of the grand methods of later, more expansive studies, which would include large-scale samples and sophisticated questionnaires of citizens of Japan and other advanced industrial societies. Nevertheless, its authors made determined efforts to engage in some reasonably comparative assessments of "images of leisure" in Japan and other countries, interviewing 25-person groups of Americans, French, British, West German, and Italian citizens, each of whom had spent a year or more living in Japan. They also interviewed identical numbers of Japanese with experience living in each of those countries. The purpose of the study was to generate a "frame of reference" for understanding leisure in advanced societies.[5]

It goes without saying that such a study was almost certainly too small to be of much value in doing any more, as the authors were no doubt aware. What is somewhat more striking than the budget-minded methods, however, is the way in which the report reinforced a frame of reference that already existed. The study self-consciously compared Japanese leisure activities not to those in the other countries of Asia or a global sample but to those in the industrialized countries of western Europe and North America. Economic policymakers in 1970s Japan had begun to latch onto the idea that leisure could lead the way for the nation's continuing growth. "The West" seemed to display the natural progress of economic change, and leisure development represented part of a crucial shift toward a mass consumer society.

Moreover, leisure could be politically useful. A nation dotted with leisure resorts, particularly if they were profitable, seemed like an appealing goal—especially considering the apparent alternative: a dystopian collection of smog-belching factories connected by freeways and parking lots. With a variety of pollution scandals and industrial crimes starting to rouse opposition to Japan's conservative leadership in the early 1970s, roller coasters and golf must have seemed like attractive issues to emphasize in government initiatives. Increased leisure has often been used as a "feel good" proposal for a nation frequently characterized as workaholic. This was perhaps most pointed in 1991, when Prime Minister Miyazawa Kiichi—facing the financial meltdown that followed the explosion of the Japanese bub-

5. YKC, *Yoka Oyobi Yoka Katsudō ni Kan Suru Imēji ni Tsuite no Kokusaiteki Hikaku Chōsa Hōkokusho* (Report on the International Comparative Study of Images of Leisure and Leisure Activities) (Tokyo: YKC, 1973).

ble economy—gave a speech promising to make Japan a "lifestyle superpower" (*seikatsu taikoku*). What specifically could he have meant?

The Japanese word *seikatsu* means something different than *lifestyle* conventionally does in American political usage. Where "lifestyle politics" in the United States generally refers to morality issues (e.g., whether "alternative lifestyles" such as single parenting and gay marriage ought to be institutionally protected), in Japan it is more closely related to what we might call "quality of life." Although *seikatsu* might refer to anything, from time spent commuting to the size of one's living quarters, when used generally in political discussions, "leisure" is almost invariably a significant component of any discussion of what Japanese lifestyle ought to be.[6] And a number of the catch phrases of the past two decades in Japan—such as *yutaka na shakai* (wealthy and happy society) and *yutori no aru shakai* ("a society that gives me space to do my own thing," to use Gavan McCormack's accurate rendering of this difficult term)[7]—cannot be understood without reference to leisure. "Lifestyle" appears to be in part the government's responsibility, and the term in Japan connotes opportunities for people to enjoy themselves in productive and meaningful ways.

Even if we understand the first part of the term "lifestyle superpower," the latter half—in Japanese, *taikoku*—is mystifying. What does it mean to be a lifestyle "superpower"? Is there a competition that governments keep secret from the rest of us? Does a government get bragging rights at international conferences if its citizens use jet skis more often than their foreign counterparts? Odd as it was, Miyazawa's promise was met with generally positive reactions, and no observers in Japan seem to have noticed how unusual it would be that the word "superpower" would be used just as in its more common way—that Japan is an "economic superpower" (*keizai taikoku*). Elsewhere, the phrase would have made little sense, but in Japan it had a meaning that was nearly instinctive.[8] To many Japanese observers,

6. On this topic, see Suga Yukiko, "Watashitachi no Jidai no 'Seikatsu Bunka' to Wa" (What "Lifestyle Culture" Means in Our Times) in *Kurashi no Tetsugaku to shite no "Seikatsu Bunka"* ("Lifestyle Culture" as a Philosophy of Living), ed. Matsuda Yoshiyuki (Tokyo: PHP, 1997), 170–201.

7. Gavan McCormack, *The Emptiness of Japanese Affluence* (Armonk, N.Y.: M. E. Sharpe, 1996), 85.

8. To give a counterexample, the phrase "family values" (which means different things to different people in the United States but always means something) would make little sense in Japan.

the nation has been deficient in leisure, with citizens who work too hard and have too few opportunities to take it easy or experience *yu-tori* (that "space to do my own thing").[9] In their view, Miyazawa was only acknowledging the obvious and suggesting that it would be the government's role to do something about it.

Japan would have to catch up to nations that already qualified as leisure superpowers; a country can be a lifestyle superpower only if leisure is something that can be meaningfully compared across nations. One sees this notion prefigured in the choice of nations for the YKC's 1973 report (and the choice would be explained in detail in other policy documents from the era, which I discuss in chapter 4). The appropriate references were rich countries; those that might at the time (with the possible exception of Italy) have been described as "economic superpowers." The problem, this suggests, was not just that Japanese were not enjoying themselves; rather, they were not enjoying themselves in the same way as citizens of the club of rich nations to which Japan ardently sought membership. And despite the obvious bureaucratic machinations and crude political goals that typify many of Japan's leisure policies, as they do policies in most countries, it is this comparison that has persisted. The effort to make Japan look like the nations of western Europe and North America has continually defined the myriad initiatives to create a lifestyle superpower in Japan, to make it a nation of golf courses, ski resorts, and water parks.

Explaining the Lifestyle Superpower

The guns versus butter choice crudely captures much of what political observers analyze. It is no surprise that, in general, we have a better grasp of how to search for explanations for security and welfare policies than we do of how to start to think about what would qualify as a good lifestyle for citizens. In security politics, for example, we can be reasonably certain that states prefer to be more rather than less secure; that arms manufacturers would like to promote procurement; and that defense-related agencies pursue greater budgets and autonomy. Similarly, in welfare politics, we can examine whether governments try to incorporate or to exclude labor, how interest groups and

9. In correspondence, Leonard Schoppa has suggested that another formulation might be "the space *and time* to do my own thing" (emphasis added).

social movements pursue economic goals, and the like. This does not mean that we have all the answers; political scientists continue to disagree about what we do know and admit there is a great deal that we do not. But until recently, we have not even had a good way of researching why a government would ask whether its citizens' leisure activities were up to scratch, or why it would want to emulate behavior evident abroad. The Japanese government's use of American or European models, if noticed at all, would have been considered simply mysterious and exotic, probably the result of some kind of fundamentally unknowable Japanese culture.

Some observers, however, have recently moved to explain what they see as the development of "international norms" that define the contours for proper activity among states.[10] This research began with questions about ethical and moral behavior among states, because such behavior is so inexplicable from traditional perspectives on politics and power. For example, the international movement against apartheid encouraged domestic activists to put pressure on their governments to level sanctions against South Africa; the result, over the long run, was a nearly universal agreement among nations that helped break the back of the apartheid regime.[11] A more recent example is the transnational movement against land mines, which has succeeded in no small part because of the Internet activity of its leaders and their ability to sway the opinions of celebrities such as Princess Diana.[12] From this logic, we might surmise that a transnational "leisure movement" has pushed all nations, not just Japan, to adhere to rigorous standards for appropriate recreational practices.

Another strand of analysis looks at the ways in which international

10. There is no shortage of recent work in this branch of international relations. For the best discussions, see Peter J. Katzenstein, ed., *The Culture of National Security: Norms and Identity in World Politics* (New York: Columbia University Press, 1996); Alexander Wendt, *Social Theory of International Politics* (Cambridge: Cambridge University Press, 1999).

11. Audie Klotz, "Norms Reconstituting Interests: Global Racial Equality and U.S. Sanctions against South Africa," *International Organization* 49, 3 (summer 1995): 451–78.

12. Richard Price, "Reversing the Gun Sights: Transnational Civil Society Targets Land Mines," *International Organization* 52, 3 (summer 1998): 613–44. For a more general discussion see Thomas Risse-Kappen, ed., *Bringing Transnational Movements Back In: Non-state Actors, Domestic Structures, and International Institutions* (Cambridge: Cambridge University Press, 1995).

organizations push states to adopt similar rules.[13] By simply pursuing the enforcement of labor standards, environmental agreements, and social welfare issues, these international organizations—many related to the United Nations—encourage governments to develop similar kinds of rules and formal structures. We find, then, that virtually all nations have K–12 educational systems, ministries of labor, environmental protection agencies, and the like. This is not simply because they are functional in any independent sense but because international organizations try to make the world as "legible"[14] as possible. States increasingly look alike, so that anywhere in the world, governments resemble one another structurally, even though they behave differently. And so if international institutions with some kind of authority and monitoring ability[15] encouraged governments to create similar leisure administrations and rules, the Japanese government might be inclined to follow suit.

These approaches ask the right question but provide no real answers. No "transnational leisure movement" exists; if it did, it almost certainly would have been the envy of other social movements, which could not possibly compete for media attention with protesters demonstrating in favor of more golf courses. Although there are international leisure industry organizations (such as the World Tourism and Travel Council, the WTTC), they are not intergovernmental bodies, and no global organization tries to ensure that governments turn all their citizens into proficient skiers. Moreover—and this point is crucial—even if there were such movements or organizations, they

13. This line of thought has been heavily affected by the "world polity" literature, which emphasizes the rationalized Western state as an increasingly universal phenomenon. See John W. Meyer, "The World Polity and the Authority of the Nation-State," in *Institutional Structure: Constituting State, Society, and the Individual,* ed. George M. Thomas, John W. Meyer, Francisco O. Ramirez, and John Boli (Newbury Park, Calif.: Sage, 1987), 41–70. See also John Boli and George M. Thomas, eds., *Constructing World Culture: International Nongovernmental Organizations since 1875* (Stanford: Stanford University Press, 1999); Martha Finnemore, *National Interests in International Society* (Ithaca: Cornell University Press, 1996); John G. Ruggie, *Constructing the World Polity: Essays on International Institutionalization* (London: Routledge, 1998).

14. I take this term from James Scott, *Seeing like a State: How Certain Schemes to Improve the Human Condition Have Failed* (New Haven: Yale University Press, 1998).

15. Liliana Botcheva and Lisa L. Martin, "Institutional Effects on State Behavior: Convergence and Divergence," *International Studies Quarterly* 45, 1 (March 2001): 1–26.

would still most likely fail as explanations for Japan's leisure policies and their emulation of Western standards. The Japanese government is not trying to become like other governments, nor is it trying to make sure that its policies resemble those found abroad; leisure policymakers in Japan are well aware of the unusual nature of their fixation on recreation. Instead, they work to ensure that Japanese society becomes increasingly similar, at least in one major way, to those of western Europe and North America. The norm is not about the government; it is very much about the people. The government's goal is to make the Japanese live more *normal* lives.

Norms make sense only if there exists an accepted reference point. It is normal, for example, for university students to live in dormitories only if we have a category called "university student" and its meaning is accepted. If we enter a dorm and see a banker residing in one room and a jazz musician in the next, we are confused precisely because we have ideas about what is normal for those people and for the dorms themselves. Norms exist for doctors, wives, sons, priests, Wisconsinites, and other categories with which people can identify. To be sure, people violate norms all the time. But when they do—like a native Minnesotan wearing a Green Bay "Cheesehead" hat during a Packers-Vikings game—they need some kind of explanation (e.g., "My brother is the place kicker"). In the case of Japanese leisure policy, the relevant category is "advanced industrial nation." Japan's failure, or the perceived failure of the Japanese, to act in ways expected by membership in the advanced industrial club would call into question whether Japan really belongs, or whether it needs to find an excuse.

For a category like this to be meaningful, it has to be something that people accept in their lives without questioning; it has to be institutionalized. An "institution" is a durable set of rules or a system that people take for granted.[16] We frequently refer to institutions such as the World Bank, the Department of Education, or IBM. Although these too are institutions, we need to think more broadly than just organi-

16. The sociologist Ronald J. Jepperson describes institutions as "socially constructed, routine-reproduced (ceteris paribus), program or rule systems. They operate as relative fixtures of constraining environments and are accompanied by taken-for-granted accounts." See "Institutions, Institutional Effects, and Institutionalism," in *The New Institutionalism in Organizational Analysis,* ed. Paul J. DiMaggio and Walter W. Powell (Chicago: University of Chicago Press, 1991), 143–63. My discussion of marriage and the university as institutions draws from examples that Jepperson himself gives.

zations to get their real flavor. Other institutions include marriage and the university, both of which are taken for granted yet are extraordinarily important to our lives. Most American high school and college students, for example, simply cannot envision the rest of their lives without taking marriage into account; even if they believe they will never marry, they almost certainly can articulate a reason for this belief (e.g., "I think marriage is an outdated religious practice"). Because the university system is institutionalized, because we understand what it means and what it involves, it also provides, to people involved in it, identities and, as a result, norms for behavior. As noted above, universities have students, and on many campuses, university students live primarily in dormitories; other people, without this identity, do not. We take for granted certain constraints and rules; these tell us who we are, give our lives meaning, and tell us in subtle ways what we are expected to do.

The same holds true for national leaders embedded in a system of states. Because states are institutionalized, they come with certain norms that shape the ideas of decision makers. These are not the only norms that matter, just as a person's identity as a medical researcher might come into conflict with her identity as a Catholic if she is expected to use fetal stem cells in her work. But these norms do help to shape the ways in which government leaders understand and respond to problems. And as the leaders of an advanced industrial nation, ostensibly populated by advanced industrialized citizens, Japanese officials have taken it on themselves to encourage leisure behavior that fits.

This is, then, about more than a simple effort to get people to enjoy themselves. Japanese leisure policies have the apparent goal of encouraging people to engage in the right kind of recreation and to do it in the right way. In doing so, these policies explicitly aim at promoting a national understanding of the real meaning of leisure, which presumably has been revealed elsewhere first. This suggests that when we think about how leaders evaluate norms and proper behavior, we need to think beyond straightforward conceptions of power and objective interests and even past the more exotic issues of transnational social movements and standardizing practices of international organizations. Reflecting something that we might call a global culture, states contend also with subtle messages about what kind of lives people are supposed to lead.

Globalization and National Identity

Anyone with access to the news media will be reminded of the buzz-word "globalization."[17] Sometimes referring to the eradication of barriers to international trade and investment, the term globalization more often connotes the mixing and matching of cultures around the world. We know this intuitively in the United States, where salsa has replaced catsup as the most popular condiment. It is evident also in France, where people debate whether Muslim girls should be allowed to wear traditional headscarves in public classrooms. If Western nations have dealt with the influx of immigrants, however, other countries have been concerned about the McDonald's Effect, or the spread of Western (usually American) cultural symbols across national boundaries, raising the possibility that local cultures will be eradicated.[18] What, then, could be odder than a government's promotion of leisure behavior learned from the very countries that apparently threaten its national culture? After all, few things can be said to define a national culture more than the ways in which people spend their recreational time away from the office, the factory, or the fields. If people play golf and stop training in *kendō* (Japanese sword-fighting), would that not be a dire sign that the culture is disappearing and being replaced by another, one that is global (or rather "foreign") in nature?

17. "Globalization" itself has become a boon to academics who have produced a deluge of books on the topic. For some good examples, see Saskia Sassen, *Cities in a World Economy* (Thousand Oaks, Calif.: Pine Forge Press, 1991); Saskia Sassen, *Globalization and its Discontents: Essays on the New Mobility of People and Money* (New York: The New Press, 1998); John Tomlinson, *Globalization and Culture* (Chicago: University of Chicago Press, 1999); Roland Robertson, "Social Theory, Cultural Relativity, and the Problem of Globality," in *Culture, Globalization, and the World-System: Contemporary Conditions for the Representation of Identity*, ed. Anthony J. King (Minneapolis: University of Minnesota Press, 1997), 69–90; and Susan Strange, *The Retreat of the State: The Diffusion of Power in the World Economy* (Cambridge: Cambridge University Press, 1996). For a more popular treatise, see Thomas Friedman, *The Lexus and the Olive Tree* (New York: Farrar, Straus & Giroux, 1999).

18. Although the golden arches have something of a homogenizing effect, the McDonald's operation and its relationships with local communities differs from place to place. See James L. Watson, ed., *Golden Arches East: McDonald's in East Asia* (Stanford: Stanford University Press, 1998). Some have suggested, however, that the spread of these cultural symbols gives the United States a certain kind of power over the international system. See Bruce Russett, "The Mysterious Case of Vanishing Hegemony; or, Is Mark Twain Really Dead?" *International Organization* 39, 2 (spring 1985): 207–31. Joseph Nye writes about "soft power," which he sees as a broader phenomenon, in *Bound to Lead: The Changing Nature of American Power* (New York: Basic Books, 1991).

Few nations would likely be as concerned about this possibility as would Japan, because the nation's culture and identity have been relentlessly debated topics in the media and in political discussions for decades. To be sure, the "special" nature of the Japanese has dominated discussions of Japan by foreigners,[19] but it has been a remarkably popular theme in Japan as well. In general, these debates suggest that the Japanese are special, that their culture is "unique," and that distinctive social patterns in Japan can be used to explain a great deal of the nation's behavior.[20] Many political scientists are rightly skeptical of the idea that we should explain political outcomes with reference to Japanese culture,[21] because the claim generally obfuscates more than it clarifies. If we say, for example, that the Japanese kept the Liberal Democratic Party (LDP) in power for thirty-eight consecutive years because, as a people, they prefer consensus to conflict, we miss the ability to compare their behavior with similar dominant-party cases in Sweden and Italy and also cannot explain how the LDP lost power in 1993. Did Japanese culture suddenly change? Of course not, and the suspicion of cultural stereotypes is well placed.

The idea, for example, that the Japanese naturally are workaholics is belied both by history (in the nineteenth century, German missionaries criticized Japanese for their laziness, an equally suspect characterization)[22] and by the recent success there of leisure industries, including amazing indoor beaches and amusement parks. But just because cultural stereotypes are generally flawed and make for bad explanations does not mean that we can afford to avoid looking at them. Whether or not I, as an American, am individualistic, creative, and freedom loving in any "real" sense is probably impossible to de-

19. For the most well-known example, see Ruth Benedict, *The Chrysanthemum and the Sword: Patterns of Japanese Culture* (1946; reprint, Tokyo: Tuttle, 1988).

20. Nakane Chie, *Japanese Society* (Berkeley: University of California Press, 1986); Doi Takeo, *The Anatomy of Dependence*, trans. John Bester (Tokyo: Kodansha, 1994 reissue).

21. Chalmers Johnson, for example, argues that cultural explanations should "be reserved for the final analysis, for the irreducible residual of behavior that cannot be explained in cognitive or other more economical ways." See "The Internationalization of the Japanese Economy," in *The Challenge of Japan's Internationalization: Organization and Culture—Seminar Proceedings*, ed. Hiroshi Mannari and Harumi Befu (Tokoyo: Kwansei Gakuin University and Kodansha International, 1983), 31–58, at 36.

22. Sepp Linhart astutely makes this point in "From Industrial to Postindustrial Society: Changes in Japanese Leisure-Related Values and Behavior," *Journal of Japanese Studies* 14, 2 (summer 1988): 271–307.

termine. Whether I myself believe in the stereotype, however, is easier to check, by listening to my comments, reading my letters and articles, and talking to me about it. And this belief in the stereotype—rather than the stereotype itself—might be relevant, for example, if a candidate for office were to use it in a campaign advertisement to elicit my vote. In actuality, I might be deeply conformist and uncreative, suffering from so large a fear of genuine freedom that I might as well have agoraphobia. But as long as I believe myself, as an American, to be nearly the opposite, and as long as I value those very characteristics that "define" an American, the cultural stereotype might be useful for encouraging me to vote a certain way. It might also frame my own efforts to encourage people to do what I want them to do.

The same holds true in Japan. The "uniqueness" of Japanese society is often described as collectivistic, shame- rather than guilt-oriented, governed by relations between people rather than formal rules, preferring consensus rather than conflict, and dominated by concerns over social harmony. That stereotype is as recognizable in Japanese political discourse as the word "freedom" is in America's. In Japan, these discussions might have played an even greater political role than corresponding debates elsewhere, because in the absence of national symbols such as a flag and an anthem (neither was recognized officially until the late 1990s), conceptions of who the Japanese are occupied a central legitimating role.[23] In chapter 2, I touch on how the idea of Japanese uniqueness has become politically relevant and how its meaning has shifted over time and across the political landscape. But the idea has been so dominant that it has operated as a brake on any straightforward government effort to turn the Japanese into Americans, Europeans, or anyone else. Even if these places and the people living there loom large in the Japanese popular imagination, the timeless uniqueness of the Japanese is as "taken for granted" as is the belief that membership in the club of advanced industrial nations requires certain social changes.

The issue, then, is not whether the Japanese are "different" enough (whatever that might mean) to require policies to help them better understand the importance of leisure. Instead, the question revolves around Japanese officials' views of themselves, their society, and their place in the world. The idea of national uniqueness provides to deci-

23. Harumi Befu, "Symbols of Nationalism and *Nihonjinron,*" in *Ideology and Practice in Modern Japan,* ed. Roger Goodman and Kirsten Refsing (London: Routledge, 1992), 26–46.

sion makers both an explanation and an ideal; they can start from the assumption that the Japanese have special needs because they have a distinctive national character, one that should in some sense be preserved. Even as these officials consider what "normal" people are like in other nations, no one either believes or wants Japanese to simply become American, French, or Australian. Instead, they have to contend with two ways of thinking about what Japan is: an advanced industrial nation like any other and yet a unique place populated by a unique people. The key documents in the history of Japanese leisure policy demonstrate that this tension played a fundamental role in the government's efforts to affect the way people spend their leisure time. These reports show that Japanese policymakers were concerned about Japanese behaving differently than Americans and Europeans in their leisure time. This was considered evidence that they were somehow lagging, that they were not advanced, that they needed to catch up. On the other hand, if the Japanese were to adopt Western practices wholesale and uncritically, Japan's cultural essence might dissipate. This book explores the tension between these two ideas.

Studying Leisure, Identity, and Japan's Place in the World

This book thus aims to do more than to tell the story of Japanese leisure policy. To be sure, the growing economic importance of leisure industries makes a study of leisure policy worthwhile, if only to show that there are still significant topics that political economy has left unexplored. But Japanese leisure policy can tell us much more about Japan, the relationship between nations and "global culture," and problems of identity in international relations than the topic might at first suggest. When the Japanese government creates, as it did in 1987, public relations campaigns designed to tell adults that they can travel abroad—that they *should* travel abroad—it is not just capitulating to international criticism of the country's trade surplus. It also indicates to Japanese citizens what kind of people they are supposed to be, or what kind of behavior they ought to consider normal. Sometimes the policies have been a spectacular failure, as in the 1973 Ministry of Transport plan to promote "nightlife" tourism in the Republic of Korea, a plan immediately criticized by leftists as an effort to promote a sex tourism spot in a former colony. At other times, citizens have seemed to be completely unaware or uninterested in what the government tries to tell them. But the fact that policies sometimes work—that they do affect the nature of leisure industries in Japan and therefore the choices people make—indicates that the fight over identity carried out in these policies has real, practical consequences.

Leisure policy history in Japan is not particularly hard to reconstruct. The documents, though scattered and often buried in archives, are hardly state secrets, and many tourism- and leisure-related organizations have produced official histories neatly summarizing their development. More challenging to a researcher is uncovering the crucial tension over Japanese identity, as well as the role it plays in leisure policy. As noted above, when something is "institutionalized" (as is Japan's status as an "advanced industrial nation" but also a "unique nation"), it is "taken for granted," as is marriage. In many cases, it is difficult to evaluate the effects of institutions on people, because we ourselves do not question that which we take for granted. In general, I find it easier to evaluate the hidden, taken-for-granted aspects of debates in Japan than in the United States. As an American, I have trouble uncovering what I unconsciously accept in conversations, in the media, and in my work. Although I read and speak Japanese, I *have to* think about it when I do either, which gives me some of the distance necessary, while reading policy documents for instance, to ask what the authors are unquestioningly accepting as true and self-evident.

This distance has also proved useful, though personally frustrating, in interviews. When I determined, for example, that the YKC's researchers were sent only to advanced industrial nations for their comparative studies (which is not an official policy but is generally the case in practice—and it makes for a great job for researchers who sometimes get to travel the world and go to amusement parks), I guessed that this resulted not so much from a conscious decision to look only at the leisure behavior of Westerners, as opposed to Asians, Africans, or people elsewhere, as from a general assumption that this was the only sane way to do it. In an interview with a YKC official, I asked about the destination of YKC researchers, and he answered quickly, moving on to what he thought was more important territory. I interrupted and asked him, "But why do you send people there, as opposed to the other countries?" No doubt believing that I was either not very bright or unable to understand simple Japanese, he paused and then said slowly, "Because those are the advanced industrial nations." He did not need to say that advanced industrial nations have advanced leisure and that Japan—as such a nation—needed to learn from the others. He took this for granted and assumed that I would too.

This book is, then, an exploration of what people take for granted and how it becomes politically important. It will not, of course, skimp on the more remarkable aspects of Japanese leisure policy history, such as the Ministry of Education's early complaints that playing baseball would lead schoolchildren to become alcoholics with misshapen bodies, or the instructions given to tourism authorities in Asia regarding how they can make their nations look appropriately authentic for Japanese visitors. But beyond that, it aims to articulate a new way to study how political leaders are affected by their views of the outside world and of what constitutes proper behavior for their people. To be sure, this represents only one part of the puzzle of globalization—how the world seems to be getting smaller—but it is an aspect that has been neglected.

In using Japanese leisure policy, the book also will attempt to challenge something that most Americans, including American political scientists, take for granted: that leisure is "personal," not "political." What the state does, and how it becomes involved in people's lives, differs from place to place,[24] and even when Japanese leisure policies seem odd to foreign observers, they reflect a state-society relationship that feels natural and normal to citizens of that nation.[25] The Japanese case may well be both distinctive and illustrative; if it were not, there would be little reason to write a book about it. But it is neither aberrant nor especially dysfunctional, and it ought to challenge us to think more broadly about what politics is. Japanese leisure policy reflects a

24. Timothy Mitchell argues that the size and role of the state differs across nations, suggesting a major flaw in political science research on the role of a generalized "state." See "The Limits of the State: Beyond Statist Approaches and their Critics," *American Political Science Review* 85, 1 (March 1991): 77–96. Feminists have been at the forefront of the debate over the artificial distinctions between the public and the private. See Susan Moller Okin, *Justice, Gender, and the Family* (New York: Basic Books, 1989), especially 110–33; Iris Marion Young, *Justice and the Politics of Difference* (Princeton: Princeton University Press, 1990). Robin LeBlanc's *Bicycle Citizens: The Political World of the Japanese Housewife* (Berkeley: University of California Press, 1999) discusses this issue (and many others) with regard to Japanese women and politics.

25. Other recent works that provide broader historical accounts of Japanese state intervention in the "private" lives of citizens are Narusawa Akira, "The Social Order of Modern Japan," trans. Timothy S. George, in *The Political Economy of Japanese Society*, vol. 1: *The State or the Market?* ed. Junji Banno (Oxford: Oxford University Press, 1997), 193–236; and Sheldon Garon, *Molding Japanese Minds: The State in Everyday Life* (Princeton: Princeton University Press, 1997). Narusawa focuses especially on comprehensive shifts toward modernity in the late nineteenth century, while Garon is especially interested in moral suasion campaigns in the twentieth century.

tension that affects all governments: how to remain distinctive in an international system of states that seems increasingly to include assumptions and expectations for proper behavior and development. In a way, this recasts our opening question about why a government would be interested in paragliding. The Japanese government may not itself be particularly enamored of the activity. Officials, however, would like to see citizens become paragliders, particularly if they can find a Japanese way to do it.

A Japanese tourism promotion guide for Manchuria, 1930s. Photo by permission of the Harvard-Yenching Library.

Leisure, Policy, and Identity

I worry a bit about having revealed in chapter 1 that I play video games more than golf. Who, other than adolescents, plays video games? Socially maladjusted loners, perhaps; certainly not professors of political science, in spite of the staggering overlap between these categories. I have friends who go salsa dancing (on occasion, I go with them), which seems somehow more appropriate. It is reasonably trendy, reflects an openness to other cultures, and requires some skill. Other friends belong to the coffeehouse set. Certainly I could fit as a certain type of scholar if I could reliably be seen on Thursday evenings, alternately grading papers and reading poetry by Seamus Heaney or Nikki Giovanni, while sipping my decaf cappuccino and listening to a postfolk performer. Still other friends are more outdoorsy. On weekends, they go for long bicycle rides or long hikes, at least as long as the unforgiving Wisconsin weather permits. I do not know what they do at night; I have not asked, and I suspect that they would not tell me, though I worry that the answer is that they work.

Although my career would probably best be served by overcoming my compulsive need to confess, I see the problem as something larger. Ultimately, it would be better if I were the sort of person who prefers to do something other than twitch my thumbs on a PlayStation2 controller. Perhaps if I go salsa dancing often enough, I sometimes tell myself, I will become good at it and will want to do it more often. After all, I started listening to rap music specifically because cool friends in college did; now I genuinely like it. By self-consciously taking part in these more respectable leisure activities, perhaps I will become the kind of person who does them convincingly and without affect. Like many people, I shift uneasily between those leisure activities that I genuinely enjoy and those that I would like to enjoy more, because they somehow seem right for a person like me. I simply cannot imagine how best to spend my leisure time without taking note of how people around me—especially the people I like, respect, and emulate— behave. And I realize that my listening to rap music, which was originally something of an affectation, has made me think of myself differently and maybe made me a different person.

Japanese leisure policies reflect government concerns over what kind of people the Japanese are supposed to be. This chapter examines leisure policy more generally, showing that the issue of identity permeates state intervention in leisure. Regardless of government motives for trying to affect citizens' recreational choices (and these motives can range from regime security to environmental protection), they often tell us a great deal about leaders' views of the qualities that make for a good citizen or a healthy lifestyle. Leisure invites this kind of concern because it ostensibly represents the area of activity in which people can most be themselves. Any public effort to affect people's leisure decisions will likely take into account what kind of "selves" people are supposed to become. What distinguishes Japan's approach, at least among democratic states, has been the relative durability of the government role in leisure, as well as the consistency of the standard for evaluating whether citizens are leading good or bad lives.

Leisure, Meaning, and Identity

No one would dispute that our tastes are shaped by our environment, that a podiatrist in Brookline, Massachusetts and a militia member in Kandahar, Afghanistan, will probably have different hobbies. But this raises a daunting question: how do we explain these differences? On one level, most would agree that tastes and preferences are "socially constructed" when they are obviously cultural in nature,[1] and newer scholarship on leisure has aimed at teasing out those elements of a cultural

---

1. Paul J. DiMaggio, "Culture and Economy," in *The Handbook of Economic Sociology*, ed. Neil J. Smelser and Richard Swedberg (Princeton: Princeton University Press, 1994), 27–57, especially 41–46.

or institutional environment that make us want to spend our leisure time in different ways.[2] The classic research on people's recreational choices has handled these differences primarily by taking a critical stance toward those people or leisure patterns that the authors find distasteful. Thorstein Veblen's classic *Theory of the Leisure Class* argued—with no small amount of satire[3]—that the wealthy could distinguish themselves from the riff-raff through "conspicuous consumption" of certain goods and services that would mark them as different, possessed of proper breeding.[4] German social theorist Theodor Adorno examined the ways in which late capitalist societies homogenize tastes to center them around markets and the "culture industry."[5] Each of these accounts points to something crucial about leisure, though the main target of each is the hatefulness of modern life, whether of its soul-crushing banality and subservience to corporate interests or of its ostentatious class-consciousness. It is more difficult and uncomfortable to turn the critical gaze toward one's own recreational pursuits.

Rendered in prose so daunting that it masks the argument's relevance and intuitiveness, Pierre Bourdieu's widely read book *Distinction: A Social Critique of the Judgement of Taste* provides a useful way to approach the issue. In this book, Bourdieu's central claim is that societies feature largely unexamined but widely accepted cultural markers for distinguishing between classes. In his view, class is more than simple economics; it is an entire social system in which citizens operate in a "field" of forces, with some limited ability to move upward in influence, power, wealth, and control. People's social tastes indicate their position in the *habitus,* a map of social practices and cultural phenomena, which is broadly related to the field of forces. In other words, people's cultural choices, leisure practices, and social tastes can tell us a good deal about who they are and, to use more con-

2. For a helpful overview, see Nicole Woolsey Biggart, "Labor and Leisure," in *Handbook of Economic Sociology,* ed. Smelser and Swedberg, 672–90.

3. Clarifying Veblen's intellectual lineage, Joseph Dorfman emphasized that Veblen's work, while written in a satirical voice, should be seen as a rejection of social Darwinism. Joseph Dorfman, "The 'Satire' of Thorstein Veblen's *Theory of the Leisure Class,*" *Political Science Quarterly* 47, 3 (September 1932): 363–409.

4. Thorstein Veblen, *Theory of the Leisure Class: An Economic Study in the Evolution of Institutions* (New York: Penguin Classics, 1994).

5. See, for example, Theodor Adorno, *The Culture Industry: Selected Essays on Mass Culture* (London: Routledge, 1991). J. M. Bernstein's introduction to the collection is a useful overview of Adorno's essays. See also the excellent discussion in Claus Offe, "The Utopia of the Zero Option: Modernity and Modernization as Normative Political Criteria," translated by John Torpey, reprinted in Claus Offe, *Modernity and the State: East, West* (Cambridge: MIT Press, 1996), 3–30, especially the passage on 14.

ventional language, the "class" to which they belong.[6] Because people instinctively know this, they can try to adopt the tastes, styles, and behavior of people in a class to which they want to belong. This is hardly a new or unique idea in itself; after all, there are countless literary works, from *The Prince and the Pauper* to *Six Degrees of Separation*, that focus on imposters who must feign comfort with certain social activities that do not match their "real" class or station. By dealing with this type of question in social theory, however, Bourdieu aspires to do more than provide a cultural critique of the elites; he reshapes the way that we think about class as well as the relationship between culture and power throughout a society.

Bourdieu's perspective resembles the institutional logic advanced in chapter 1, because it implies that people take for granted a relationship between what people do, who they are, and who they want to be.[7] It also offers a new way to think about leisure and norms. I want to hike, dance to salsa music, or read Jonathan Franzen novels because I want to be the kind of young professor who does those things—not because I have any clear reason to believe I will like any of them. And I do not want to admit that I play video games because I know that it is taken for granted that people who do are simply not "scholars."

Leisure and Politics

These concerns permeate politics as well, because cultural tastes involving leisure choices become significant political markers. Recent choices by America's Republican Party demonstrate this well. At the 2001 inauguration ceremonies for President George W. Bush, a young Latino musical superstar performed, a choice that would have been

6. Pierre Bourdieu, *Distinction: A Social Critique of the Judgement of Taste*, trans. Richard Nice (Cambridge: Harvard University Press, 1984). For a clear introduction to Bourdieu's work, see Cheleen Mahar, Richard Harker, and Chris Wilkes, "The Basic Theoretical Position," in *An Introduction to the Work of Pierre Bourdieu: The Practice of Theory*, ed. Mahar, Harker, and Wilkes (London: Macmillan, 1990), 1–25.

7. Although there are some significant differences, Bourdieu's views resemble the institutional logic, the "taken for grantedness," discussed in chapter 1. Although people might make deliberate choices about leisure activities, these choices must rely on a taken-for-granted standard of what makes for appropriate and inappropriate leisure. That people take things for granted does not mean they do not make choices; it only means their choices are constrained by what they believe they can and cannot do. On these connections, see Paul J. DiMaggio and Walter W. Powell, introduction to *The New Institutionalism in Organizational Analysis*, ed. DiMaggio and Powell (Chicago: University of Chicago Press, 1991), 1–40, especially 25–26.

unthinkable at Ronald Reagan's inauguration. This was immediately taken as a symbol of the Republicans' courting of the Latino vote in future elections, but it represented something else as well. It indicated that the party sometimes viewed as the defender of predominantly white American conservatism was at least nominally interested in portraying itself as authentically multicultural, partly because many whites would find this openness appealing. No doubt, many of the guests at the ceremonies felt vaguely out of place listening and dancing to the salsa-inflected beats, including the visibly awkward new president, who seemed to make the wise last-minute decision not to attempt a few dance steps when invited on stage by the singer.

American presidential candidates know that their leisure choices provide information to the public. None, for example, would appear at a modern dance performance by Pilobolus or on the dais at the medals ceremony of the X-Games, because neither seems like a comfortably middle-American decision. And when the candidates are asked in an interview who their favorite authors are, answers such as "I don't like to read" and "Don DeLillo" are bad choices. "John Grisham" is a better one. The answer matters, because it tells the audience reading the interview that the president is literate but normal, not inclined to read something foreign to the average voter. When governments pursue policies designed to affect people's access to or restriction from leisure practices, they are often confronted by debates over what kind of a society a government is supposed to lead.

This is not necessarily the first thing one thinks of when looking at given leisure-related initiatives, which in general aim at more obvious goals. Tourism promotion schemes seek to increase travel-related revenues, usually to specific regional destinations. Legislated limits on working hours can demonstrate capitulation to or cooperation with labor unions. Restrictions on open hours for taverns might be in the interest of safety or might demonstrate the political power of temperance organizations. And concerns over public morality might encourage leaders to enact limits on sex or foul language in popular entertainment. None of these motives seems particularly surprising, and all have been relevant in government intervention in citizens' recreational choices. But leisure policies are often conditioned by larger questions over identity, over what kind of people go hiking, visit health spas, or stay out until 4 A.M., drinking while listening to country music.

In 1953, American Joseph Pendergast, the executive director of the

National Recreation Association,[8] neatly summed up these tensions in a description of what recreation is and how it would need to be in part a public phenomenon:

> The chief value of recreation, i.e., the creative use of leisure time lies in its power to enrich the lives of all individuals. It also has many valuable "by-products" in the fields of physical and mental health, safety, crime prevention and citizenship. Because recreation contributes to rich and satisfying living and social cooperation, it should play an important part in the life of everyone, everywhere. It is not merely for those who have suffered misfortune, nor simply to prevent man from encountering misfortune. *It is to give all men opportunity for growth, opportunity to be and become themselves.*
>
> Children *need* happy, healthful social play to attain their fullest development; young people *require* wholesome recreation opportunities to replace questionable amusements which might lead to delinquency; workers *need* recreation during their off-duty hours in order to keep their spirits and production high; adults and the aged *need* opportunities to find the most satisfying use of their expanding leisure time. Furthermore, people who play together, sing together, make things together, *achieve* in its truest sense a community of feeling. Recreation programs also help to preserve local, state and national traditions [emphasis added].[9]

In this view, people "become themselves" through recreation, and a government might well want them to be the kinds of selves that sing, play, and make things. These selves are a nice, agreeable lot, the kind idealized in the television programs of the era. They will not, one hopes, become the kinds of selves who engage in "questionable amusements," commit crimes, or simply become slothful. And Pendergast's vision captures something central about the goals for public management of leisure and recreation: leisure policies—whatever their other goals—also involve state efforts to ensure that people do the "right" thing in their leisure time. Below, I identify some of the motives governments might have in trying to regulate leisure policies. The list is neither exhaustive nor conceptually pure, because governments often have several goals for given initiatives. My aim here is simply to demonstrate that all governments are in some way inter-

8. Funded by philanthropists, the National Recreation Association had, as early as 1906 when it was known as the Play and Recreation Association of America, pushed for the creation of new playgrounds and facilities that were now "known" to be important and valuable. In the postwar period, it continued to push for the creation of socially responsible recreation practices under public auspices. George Hjelte, *The Administration of Public Recreation* (New York: Macmillan, 1940), 7.

9. Quoted in Lynn S. Rodney, *Administration of Public Recreation* (New York: Ronald Press, 1964), 6.

ested in citizens' use of leisure time, and that their efforts to shape recreational choices reflect predominant concerns over the kinds of people citizens are supposed to become.[10]

Controlling Leisure Time

Above and beyond any other goals a state might have, its most obvious motive in creating leisure policies might be to control the period of time in which citizens might otherwise behave in ways that could threaten state or public safety. In the most depressing cases, the citizens of some authoritarian states have had to undergo "compulsory leisure," which would seem to defeat the purpose of having leisure in the first place. In more benign versions, leisure activities might be designed to offer opportunities that can distract participants from other, more potentially threatening choices, such as crime.

This latter goal was clearly visible in the English political elite's efforts to create leisure distractions for a possibly menacing population of the urban poor, especially after the Enclosure Act of 1793 formalized and accelerated the trend toward British urbanization. Although Tories tolerated a somewhat rowdy popular culture among landowners and their tenants, increasing concerns about the apparent threat to social order in urban bars, brothels, and the like led to a movement to control leisure more effectively. Combined with the growing role of Methodism at the turn of the nineteenth century, popular attitudes and public decrees began to reflect genuine fears of unrestrained debauchery. The 1787 "Royal Proclamation for the Encouragement of Piety and Virtue" was not itself particularly effective, but the Society for the Suppression of Vice began by the early nineteenth century to press heavily for restraints on behavior on the Sabbath, which presumably shut down even more recreational options.[11] Charles Dickens noted that the restrictive work by the Sabbatarians had done perhaps more harm than good: "In some parts of London, and many of the manufacturing towns of England, drunkenness and profligacy in their most disgusting forms, exhibit in the open streets on Sunday, a sad and a degrading spectacle."[12]

---

10. John Wilson also categorizes leisure policies in *Politics and Leisure* (Lexington, Mass.: Lexington Books, 1988), though he does so primarily by linking policies and regime types.

11. John Clarke and Chas Critcher, *The Devil Makes Work: Leisure in Capitalist Britain* (London: Macmillan, 1985), 53–55.

12. Charles Dickens, "S. C. on the Observance of the Sabbath Day," cited in Hugh Cunningham, *Leisure in the Industrial Revolution* (New York: St. Martin's, 1980), 86.

The goal of eradicating troublesome forms of leisure behavior inspired new efforts to offer better opportunities in their absence. In nineteenth-century Britain, the state's role in leisure began as the "suppression of popular recreation" before shifting toward the "promotion of acceptable forms of leisure."[13] The political promotion of better recreation had something of an evangelical quality to it, especially as it reflected the nearly missionary zeal of members of the leisure class who extolled the civilized virtues to those less economically fortunate. And although much of their concern stemmed from fears of an uncontrolled, unrestrained labor class, middle-class guilt revolving around differential access to "proper" recreation fed into efforts to promote more public space for reflective, rational leisure: parks, public libraries, and public museums. Indeed, by the middle of the nineteenth century, Parliament was establishing parks for the enjoyment of all (even as other lands were rendered private), setting aside substantial sums of money for public park maintenance.[14] One journalist summed up perfectly the view that leisure was a necessity but also something that could and should be tamed:

> There must be safety valves for the mind; that is, there must be means for its pleasurable, profitable, and healthful exertion. These means it is in our power to render safe and innocent: these means in too many instances have been rendered dangerous and guilty.[15]

Other governments have also constructed leisure policies partly in the hope of constraining people's use of leisure time. This has, of course, been most notable in the cases of authoritarian and totalitarian regimes. During the Third Reich, for example, Hitler's regime organized leisure and sport competitions through approved social organizations in part because of their ability to draw citizens into government-sponsored groups, where their activities and utterances could be more easily monitored.[16] Under Joseph Stalin, the Soviet gov-

---

13. Ian Henry and Peter Bramham, "Leisure Policy in Britain," in *Leisure Policies in Europe*, ed. Peter Bramham, Ian Henry, Hans Mommaas, and Hugo van der Poel (Wallingford, U.K.: CAB International, 1993), 101–28, at 106.

14. Cunningham, *Leisure in the Industrial Revolution*, 76–109.

15. W. Cooke Taylor, "Notes of a Tour in the Manufacturing Districts of Lancashire" (Manchester, U.K.: n.p., 1842), 132–36, quoted in Peter Bailey, *Leisure and Class in Victorian England* (London: Routledge, 1978), 37.

16. On the role of social organizations in the "denunciations" that were important to Nazi discipline, see Robert Gellately, "Denunciations in Twentieth-Century Germany: Aspects of Self-Policing in the Third Reich and the German Democratic Republic," *Journal of Modern History* 68, 4 (December 1996): 931–67.

ernment pursued an even more extensive organization of all social life, including leisure. With compulsory mass entertainment and leisure activities aimed at "cultural enlightenment," the Stalinist regime sought to "absorb" as much of the citizens' free time as possible, under the assumption that unobserved hands might make the devil's work.[17]

The fate of "midnight basketball" programs in the United States offers a look at some of the limits a democratic state can face in promoting leisure in order to reduce the risks of more dangerous behavior. Started in Glenarden, Maryland, in 1986, "midnight basketball" leagues soon sprouted in major cities around the United States, attracting federal funding as part of the government's anticrime efforts. By providing an alternative to drugs and violence, the programs aimed at protecting "at risk" youth (a euphemism for predominantly poor, urban, African Americans) from the other temptations of night in the city—and, quietly, at protecting other citizens from the "at risk" youth. The program's apparent success rested in part on its putative ability to channel African American efforts into an area in which they felt they could excel: basketball.[18] Even so, conservative critics seized on the program as an absurd waste of taxpayer dollars, arguing that the money should go instead to law enforcement and punishment of offenders.[19] The government, in this view, was supposed to lock criminals up, not offer recreational opportunities to "at risk" children who could be studying or, even better, working in low-wage jobs in the service sector.[20]

Propaganda and National Culture

Closely related to the issues of discipline and order is, of course, the government's intervention in leisure to generate national pride and loyalty to the regime. This is, of course, most widely evident in government support for national sports teams performing in international events such as the World Cup or the Olympics. Another avenue has been support for the arts, or at least those with a distinctively national heritage. For example, the French government's postwar leisure policies have been quite limited but have consistently promoted the exposure of French citizens to the nation's high culture. Following an initial postwar period of reconstruction of basic leisure opportunities

17. Anne White, *De-Stalinization and the House of Culture: Declining State Control over Leisure in the USSR, Poland, and Hungary* (London: Routledge, 1990), 21–23.
18. Gary A. Sailes, "Basketball at Midnight," *UNESCO Courier* 52, 4 (April 1999): 25–26.
19. "Order on the Court," *Time*, 29 August 1994, 35.
20. Ralph R. Reiland, "Let's Promote Midnight Dishwashing," *Restaurant Hospitality* 78, 11 (November 1994): 28.

(vacation sites, parks, and the like), from the 1960s to the 1980s the government reduced working hours and began a series of "cultural" initiatives that were supposed to instruct citizens in how to learn more about their French heritage. Until the early 1980s, when budget cuts began to bite into some arts and culture programs, the French government's generous funding for the preservation and display of visual arts and music by French artists was designed, at least in part, to define and strengthen a French national identity.[21]

The propaganda possibilities of the occasional trip to the museum, however, pale in comparison to the rich potential of popular entertainment. Authoritarian regimes have long used their control over the mass media to engender loyalty to the state and its stated values. Even so, the fact that modern media, including television, radio, and films, can be enjoyed by individuals as well as groups has made it difficult for authorities to monitor the audience's receptiveness to propaganda messages. The Nazi regime, for example, tried to ban jazz because of its African American origins and its reliance on improvisation—a dangerous artistic concept for a polity based on regimentation and control. The regime met with only limited success in this regard because of the difficulty of defining precisely what jazz is. The music served as something of a bone of contention for regime critics like Hamburg's "Swing Youth."[22] The Soviet government's insistence on proregime propaganda in television made Russian programming blandly subservient to political interests, even when talented artists became involved. In one case, producers decided to film an adaptation of Robert Penn Warren's classic novel *All the King's Men*, about Huey Long, but set it in the contemporary United States in order to indicate that there was no difference between the Washington of 1974 and the Louisiana of the Great Depression.[23] Even in democracies, governments can try to influence the spirit of popular culture. In the United States, the second Bush administration publicly sought the assistance of Hollywood leaders in producing more patriotic films and television programs in the wake of the September 11 terrorist attacks.[24]

21. Genevieve Poujol, "Leisure Politics and Policies in France," in *Leisure Policies,* ed. Bramham et al., 13–40.

22. Michael H. Kater, "Forbidden Fruit? Jazz in the Third Reich," *American Historical Review* 94, 1, supplement to vol. 94 (February 1989): 11–43.

23. David E. Powell, "Television in the USSR," *Public Opinion Quarterly* 39, 3 (autumn 1975): 287–300, at 288–89.

24. Rick Lyman, "Hollywood Discusses Role in War Effort," *New York Times,* 12 November 2001, B2.

Revenues, Conservation, and Other Public Policy Goals

Beyond the benefits that propaganda and control of free time can provide to regime security, governments have intervened in citizens' leisure time in the pursuit of a variety of other goals. Most obvious have been the efforts to use the economic advantages of leisure consumption to enhance tax revenues or to engage in redistributive schemes that bring money to disadvantaged regions. Dutch leisure policy, for example, is marked by efforts to encourage Dutch vacationers to spend their time and money in the Netherlands, as well as to increase the number of visitors from abroad;[25] the latter mission has been nearly ubiquitous for national tourist organizations. In nineteenth-century Great Britain, successive efforts to promote seaside holidays corresponded with the growing role and economic importance not only of the resorts themselves but also the train lines that connected them.[26] And in his efforts to rescue a staggered U.S. airline industry after the September 11 attacks, President Bush went about as far as America's limited leisure policy stance allowed, by exhorting Americans to travel again: "Get on board. Do your business around the country. Fly and enjoy America's great destination spots. Get down to Disney World in Florida. Take your families and enjoy life, the way we want it to be enjoyed."[27]

Tourism is also regarded as a good reason to promote environmental conservation. Indeed, to the extent that the U.S. federal government maintains a genuine set of policies regarding leisure, they involve protection of national parks through the National Park Service. This mission formally began in 1916—even though Yosemite had been named a national park over twenty-five years earlier—when the national government created the National Park Service within the Department of the Interior, mainly so that it could protect Yosemite in ways the state government of California had failed to do. This has never been labeled "recreation policy" or "leisure policy," though America's national parks clearly constitute the main part of its efforts to provide leisure opportunities to citizens. The government's only ex-

25. Hugo van der Poel, "Leisure Policy in the Netherlands," in *Leisure Policies*, ed. Bramham et al., 41–70.

26. See Cunningham, *Leisure in the Industrial Revolution*, 160–64, on the importance of railroads in simultaneously improving access of middle-class English to resorts, as well as in driving the wealthier travelers to take ever-longer trips to avoid the middle-class mobs.

27. George W. Bush, speech to workers at O'Hare International Airport, Chicago, 27 September 2001. Full text available online at: http://www.whitehouse.gov/news/releases/2001/09/20010927-1.html. Accessed 7 March 2002.

plicit foray into leisure policy was the brief existence within the Department of the Interior of the Bureau of Outdoor Recreation, created by President Kennedy in 1963 and later cut by the Nixon administration.[28] Leisure itself turned out to be an insufficient reason to maintain a policy, but it could be mobilized as a factor in encouraging conservation.

When democratic governments have sought to use leisure for explicitly political purposes, they have largely aimed at garnering support from labor unions and others who might applaud the extension of the welfare state to provide for improved recreational environments. In part because of memories of the Third Reich's control of leisure, for twenty-five years after World War II, West German conservative governments displayed little interest in becoming involved in leisure; it was not only understood as a quintessentially private activity but was also eschewed as a dangerous tool of state authorities. In 1973, however, Willy Brandt declared that "the quality of life is more than merely the standard of living. It means enrichment of life and more than income and consumption . . . the improvement of standards of living, the improvement of work, or leisure and of recreation have to be focused upon." For much of the next fifteen years, the West German government would sponsor committees for developing leisure policy, though, as noted below, most of the important work would go on at the local level.[29]

And leisure policy can turn the average citizen into a crime fighter, or at least make him think he is. France has the distinction of having created one of the more ghoulish leisure policies on record. In the early nineteenth century, a police decree opened up the local morgues to the public, in the hopes of having bodies identified, which would be useful to "the social order." By 1895, in part because of governmental encouragement, huge crowds were appearing at the morgue to see the corpses of young babies fished out of the Seine. Hoping to attract more visitors, the administration of the Paris morgue turned the display of

---

28. A good (though biased) history of the bureau and its relationship to the Park Service appears in Edward M. Fitch and John F. Shanklin, *The Bureau of Outdoor Recreation* (New York: Praeger, 1970).

29. Wolfgang Nahrstedt, "Leisure Policy in Germany," in *Leisure Policies*, ed. Bramham et al., 129–48, quotes on 136 and 145. The administrative breakdown of responsibilities for leisure in Brandt's time can be found in Felizitas Lenz-Romeiss, *Freizeitpolitik in der Bundesrepublik* (Göttingen: Verlag Otto Schwartz, 1975), 65–78, with a helpful chart on 79. A collection of some of the main documents of the 1970s leisure policy can also be found in the appendix of Heribert Kohl, *Freizeitpolitik* (Frankfurt: Europäische Verlagsanstalt, 1976), 152–86.

the bodies into something of a public show.[30] In a more recent and less gruesome example, the September 11 attacks prompted the U.S. government to ask the Fox television network to preempt its regular programming to allow a special episode of *America's Most Wanted*, a program that features vignettes on unsolved murders and asks viewers to call a help line with tips.[31]

Making the Ideal Society

I have offered these goals to highlight the reasons that governments might intervene in the leisure, recreation, sports, and entertainment choices of their citizens. But accompanying these motives is usually the vision of the country's recreation theorists and advisors of what kind of a society the government should be ruling. Communist states, for example, might have more effectively occupied people's private time by holding mandatory viewings of recent Hollywood films, though of course this might have encouraged American-style materialism. Conversely, if nineteenth-century British governments had been interested only in crowd control, they might have more profitably limited damage caused by unruly lower classes by policing pub districts more tightly. Instead, each of these countries chose leisure initiatives that reflected prevailing beliefs among the leadership about what constituted good and bad leisure. And these beliefs tie directly into assumptions about the kind of people that citizens are supposed to be when they are being themselves.[32]

Nowhere has this been clearer than in Great Britain, the nation that has spawned, by my unscientific estimates, the largest amount of research on what leisure is and how it can best be pursued. In Britain, we see the earliest political articulation that leisure is an objective social *need*, and the limited state role has partly been shaped by a belief that some kinds of recreation fulfill that need more effectively and safely than do others. Even in the nineteenth-century conception of "rational recreation," we see the belief that leisure itself can be understood and that it is proper to judge what kind of activities people need. In discussing what was meant by the term, Hugh Cunningham argues:

30. Vanessa R. Schwartz, *Spectacular Realities: Early Mass Culture in Fin-de-Siècle Paris* (Berkeley: University of California Press, 1998), 45–88, quote on 49.

31. Alessandra Stanley, "President is Using TV Show and the Public in Combination to Combat Terrorism," *New York Times*, 11 October 2001, B2.

32. Shirley Tillotson makes this point well in reference to Ontario's recreation policies in the 1950s. See *The Public at Play: Gender and the Politics of Recreation in Post-war Ontario* (Toronto: University of Toronto Press, 2000), especially 20–43.

Rationality implied both order and control. Jane Austen conveys to us its early-nineteenth-century meaning in writing of Charles Musgrove in *Persuasion* that ". . . a woman of real understanding might have given more consequence to his habits and pursuits. As it was, he did nothing with much zeal, but sport; and his time was otherwise trifled away, without benefit from books, or anything else."[33]

To a large degree, this meant the categorization of middle-class tastes as proper or safe and the civilizing of coarse manners and social preferences. Only in the area of music did nineteenth-century middle-class social reformers find that the matter was as simple as providing facilities, since it became clear that Handel was, for example, as popular among northern factory workers as he was among members of the aristocracy. With this important exception, however, rational recreation implied not only the extension of opportunities and facilities to the poor but also the teaching of what they really should want to do in their leisure time.[34] The links between good/bad leisure on the one hand, and high/low class on the other, show an extraordinarily close fit with the kind of generally accepted standard for measurement that Bourdieu emphasizes in *Distinction*. After all, it was known—and taken for granted—that one could distinguish between the kind of leisure that would make one a better person and the kind that would not; to the extent that the state could get involved, it would clearly be on the side of making people better.

For governments in the colonial and postcolonial periphery, the drive to improve leisure would take different forms. From the late 1920s until the 1949 revolution, the Chinese Nationalists struggled to control leisure practices in Shanghai through a strict system of licenses. Here, distinctions between good and bad leisure rested uneasily on the lionization of "modern" entertainment (such as films) and criticism of purportedly foreign-influenced vices, such as prostitution and alcoholism. To the Nationalists, leisure would help to make China a modern society without capitulating to the moral licentiousness of the West.[35]

The white authorities in 1940s South Africa adopted a different stance with regard to appropriate leisure, believing that "native"

33. Cunningham, *Leisure in the Industrial Revolution*, 90.
34. Ibid., 76–109.
35. Frederic Wakeman Jr., "Licensing Leisure: The Chinese Nationalists' Attempt to Regulate Shanghai, 1927–1949," *Journal of Asian Studies* 54, 1 (February 1995): 19–42.

recreational practices might fit the locals better than would European forms. Gold mine owners cooperated with political authorities to discourage the black African workers from presumably unhealthy practices as consuming narcotics and consorting with prostitute. But in trying to develop organized leisure that would sway the workers away from these vices, the Chamber of Mines idealized African life, creating tribal dance competitions and the like, which—understandably, at least with the benefit of hindsight—failed to draw many spectators. As Africans, the Chamber's intellectuals argued, the workers would prefer these practices to European games such as soccer, in spite of direct evidence to the contrary.[36]

Under state socialism, the compulsory leisure sessions might simply be regarded as efforts at control, domination, and propaganda, but in addition to these more cynical motives, leaders genuinely believed that these practices would provide "cultural enlightenment." People really wanted to live in a workers' paradise; they simply did not know it, and the use of entertainment pushing this dogma would enable them to become the ideal proletarians they were supposed to be.[37] Even socialist labor competitions, meant to combine the thrill of a sporting event with feverish productive output (and often accomplishing neither), grew out of a genuine sense on the part of policymakers that these activities would make people *want* to be better workers; what kind of self-improvement could possibly be more worthwhile than that?[38]

In the United States, most public debates over leisure in recent years have targeted the content of popular entertainment. To a degree, criticism of violence in the media has been motivated by concerns over the possibility that watching violent behavior inspires violent behavior, especially by children. But beyond this, the concerns deal to a large degree with questions of values. After all, liberal groups have been more likely to criticize the macho fantasy films with largely white male audiences, especially those movies starring Sylvester Stallone or Arnold Schwarzenegger. Conservative groups, in contrast, have focused much of their ire on the ostensibly satanic lyrics of singer Mar-

36. Cecile Badenhorst and Charles Mather, "Tribal Recreation and Recreating Tribalism: Culture, Leisure, and Social Control on South Africa's Gold Mines, 1940–1950," *Journal of Southern African Studies* 23, 3 (September 1997): 473–89, at 485–88. The Chamber's advisors, however, also suggested showing films, especially westerns that demonstrated the importance of humans' taming of the natural world.

37. White, *De-Stalinization*, 31–68.

38. Padraic Kenney, "Remaking the Polish Working Class: Early Stalinist Models of Labor and Leisure," *Slavic Review* 53, 1 (spring 1994): 1–25.

ilyn Manson or the disconcertingly unpatriotic worldview expressed in gangster rap music.[39] This is more than mere propaganda about regime loyalty. From both sides, the argument about entertainment is an argument about what kind of people citizens are supposed to be and what leisure pursuits best exemplify this stance.

I offer this brief and necessarily incomplete discussion of leisure and politics in order to demonstrate that above and beyond the instrumental goals that political leaders might have for intervening in leisure, they are usually motivated as well by concerns over what different leisure and entertainment choices mean. A person's leisure choices tell us something about her as a person, perhaps in ways that she intends. A government that encourages citizens to attend or to perform in classical music concerts has a different view of their people than would a government that provides support to country-western or jazz music. Knowing, as we do, what some of the goals of Polish leisure policies were during the socialist era provides us with additional insight about the nature of postwar Polish national identity; the fact that these leisure policies are now unthinkable provides additional information on the changes in Polish citizenship since the collapse of that regime. Leisure choices can provide useful information about constructions of identity, and leisure policies are never free from governments' concerns about the kind of societies they want to lead, whether they are composed of readers, tourists, or video game players.

Japan in Comparison

Japan's stance on leisure policy is marked by two related differences from other advanced industrial nations. First is the durability of Japanese leisure policy institutions. As I will discuss in chapters 3 and 4, Japan's leisure policies can be traced to the late nineteenth century but are best understood in their present form as originating in the early 1970s, when they became a component of industrial policy. Although policymakers have made use of leisure policy primarily to solve specific problems at specific times (e.g., encouraging international tour-

---

39. For one instructive example, see Robert H. Bork's exegesis of the lyrics of Snoop Doggy Dogg's song "Horny": "The music is generally little more than noise with a beat, the singing is an unmelodic chant, the lyrics often range from the perverse to the mercifully unintelligible. It is difficult to convey just how debased rap is." From Robert H. Bork, *Slouching towards Gomorrah: Modern Liberalism and American Decline* (New York: HarperCollins, 1996), excerpted as "The Collapse of Popular Culture and the Case for Censorship," in *Mass Politics: The Politics of Popular Culture,* ed. Daniel M. Shea (New York: St. Martin's, 1999), 122–34, at 122.

ism in order to redistribute Japan's heavily criticized trade surplus in 1987), its place on the "map" of Japanese political options has enabled leaders to choose this option more often than leaders of other democracies have. In Japan, leisure policy is institutionalized, at least when compared to the other advanced industrial democracies. It is taken for granted as an area of administrative concern for the national government in a way that it is not elsewhere.

In other democracies, patterns of state intervention in leisure have shown remarkable variety (and not a little creativity), from morgue shows to the establishment of national parks. But the idea of "leisure policy" as a long-term, institutionalized prospect has in general found itself confronted by concerns over a properly limited role for the state. Proponents of leisure policy have thus generally been advocates of expanded social welfare, from the United Kingdom's Labour Party to West Germany's Willy Brandt. But wide distrust of state control on "private" activity, combined with only minimal interest from the labor unions that might otherwise be important allies of the social welfarists, have together meant that leisure has been an area of only sporadic and uninstitutionalized activity by democratic states. Despite Brandt's hopes, for example, the West German government dealt with public concerns about state control of leisure by shifting responsibility for actual legislation and implementation to local authorities. Even the Social Democrats neglected the extent to which the leisure industries in the service sector might contribute to growth until the late 1980s. Since the reunification of the East with the West, moreover, leisure policies have focused on the extension of leisure facilities and opportunities to those in the East. The discussion of leisure's importance in Germany notwithstanding, "no comprehensive approach to leisure policy has ever been developed."[40]

In Great Britain and the United States, conservative governments have cut national leisure programs and shifted them to the local level. As might be expected, Margaret Thatcher's administration provides the best example of the dim view a promarket government would take of the public management of leisure. In response to a House of Commons debate over whether the government should create a Ministry of Leisure, the Conservative spokesperson, John Page, remarked:

> The idea of a new Cabinet Minister and a Department of Leisure is totally unacceptable. . . . I believe that the Prime Minister would have nothing to do with a motion such as this. She believes in letting in the

40. Nahrstedt, "Leisure Policy in Germany," 145.

icy, gusty, lusty, thrusty winds of reality and competition to blow away
the sleep from people's eyes and the cobwebs from the machinery of
our industrial life.[41]

President Nixon's elimination of the Bureau of Outdoor Recreation
was based on a similar logic, and so, as in Britain, most government
recreational initiatives in the United States are handled by state and
local governments.[42]

In contrast, Japan's leisure policies have largely been the province of
economic bureaucrats seeking to integrate consumption of recreational services into plans for the nation's overall financial health.
Rather than finding conservative forces arrayed against the idea of state
interference in a private matter, the leisure policymakers have always
taken it as their duty to improve Japanese lifestyles while making them
serve larger national interests. This is a fundamentally different notion
of public and private than the classical liberalism espoused by John
Page. This is not because of a social welfarist bent or crypto-fascism in
Japanese politics; Japan is neither 1970s Sweden nor Nazi Germany. Instead, it reflects a desire to use noncoercive power to change people's
behavior in ways that might benefit political goals, while also making
the people happier, more whole, and, in a word, "normal."

I use "normal" here because it points to the second and, in many
ways, more instructive difference between Japan's leisure policies and
those of the other democracies. Like other governments, Japan's has
distinguished between "good" and "bad" leisure by making judgments
about what kind of people their citizens are supposed to be. In Japan's
case, however, the distinction rests on an international standard that
Japan is supposed to meet: the Japanese, as citizens of an advanced
industrial nation, should behave in ways that broadly resemble activities of citizens elsewhere. This impetus flies in the face of the often-
repeated assertion, particularly popular among Japanese leaders, that
the Japanese are culturally unique. Japanese leisure policies thus engage the most central and sensitive questions of whom the postwar
Japanese are and are not supposed to be.

41. Official Report of the House of Commons, 24 January 1980. Quoted in Ian P.
Henry, *The Politics of Leisure Policy* (Houndmills, U.K.: Macmillan, 1993), 38.
42. See, e.g., Rodney, *Administration of Public Recreation*; Martin H. Neumeyer
and Esther S. Neumeyer, *Leisure and Recreation: A Study of Leisure and Recreation
in their Sociological Aspects* (New York: Ronald Press, 1958).

Cultural Uniqueness and International Norms in Japanese National Identity

As many people, I could have something at stake in the claim that "the Japanese are unique," which is the hallmark of *nihonjinron*, or "theories of Japaneseness." After all, if the Japanese really are like no other countrymen—especially not Americans—it stands to reason that universities really need someone like me to divine what the otherwise inscrutable Japanese are up to. In fact, I reject the claim not because it is demonstrably untrue (I have no idea how one would demonstrate that it is right or wrong) but rather because it seems to me to be a political, not analytical, statement—one used to simplify Japan in order to praise or to condemn it. Many Japanese political leaders themselves have engaged in efforts to prove systematically and empirically that the Japanese are a people like no other. Definitely recognizing, and almost certainly believing himself in some of these cultural stereotypes, conservative Prime Minister Nakasone even created in 1987 Nichibunken (The International Center for Japanese Studies), a thinktank under the Ministry of Education. Employing some of the most renowned scholars of Japan's "special characteristics," this institute is well known as an environment for research on Japan's cultural uniqueness and its effect on social and political behavior.[43] The increasing dominance of these views in the 1970s and 1980s provoked a backlash, with some observers working to show that Japan's "uniqueness" is a "myth,"[44] and that Japan is not "uniquely unique."[45]

These theories have grown more because of political need than because of their intellectual value. After the nation's political unification under the Tokugawa military government in 1600, authorities decided to close Japan to foreign contact, immediately concerned about the possible influence of Christian missionaries and also with the threat of possible attacks by European armies. During this "closed" period (*sakoku*),[46] an intellectual tradition known as *koku-*

43. Chapter 5 discusses Nichibunken in more detail.
44. See Peter N. Dale, *The Myth of Japanese Uniqueness* (New York: St. Martin's, 1986), who blames Ruth Benedict's *The Chrysanthemum and the Sword: Patterns of Japanese Culture* (Tokyo: Tuttle, 1988) for much of the problem, especially on 30–31, 117–87.
45. Ross Mouer and Yoshio Sugimoto, *Images of Japanese Society: A Study in the Social Construction of Reality* (London: Kegan Paul, 1986), 11.
46. *Sakoku* was never quite complete, and certain ports were left open to trade with

gaku (national learning) developed, fueled by the political effort to separate the country from an earlier tradition of idolizing China. These theories emphasized the indigenous roots of Japanese culture and played down the influence of China.[47] After the forced opening of Japan in 1853 by American Commodore Perry, the new Meiji government struggled to create an idea of Japan as a real nation, or national family, headed by the emperor. The idea that Japan had a special *kokuminsei* (national character) proved to be a durable legacy of the work of intellectuals such as Fukuzawa Yukichi, who sought to imbue the new regime with as much legitimacy as possible, in what was a terribly uncertain period. Although scholars such as Nishi Amune were at the time trying to determine precisely what it was that made the Japanese "different," the logic had not yet become an enveloping theory of national culture.

According to the psychology scholar Minami Hiroshi, the defining feature of *nihonjinron* is their effort to explain why some national characteristics can found in Japan *and nowhere else.* Minami locates the real beginning of *nihonjinron* as Ariga Chōnan's 1888 book *Kokka Tetsuron* (Philosophical Discourses of the State). The differences between Japanese and Westerners (which was the operative concern) were seen not merely as being the outcome of a mystical, timeless character, nor as the simple result of relative backwardness. Instead, Japan's "lagging" individuality was a consequence of three hundred years of Tokugawa rule, in which the regime had used various forms of social and political control that had affected the structure of society. To Minami, this is what constitutes the beginning of *nihonjinron*, in that it was a genuine effort to explain in rational terms the development of a different kind of social system.[48]

What gives *nihonjinron* their popularity is, at least in part, their reliance on "scientific" ways of explaining why the Japanese are the way they are. Oguma Eiji's recent work on *nihonjinron* argues that they began to a significant degree not with Japanese intellectuals themselves

---

other Asian nations and with the Netherlands. Even so, the term is still used today to symbolize Japan's apparently closedness to foreign influence, and sociologist Mayumi Itoh refers to a "*sakoku* mentality" among Japanese bureaucrats. See Mayumi Itoh, *The Globalization of Japan: Japanese Sakoku Mentality and U.S. Efforts to Open Japan* (New York: St. Martin's, 1998).

47. See Tetsuo Najita, *Japan: The Intellectual Foundations of Modern Japanese Politics* (Chicago: University of Chicago Press, 1980).

48. This discussion is based largely on Minami Hiroshi, *Nihonjinron: Meiji kara Ima Made* (Nihonjinron: From the Meiji Era to the Present) (Tokyo: Iwanami, 1995), 15–43.

but rather with foreign scholars who traveled to Japan and attempted to capture *in scientific terms* the differences observed between Japan and their home countries. *Nihonjinron*, never particularly reliable to begin with because of their categorical definition of what is Japanese and what is not, became useful tools to political authorities. Descriptions and explanations of Japanese behavior would change over time in response to political agendas and perceived needs.[49] To give an example based on cases that appear later in this book, Japanese authorities complained to the International Labour Organization in 1919 that the nation needed long working hours because the Japanese were naturally unproductive and even somewhat lazy; by the 1970s and 1980s, however, Japanese authorities used nearly the opposite cultural arguments to explain why the nation should not alter its labor practices, because the Japanese are hard workers and essentially enjoy it. The idea that the Japanese are culturally unique remained, but the content of that uniqueness changed over time.

The idea that the Japanese are culturally unique is now taken for granted in ways that transcend mere politics. In her well-regarded ethnographic study of Tokyo, the Japanese-American scholar Dorinne Kondo writes eloquently of reactions to her position in Japan:

> Most Japanese people I knew seemed to adhere to an eminently biological definition of Japaneseness. Race, language, and culture are intertwined, so much so that any challenge to this firmly entrenched schema—a white person who speaks flawlessly idiomatic and unaccented Japanese, or a person of Japanese ancestry who cannot—meets with what generously could be described as unpleasant reactions.[50]

Even today, the idea that the Japanese are culturally unique (usually meaning collectivistic, motivated by relationships rather than rules, etc.) motivates the publication of new books and articles in Japan on what kind of people the Japanese really are.[51] Of course, the precise content of these stereotypes varies, and most analysts who use *ni-*

---

49. Oguma Eiji, *Tan'itsu Minzoku Shinwa no Kigen: 'Nihonjin' no Jigazō no Keifu* (The Myth of the Homogenous Nation: A Genealogy of the Meaning of Japaneseness) (Tokyo: Shin'yōsha, 1995). Although it might someday be matched by one of the new books appearing in English and Japanese on the issue of Japanese national identity, this excellent work ought to be the primary reference for any readers interested in the topic.

50. Dorinne Kondo, *Crafting Selves: Power, Gender, and Discourses of Identity in a Japanese Workplace* (Chicago: University of Chicago Press, 1990).

51. Soeda Yoshiya's *Nihon Bunka Shiron* (An Essay on Japanese Culture) (Tokyo: Shin'yōsha, 1993) is a good case in point. This work traces the development of theories

honjinron have slightly different takes on who the Japanese are. But the reference point for understanding uniqueness is a ubiquitous one, for Japanese and foreign users of *nihonjinron* alike. When people use different kinds of cultural explanations of Japanese behavior, they never compare Japan to, say, Peru or Uzbekistan, and only very rarely to China or Korea. Instead, Japan is collectivistic while America is "individualistic," or Japan is a "relation-based society" rather than a "rule-based society" like the countries of "the West."[52] In other words, the comparative standard against which Japanese distinctiveness can be measured and evaluated is "the West" and often the United States.[53]

This raises an interesting question. How can Japan's distinctiveness be fully acceptable if there is a norm from which it deviates? Since the 1970s, it has not been. In fact, in a series of policies issued since that time, the Japanese government has extolled "internationalization," or openness to foreign—usually Western—phenomena and usually in ways that would be seen as "normal" in the ostensibly cosmopolitan West. Chapter 6 will discuss some of these initiatives in more detail. This does not mean that *nihonjinron* are waning; in fact, these policies tend to build from the assumption that the Japanese are and should remain culturally unique in many ways.[54] But they illustrate one way in which issues of identity have crept into the very fabric of Japanese and social life, beyond obvious areas of concern such as immigration and citizenship policy. They reflect the acceptance of social and political standards drawn from the other advanced industrial na-

---

of Japanese culture, based largely on the durability of Benedict's book, but ultimately reflects on how Japan will somehow need to shift toward a more "individualistic" society, one based on "guilt" as much as "shame." See 377–81. For a more recent and fascinating example, see Machizawa Shizuo's comparison of the scandals of Bill Clinton and Osaka Mayor Yokoyama "Knock" as a way of understanding the differences between Americans and Japanese. In Kishida Shu and Machizawa Shizuo, *Naze Nihonjin wa Itsumo Fuan na no Ka* (Why Are Japanese Always Insecure?) (Tokyo: PHP, 2000), 154–58.

52. This latter characterization turns up unexpectedly but significantly in David L. McConnell's award-winning study of the JET Program, a program to bring English-speaking teachers to Japan. See *Importing Diversity: Inside Japan's JET Program* (Berkeley: University of California Press, 2000), especially 268–75.

53. Following the comparative literature scholar Sakai Naoki, Tessa Morris-Suzuki makes this point in her excellent *Re-Inventing Japan: Time, Space, Nation* (Armonk, N.Y.: M. E. Sharpe, 1998), 154.

54. In a brief but commanding study of *nihonjinron*, Aoki Tamotsu argues that internationalization is a crucial reflection of the belief among policymakers that the Japanese are unique. See Aoki Tamotsu, *'Nihon Bunkaron' no Hen'yō* (The Transformation of Theories of Japanese Culture) (Tokyo: Chūō Kōronsha, 1990), 156–72.

tions and used as ways of redefining what the Japanese are doing right and what they are doing wrong.

What Leisure Policy Means For Japan

The Japanese government, then, walks a tightrope between emphasizing the uniqueness of the Japanese and encouraging them to be more "normal." Why get involved in leisure at all? The remainder of this book explores how leisure became a public and political phenomenon in Japan and argues that there have been important motives and incentives for officials to get involved in leisure: to develop the economy, to build broad public support for other programs, and to capitulate to heavy pressure from abroad regarding Japan's trade surpluses. The leisure policies themselves, as well as the policy processes involved, reflect, however, that Japanese officials are themselves trapped in conceptual cages from which they cannot escape. They *know*, because they take it for granted, that Japan is supposed to be an advanced industrial nation, and therefore the Japanese should behave like citizens of other nations. They also *know*, because they take it for granted, that the Japanese are unique, and that the uniqueness should be valued and protected.

And so the remainder of this book provides an empirical investigation of the broad transformations in Japanese lifestyle over the past century, focusing especially on the state's role in trying to effect major shifts. There are differences, of course, in the political motivations for early-twentieth-century tourism policy, the 1970s efforts to shift toward "greener" service industries such as leisure, and former Prime Minister Miyazawa's 1991 declaration that Japan should aspire to become a "lifestyle superpower." Yet the consistent motif has been an acceptance that the West is somehow ahead of Japan in leisure and lifestyles and that Japan needs to catch up if it is to show progress, tempered with the knowledge that the Japanese are different. The goal recently has been to create a *yutori no aru shakai* (which we once again, following Gavan McCormack, define as "a society that gives me the space to do my own thing"). It would be better still if Japanese people's "own thing" were to resemble those of Westerners while still maintaining some clear and undeniable marks of "Japaneseness" and difference. *That* would be progress.

The cover of an 1897 map by Japan's Welcome Society for foreign tourists. Photo by permission of the Harvard-Yenching Library.

Prewar Leisure and Tourism as "Politics by Other Means"

When rebellious samurai from the Satsuma and Choshu provinces of Japan defeated the waning Tokugawa shogunate and in 1868 "restored" the emperor as the official center of Japanese authority, they instigated one of the most dramatic and rapid national transformations ever witnessed. In their efforts to ward off the threat of colonization by Western powers hungry for empires, they established a modern state that bore almost no formal resemblance to anything Japan had yet experienced. In addition, they promoted industrial growth at an astonishing pace. Perhaps most reflective of state goals, Japanese military forces developed so rapidly that within forty years of the Meiji Restoration, Japan would be able to defeat Russia in naval warfare. A great number of government initiatives aimed precisely at this kind of military development; in a period of revolutionary insecurity, the early Meiji samurai had erected a government system designed in part to protect over the long term their goal of national strength and defense.[1] But the political, social, and cultural epiphenomena of this

1. On the establishment of the Japanese bureaucracy and the goals of Meiji samurai, see Bernard Silberman, *Cages of Reason: The Rise of the Rational State in France, Japan, the United States, and Great Britain* (Chicago: University of Chicago Press, 1994).

drive fall far beyond the simple establishment of Japan as a "rich nation with a strong army."[2]

Improving the leisure lives of Japanese was hardly an important consideration for political elites between the late nineteenth century and the beginning of World War II. I will argue, however, that the prewar period is crucial for understanding Japan's later leisure policies, because the era witnessed the creation of government organizations for the management and use of recreation and leisure travel. Additionally, largely for economic reasons, the Japanese government began to use the countries of Europe and North America as the appropriate reference points for understanding how Japan's leisure and tourism industries should develop. Because of tumultuous upheavals in Japanese politics in the first half of the twentieth century, these efforts were not fully institutionalized, in that they were heavily contested and not taken for granted. But they did leave in their wake a framework that would enable postwar leisure and recreation initiatives designed to further state goals.

Conflicts over Leisure in the Late Nineteenth and Early Twentieth Centuries

Political control over leisure in pre-nineteenth-century Japan often meant little more than the ringing of bells by feudal authorities to tell the peasants when to begin and when to end work. The actual use of leisure time was of considerably less importance than the management of time itself.[3] Few data exist regarding the actual consumption of leisure products before the twentieth century, with household accounts—the standard source for Japanese historians dealing with the daily lives of Japanese citizens, at least the middle class, in the late nineteenth and early twentieth centuries—including no special categories for *yoka, goraku,* or the phoneticized English word *rejā* (leisure) for evaluation. There are figures for *kōsai,* or "associating with others," though this is an imprecise fit.[4]

---

2. *Fukoku kyōhei* (rich nation, strong army) was one of the main rallying cries of Meiji elites. Richard Samuels recently used it as the title of his book *"Rich Nation, Strong Army": National Security and the Technological Transformation of Japan* (Ithaca: Cornell University Press, 1996), which examines the intellectual and institutional legacies of "technonationalism" among Japanese political and military elites.

3. Maki Yūsuke, *Jikan no Hikaku Shakaigaku* (The Comparative Sociology of Time) (Tokyo: Iwanami, 1995), especially 116–29.

4. There are a number of Japanese language materials that analyze household ac-

By the late nineteenth century, however, the government would be hotly debating the issue of leisure, in general arguing forcefully that people should not be entitled to much of it. Fortunately, the ostensible demands of cultural uniqueness and the needs of industry seemed conveniently aligned. The government weighed in repeatedly on traditional "Japanese values" to make the case that the country's citizens should be worked as hard as possible. Although the late-twentieth-century tendency to claim that the Japanese are "workaholics" has hardly been limited to foreign observers,[5] the Japanese political view of Japanese workers in the prewar period was that they were naturally lazy and indolent, a view shared by Western visitors during the Meiji Era. Indeed, one European missionary visiting in Japan in the late nineteenth century wrote of the Japanese worker, "His impulsive, restless, easily distracted manner tempts him to inconsistency, superficiality, and therefore to unreliability. We search in vain for a quiet, coordinated procedure, for constancy and continuity. The Japanese goes to work very quickly but soon loses interest."[6] Another added, "Until now, constant work has hardly been known in Japan. This seems to be the main reason, acknowledged by all foreigners, that Japanese workers achieve relatively little, because all work advances only very slowly."[7]

Japanese managers and policymakers would take advantage of the stereotype. Meiji intellectuals argued against the importation of "Western" standards for work and leisure, with one of the most famous, Fukuzawa Yukichi, stating that such reform would cramp the tradi-

---

counts from the late nineteenth century into the twentieth century as a marker for lifestyle change. Indeed, the categories used within the accounts are frequently more interesting than the data contained within the records. Among the more recent examples is Nakamura Takafusa, ed., *Kakeibo kara Mita Kindai Nihon Seikatsushi* (The History of Modern Japanese Lifestyles as Seen through Household Accounts) (Tokyo: University of Tokyo Press, 1993). This book's chapters focus on single households, which are chosen as emblematic of an era or class, and the writers ultimately use anecdotal evidence to provide a "slice of life" in a given setting.

5. For one example of the "Japan as workaholic" logic, see Sampei Koseki, "Japan: Homo Ludens Japonicus," in *Leisure and Life-Style: A Comparative Analysis of Free Time*, ed. Anna Olszewska and K. Roberts (London: Sage, 1990), 115–42.

6. Statement by Carl Munzinger cited in Adolf Freitag, *Die Japaner im Urteil der Meiji-Deutschen*, Mitteilungen der deutschen Gesellschaft für Natur and Völkerkunde Ostasiens, vol. 31/C (Tokyo: OAG, 1939). This citation (and English translation from the German) is found in Sepp Linhart, "From Industrial to Postindustrial Society: Changes in Japanese Leisure-Related Values and Behavior," *Journal of Japanese Studies* 14, 2 (summer 1988): 271–307, at 271.

7. Comment by economist Karl Rathgen, cited ibid., 271.

tional and beneficial relationship between employer and laborer. According to Kyoko Sheridan, Fukuzawa opposed the introduction of such labor legislation to provide more leisure time to workers largely on the grounds that it would be inflexible, would limit the opportunities for workers, and would violate Japanese industrial traditions.[8] When the International Labour Office (ILO) proposed in 1919 that member nations stipulate a 48-hour workweek, the Japanese delegate responded that the Japanese worker "is not accustomed to educating himself or to devoting himself to sports and play. Therefore, the time gained by reducing working time would not be used by workers and would have bad consequences. . . . For us Japanese ten or twelve hours a day is by no means an excessively long working time." Sepp Linhart notes that in spite of this response, Japanese working hours did in fact drop in the following years.[9]

The most widely known effort to grasp the essentials of leisure behavior from the era is *Yoka Seikatsu no Kenkyū* (Research on Leisure Lifestyles), a study published by the Osaka city government in 1923. The written text of the report demonstrates clearly its role as part of a broad follow-up to Japan's uneasy response to the ILO over the issue of working hours. It reminds readers, for example, that Japan had adopted a series of institutions from the West in rapid succession, including the creation of weekly vacation days, and that there were still lingering questions over what kind of responsibilities Japan should face as a late developer in terms of concessions to workers.[10] What helps to distinguish this early effort of the Osaka city government is not merely the comprehensiveness of the research, though it is impressive, but also its *mondai ishiki*, or its understanding of the issues to be addressed. Rather than merely finding out what people were doing for fun, this report actually followed some of the oddly utopian logic about leisure evident in the ILO's reports of the era. As Ujihara Shōjirō notes, the feeling seemed to be that increased leisure time and behavior would "unleash creative energy" and would promote a more "civilized" populace.[11] This does not mean that state authorities im-

---

8. Kyoko Sheridan, *Governing the Japanese Economy* (Cambridge, U.K.: Polity, 1993), 96–97.

9. Linhart, "From Industrial to Postindustrial Society," 279. For statistical tables on the history of working hours in Japan, see the National Institute of Research Advancement (NIRA), *Seikatsu Suijun no Rekishiteki Suii* (Historical Progress in Lifestyle Standards) (Tokyo: NIRA, 1985).

10. *Yoka Seikatsu no Kenkyū* (Research on Leisure Lifestyles), with an introduction and "interpretive essay" by Ujihara Shōjiro (Tokyo: Kōseitan, 1923, 1970).

11. Ujihara Shōjirō, "Kaisetsu: Dai-ichiji Taisengo no Rōdō Chōsa to *Yoka*

mediately embraced the value. Indeed, government leaders (including many of the Osaka municipal authorities not associated directly with this research project) and industrialists remained staunchly opposed to efforts to limit working hours or to constrain their abilities to extract labor from Japan's working population. And the Great Kantō Earthquake of 1923 brought so many other serious problems to Japan that the attention of leaders remained focused on topics somewhat hotter and more immediately troublesome than whether or not a certain neighborhood needed another park. The existence of *Yoka Seikatsu no Kenkyū* suggests, however, that even in some public documents at the time, leisure gained some purchase as a keyword in understanding how normal, modern societies were supposed to operate.

Another report from this era shows that the national government too was beginning to consider how leisure space might best be integrated into a modern city. In 1902, Ebenezer Howard published his classic work on the development of cities,[12] a work that argued for more planning in cities to take into account and to provide for the lifestyle and health needs of its citizens. Perhaps its influence in Japan need not be taken as striking or peculiar, but its selection by the Regions Bureau of the powerful Ministry of Home Affairs (MHA) as the foundation of a 1907 report entitled *Den'en Toshi* (Garden Cities) suggests the extent to which the Meiji state planners and political authorities of the era used the West as a model—even in some unexpected ways—for generating ideas about what they should do to make Japan a more manageable, normal society. The incorporation of the leisure lifestyle suggestions in Howard's book into the new MHA conception suggests that these ideas had begun to take on an important role for bureaucrats in determining what Japanese society was supposed to look like as it became modern.[13]

Leisure development in Osaka illustrates the utility of Western models for entrepreneurs as well as the threat these entrepreneurs posed to practitioners of traditional Japanese entertainment forms.[14] The Japanese government and local authorities were not the first or even the most important figures in the development of leisure in early-

Seikatsu no Kenkyū" (Introduction: *Yoka Seikatsu no Kenkyū* and Studies of Labor after World War I), in *Yoka Seikatsu no Kenkyū*, especially 80–87.

12. Ebenezer Howard's famous 1902 work is reprinted in *Garden Cities of To-Morrow*, ed. and with a preface by F. J. Osborn (Cambridge: MIT Press, 1970).

13. Takemura Tamio, *Shōraku no Keifu—Toshi to Yoka Bunka* (The Genealogy of Fun: The City and the Culture of Leisure) (Tokyo: Dōbunkan, 1996).

14. The following discussion draws heavily on Takemura, *Shōraku no Keifu*, especially 171–207.

twentieth-century Japan. Private entrepreneurs began to take advantage of the rapid development of Japan's cities by offering expanded leisure services and large-scale amusement parks. But Japan, with its traditional forms of entertainment such as *rakugo* (comic storytelling) and *bunraku* (puppet theater) did not offer immediate ideas to industrialists trying to attract growing masses into large arenas and take advantage of economies of scale to increase revenues rapidly. Founded in 1901 by thirteen wealthy financiers including Itō Kijūrō, Iwamoto Einosuke, Obayashi Yoshigorō, Nōmura Tokuschichi, Fujimoto Kiyobe, and Kobayashi Kazumi,[15] one company, the Osaka Land Development Corporation (Osaka Tochi Kembutsu Kabushiki Kaisha) began its plans for mass leisure development with its initial financial base of three million yen. Settling on the establishment of an amusement park, the group used Coney Island as the model and developed Lunar Park, which opened in 1912. Although before this time, Osaka had *yūenchi* (broadly meaning "amusement parks" but perhaps more akin to state fairs in the American example), it had never had something approaching the grand scale of Lunar Park.

Even traditional performers were forced to conform to the new market logic available in mass leisure. Another company, Yoshimoto Development, established what was virtually a chain of entertainment facilities, even offering *rakugo* performances at discount prices in order to lure customers. This strategy proved more successful for Yoshimoto than for the comic storytellers; by 1930, the storytellers had become so overwhelmed by the competition from music halls, movie theaters, amusement parks, and other new forms of entertainment that they formed the Goraku Preservation Society in order to protect their craft (and their livelihoods) from the encroachment of new and, significantly, foreign leisure practices. Yoshimoto Development, meanwhile, rapidly became one of the premier leisure spot owners in Japan and survives today as an entertainment firm.

The tension between traditional leisure and sports on the one hand and foreign-influenced forms of play on the other became a matter of concern to national policymakers as well.[16] For example, the Ministry

15. In conveying these names in English, I am using my best guess regarding the proper readings of the characters involved. I have consulted with Japanese as well, but the multiple readings available to each *kanji*, particularly where names are concerned, make it difficult to be absolutely certain how the *kanji* in these names were read. In any case, the family names of all people discussed in this chapter are reasonably clear, and should provide the first step to anyone interested in pursuing future research.

16. The relationship between sports and leisure is tricky, especially as states have

of Education had initially raised concerns about the invasion of base-ball into Japan; the sport gained rapid popularity in the early years of the twentieth century, particularly with the famous rivalry of the Waseda and Keio Universities' baseball teams. And when high school and junior high school students began to play the sport more avidly, some of Japan's leading newspapers became involved in the debate. Al-though it was careful not to attack baseball as being an American sport, in August and September, 1911, the *Tokyo Asahi Shimbun* ran a story series entitled "Yakyū Sono Gaidoku" (The Evil Effects of Base-ball), based in large part on the results of a survey questionnaire dis-tributed by the Ministry of Education. Baseball, it was argued, had four principal vices: it consumed time that could be better put to use for studies; it resulted in severe fatigue among the players and prevented them from studying and pursuing other activities; its games were fre-quently followed by parties and dinners where the players (even the students) would drink alcohol; its play, such as pitching and hitting, relied on "unnatural" motions or activities. While in fact all four of these are arguably true (a glance at American baseball stars in the early twenty-first century would have been unlikely to dissuade the Min-istry of Education [MOE] and the newspaper critics), perhaps the more damning element came from the fact that baseball was identifiably an American pastime.

The financial success, however, of baseball tournaments between Japanese junior high school and high school teams convinced the MOE that it should be more open-minded. By the mid-1920s, it was coop-erating with the Ministry of Home Affairs in helping to sponsor an an-nual sports tournament, the centerpiece of which was the youth baseball contest.[17] Rather than denigrating baseball's tendency to pro-duce uneducated, fatigued alcoholics with misshapen bodies, the bu-reaucrats in both ministries chose to turn the sport to national advantage by emphasizing two more laudable features: teams that

---

used national teams and regulated sports leagues in accordance with political goals in ways that often have little to do with broader orientations toward leisure policies. I draw the link here because of the Japanese government's effort first to discourage, and then to encourage, a certain kind of recreational practice (playing and/or watch-ing sports), tying into it national myths in order to justify the different stances. For another perspective on sports as an element of leisure in Japan, see T. J. Pempel, "Con-temporary Japanese Athletics: Window on the Cultural Roots of Nationalism-Inter-nationalism," in *The Culture of Japan as Seen through Its Leisure,* ed. Sepp Linhart and Sabine Frühstück (Albany: State University of New York Press, 1998), 113–38.

17. Takemura, *Shōraku no Keifu,* 217–35.

fought together for a common goal, and a spirit of self-sacrifice and purity that derived specifically from being an amateur sport.

The point here is not that there was a consistent goal or purpose to these leisure-related policies; in fact, they were contradictory and meandering, even over narrow issues such as baseball as a sport. But at no time did the Japanese government bracket off leisure as a "private" issue, or one that ought to be off-limits to state intervention. Moreover, whatever goals policymakers had with regard to leisure, early documents show a preoccupation with the *meaning* of leisure: what kind of recreation would be good for Japanese, and whether leisure ought to be modern (i.e., Western) or traditional. Only in the area of tourism, however, would the government find a temporarily stable mix. Because of the economic potential of tourism, the Japanese government would simultaneously laud Japan's cultural uniqueness while pushing for the creation of a "modern" travel infrastructure. This push would have important consequences for Japanese travel patterns, as well as for the long-term place of the Japanese state in citizens' recreational options.

Pre-Meiji Travel and Leisure

As elsewhere, recreational travel in early Japan was traditionally a pursuit only for the wealthy. The *Man'yōshū* (a famous collection of eighth-century poetry, and one of the earliest existing examples of Japanese literature) refers to travel by using the word *tabi* (trip) but suggests that its practice was only for the nobility, who typically took short tours within Japan. During the Nara Era (710–784 A.D.), international transportation routes did exist in limited form between Japan, China, and Korea, and a place of lodging called the Kyoto *korokan* served the needs of visitors from overseas, although these routes probably favored the movement of merchants rather than nobility. And there appears to have been a center for dealing with the remains from shipwrecks, or something resembling a tourism site in Settsu, an ancient area located roughly in what is now Hyogo Prefecture. Trips by nobility to visit these areas, however, were neither common nor particularly safe. Throughout the period, the traveler risked his or her (but almost always his) life by riding through battlefields in the ongoing wars between Japan's local warlords. Typically, neutral armies had to accompany any traveling nobility in order to present a reasonable deterrent to attack.

Roads improved somewhat during the Kamakura Era (1185–1333), and Japan's palanquin system also became somewhat more advanced, which made it easier for nobility to move around, though probably did little to make the journeys safer. Indeed, perhaps the biggest advances for Japan's practice of travel—or at least that not linked explicitly to commercial or political purposes—came during the Muromachi Era (1338–1573), when the Shintō faith and worship of the Ise shrine grew to new proportions and importance. This era thus witnessed a change toward a broad acceptance of a religious value for pilgrimage, an early form of travel that has undoubtedly helped to shape the way that people around the world feel about the need (or lack thereof) to travel.[18]

This trend became more marked in the Tokugawa Period, starting in 1603. The Tokugawa *bakufu* (shogunate) not only worked to establish a genuine national road system but also to maintain control over the five national highways. Travelers had to pay for the use of such roads, and feudal authorities often tried to prohibit travel by peasants, even for religious pilgrimages. Even so, many peasants did take long journeys to the Ise Shrine, and regional political authorities generally loosened the restrictions on travel, sensing that they were ineffective and also fearing that they could become grounds for potential unrest. These pilgrimages were hardly grim affairs to see a holy site, to reflect, and then to return wiser and more pure; the *daimyō's* (feudal lords') discouragement of purely recreational travel meant in principle that any efforts to have fun had to be tied to the pilgrimage. While it would be misleading to suggest that no travelers were interested in Ise, the length of typical journeys and contemporary documentary evidence suggest that the travelers availed themselves of the "attractions" that had begun to pop up along the national routes toward the holy land. Among these were hotels, theaters, and, perhaps most important of all, brothels. Travel guides actually led the pilgrims to the proper sites, and the groups generally followed more or less fixed itineraries regarding stops at the shrine, at nearby castles, and at stalls that were surely the precursors to today's souvenir stands. Indeed, travel became so common by the early nineteenth century that regional travel guilds began to sell memberships, with which people could stay at a number of lodging sights within a given area. These guilds also produced guidebooks that enabled travelers to plan their trips in advance.[19]

Japan's religious institutions, principally its Buddhist temples, soon

18. Suetake Naoyoshi, *Kankō Jigyōron* (The Tourism Industry) (Tokyo: Hōken Bunkashō, 1984).

19. Constantine Vaporis, "The Early Modern Origins of Japanese Tourism," *Senri Ethnological Studies* 38 (1993): 25–36.

came to depend on the travelers. While regional authorities continued to fret over the disappearance of a few peasants from their farms every year (as well as the money that the peasants would be spending within the domain but were instead spending elsewhere), religious figures would capitalize on the growing interest in religious pilgrimages. As Tokugawa authorities attempted to tighten control over the temples by squeezing their funds, the temples needed to find other potential sources of revenue in order to pay for repairs and other needs. They struck on the idea of using *kaichō*, or the opening of a temple sanctuary for outsiders to see Buddhist texts and the like. Although the *kaichō* were not new phenomena (their history dates at least to the Heian Period, centuries earlier), the number of such *kaichō* appears to have exploded at this time, with over 1,500 taking place in Edo, Kyoto, Osaka, and some outlying districts as well between the mid-eighteenth and mid-nineteenth centuries, most of them in order to pay for repairs. Perhaps half of the *kaichō* were *degaichō*, or special openings in which the entire area around a given temple would be transformed into something akin to a carnival, featuring not only the usual vendors of food and souvenirs but even such attractions as freak shows.[20]

We cannot be certain what percentage of people living in Tokugawa Japan took advantage of the growing travel infrastructure, though it was surely a small minority. In an examination of the development of travel-related regulations and of infrastructure in pre-Meiji Japan, however, two trends stand out. First, regional authorities generally discouraged travel, seeing it as economically costly and thereby threatening to their coffers. They reluctantly accepted such travel, however, provided that it was linked to pilgrimages. Second, by the early nineteenth century there can be no doubt that travel itself had become commodified. Certain businesses existed solely because of the traffic of people visiting shrines or temples, or merely heading out on business. Similarly, the links between different types of travel-dependent enterprises deepened, with regional guilds controlling information about relatively distant lodging, religious figures acting as guides to local attractions, and merchants and others becoming more dependent on temples for *kaichō* or other events capable of convincing even those from far off that the trip was worth the cost and trouble involved. These two trends—political tolerance and limited commercialization—do not mean that pre-nineteenth-century Japan had a functioning tourism industry. Even with a few set schedules and some

20. Ishimori Shuzo, "Tourism and Religion: From the Perspective of Comparative Civilization," *Senri Ethnological Studies* 38 (1995): 11–24.

established sites of lodging, food, drink, and entertainment, irregularities in the flows of travelers as well as heavy burdens on visitors (in terms of departure permits, transportation costs, and the typically long duration of such trips) prevented the travel market from moving out of a relatively nascent stage of development. This shift toward a greater systemization of travel—toward something that could be called an industry—would happen only with the arrival of Westerners, fueled by the expansion of steamship and rail routes, and the creation of a modern state under Meiji authorities.

Foreigners, Hotels, and Japanese Tourism

Because authorities had been reluctant to recognize leisure travel as a legitimate pastime for any but a few members of the nobility, there had been no reason to expand Japan's (rather extensive) network of inns and boarding houses into anything resembling lodging-cum-leisure spots. Armed not only with guns but also money, however, foreigners and their increasing numbers meant that clever entrepreneurs could make a fast profit and that the industries created for foreigners would ultimately reshape understandings about how modern citizens were to spend their time.

Between the arrival of Perry and the beginning of the Meiji Restoration (1868), so few visitors arrived that efforts to create lodgings for them remained few and far between, especially given the fact that political authorities generally had more pressing concerns than the creation of luxury accommodations for the foreigners. One early effort to create a *hoterukan*[21] collapsed when the Tokugawa shogunate tried to contract for the creation of a hotel in Edo but was forced to pull out in 1867 as the *bakufu* crumbled. One British diplomat of the period lamented the apparent unwillingness of political leaders to provide for hotel construction, also remarking that while many of the visiting Westerners deplored the conditions of Japan's lodgings, they were generally unwilling to do anything about the problem themselves.[22]

This was not entirely correct. Because of inexperience in the con-

---

21. A traditional inn in Japan is known as a *ryokan*, combining the characters for trip (*tabi* or *ryo*, the same character that appeared in the *Man'yōshū*) with *kan*, meaning place or center. By replacing *ryo* with *hoteru*, or the rendering of "hotel" in the syllabary used primarily for foreign words, *katakana*, early writers created the term *hoterukan*. This has since been replaced by *hoteru*, which remains the standard term for hotel.

22. Kimura Gorō, *Nihon no Hoteru Sangyōshi* (History of the Japanese Hotel Industry) (Tokyo: Kindai Bungeisha, 1994), 25.

struction of hotels, Japanese entrepreneurs appear to have been reluctant to invest in major hospitality projects without first getting a sense of what the foreign guests would actually want. But with rapidly increasing numbers of foreign visitors and longer-term residents such as diplomats, it was perhaps only natural that a few of the travelers would become involved in the planning and creation of lodging, at least of spots capable of making them feel that they were either at home or, as a close second, in a colony. Although it is perhaps a bit imprecise to refer to it as a hotel, the first such spot in Japan appears to have been the Yokohama Club House, opened in 1869 by W. H. Smith of Great Britain. Largely serving the foreign community as a bar and restaurant, and primarily limited to club members, the Yokohama Club House was a social organization more than a hotel, at least at its inception. Its rapid burst of popularity among foreigners, however, ensured that the Club House also provided hotel services for several years.[23]

Between the 1870s and the 1920s, the nascent Japanese hotel and travel industry began to flourish. The establishment of reliable rail routes, designed originally more for business and freight travel than for leisure and tourism, throughout the period essentially created a network by which travelers could more easily plan their tours and their activities. Although the spectacular development of railroads began in Japan thirty years after it had in Europe (primarily Great Britain) and North America, its pace and effects were comparable. Japan, which was without any railroads at the beginning of the Meiji Restoration, soon had a publicly funded train route between Tokyo and Yokohama (1872). It would also have a "private" railroad firm (Nihon Tetsudō Kaisha, or Japan Railways Company, which received public support and was clearly linked with the bureaucracy), new train routes following the old Tōkaidō passage (1887), and, with a mind toward making the travel experience somewhat more entertaining, meal services on board by 1899.[24] Indeed, the development of train systems linking cities with outlying areas was the technological backbone of the noted Ministry of Home Affairs' plan to create "garden cities" (Den'en toshi), based on Howard's conception.[25]

23. Muraoka Minoru, Nihon no Hoteru Shōshi (A Short History of Japanese Hotels) (Tokyo: Chūō Shinshō, 1981), 16–20.

24. JTB, Nihon Kōtsū Kōsha no Nanajunenshi (The Seventy-Year History of the Japan Travel Bureau) (Tokyo: JTB, 1982), special appendix, 2.

25. Takemura, Shōraku no Keifu, 115–54.

Foreign tourists soon began to visit Japan in greater numbers. Although there are no reliable figures on incoming tourists for most of the Meiji Era, the Ministry of Foreign Affairs began to collect data more assiduously starting in 1910, when 15,650 visitors arrived. Their numbers increased fairly steadily for much of the next twenty years, and in fact the prewar arrival rate reached a peak in 1940, just before the American entry in World War II.[26] While there is no breakdown on nationality or on activities while in Japan, it appears that at least through the 1920s many of these visitors were from the western European countries, especially Great Britain, and from the United States, though the single largest group was from China. On occasion hundreds would arrive at once, on cruise ship tours organized by firms such as Thomas Cook, generally staying in the country for a period of roughly ten days to two weeks and visiting a number of cities, including Kyoto, Osaka, Nara, Tokyo, and Yokohama.[27] By 1930, there were fifty-three hotels in Japan that hosted one hundred or more foreigners a year apiece.[28]

As a consequence, the style of Japan's lodgings began to change rapidly. Not only were city hotels beginning to establish roots, but Japanese entrepreneurs started to modify in scope and style existing facilities in order to make them more acceptable to foreign guests and to take advantage of the new routes of transport. Of course, other than the fact that they were called *hoteru*, it can be a bit difficult to discern precisely what would be called "Western" and what would be called "Japanese." At a minimum, hotels could probably have been distinguished from *ryokan* by the use of rugs, carpets, and wood floors rather than *tatami* (traditional straw mats), Western-style furniture such as beds rather than *futon*, and the availability of European cuisine. Whereas the early days of the Meiji Era had witnessed the sporadic construction of Western-style hotels in the foreigners' quarter in Yokohama and the occasional resort cottage or spa in Nikko, between 1890 and 1930, new hotels appeared all over the country. Nagasaki alone had fifteen more hotels in 1903 than it had had in 1895, all of them with Western names (among them the Central Hotel and the rather unfortunately named Hotel de Colonie). Records also indicate

---

26. JNTO, *Kokusai Kankō Shinkōkai 20-nen no Ayumi* (The Twenty-Year Path of the Japan National Tourist Organization) (Tokyo: Kokusai Kankō Shinkōkai, 1985), 70.

27. JTB, *Nihon Kōtsū Kōsha*, 22–25.

28. Kimura, *Nihon no Hoteru Sangyōshi*, 259.

the construction of perhaps two dozen "resort hotels" around the country between 1890 and 1910, in places as far from Yokohama and Tokyo as Beppu and Shizuoka.[29] Furthermore, once established, hotels often had to deal with dramatically increasing numbers of guests. One famous resort hotel, the Fujiya Hotel, for example, saw its number of annual guests jump from roughly twelve thousand in the late 1890s to over nineteen thousand by 1915. These numbers, of course, meant that foreigners were not the only ones taking advantage of the accommodations. Indeed, by 1930, one government study revealed that no more than half of the hotel customers in Japan were foreign and that the rate of increase among Japanese tourists was greater than that among foreigners.[30]

This had two obvious ramifications. First, hotel owners could not ignore the needs of Japanese guests, without whom their occupancy rates would have fallen to dangerously low levels. Second, as more Japanese became accustomed to hotels, and as many of them began to enjoy them more than *ryokan*, the understanding of lodging during a leisure stay began to change. The hotel became the new standard for accommodations, and visitors expected private rooms, beds, and a choice of meals when they traveled. Much like the development of mass leisure and its effects on traditional forms of entertainment, the rapid spread of hotels meant not only that *ryokan* owners faced new competition but also that Japanese recreational travel itself changed. And especially after 1910, the Japanese state would become decidedly more active in shaping what a tourist or travel experience was supposed to be.

The Distinctive Nature of Japan's Prewar Tourism Policy

The state role adopted in Japan would be both innovative and anomalous. When mass international tourism became a reality in the early nineteenth century (particularly with the creation of the "package tour" and its successful marketing by Thomas Cook, the most famous of several entrepreneurial pioneers), travel was not governed by genuine policies. Even for international travel, people generally were not required to carry passports, and crossed national boundaries fairly easily. An almost completely private enterprise, the European tourist industry relied on the ingenuity of travel agents in scouting out par-

29. Muraoka, *Nihon no Hoteru Shōshi*, 134–38.
30. Ibid., 54, 259.

ticular tourist destinations, seeking appropriate lodging and transportation routes for travelers, and, most important, trying to arrange sightseeing expeditions that effectively blended a sense of the foreign and the different with the familiar and the comfortable. In the early days of the European Grand Tour, the government role was largely symbolic. British ambassadors, for example, would greet British tourists who traveled abroad.[31]

Although tourism was riven with class differences, even by the middle of the nineteenth century, middle-class citizens of England were able to travel to Scotland, France, or even to Italy for a holiday.[32] Even so, the numbers of tourists were usually so small as to make the creation of national tourist offices somewhat beside the point. Regional tourist boards occasionally operated, but for the most part, the early twentieth century witnessed little governmental effort in the area of tourism promotion, at least among the states of Europe and North America,[33] until the aftermath of World War I. In fact, after 1919, European states from England to Germany began to provide support, normally, for tourism business associations seeking to attract foreign tourists. In addition, some began to pump money into the hotel industry, but the goal of this appears to have been business support rather than national strategy.[34]

The Japanese government's role differed in three fundamental respects from those of the national tourist organizations in Europe and North America. First, while other governments engaged in promotion and financial assistance to the industry, starting in 1915 Japanese government offices actually began to take the role of the country's main travel agency, selling tours and creating links between service providers that were generally considered to be the role of private industry elsewhere. Second, its goals originated with the needs of foreign travelers, but the activities of various offices within the Ministry of Railroads soon ensured that the kind of tours it created, marketed, and guided became dominant among Japanese tourists as well. Third, and

31. John Towner, *An Historical Geography of Recreation and Tourism in the Western World, 1540–1940* (London: Wiley & Sons, 1996), 135.

32. For an overview of the development of the industry, see Lynne Withey, *Grand Tours and Cook's Tours: A History of Leisure Travel, 1750 to 1915* (New York: William Morrow, 1997).

33. See, e.g., Allan M. Williams and Gareth Shaw, eds., *Tourism and Economic Development: Western European Experiences*, 2d ed. (Chichester, U.K.: Wiley & Sons, 1995).

34. Kimura, *Nihon no Hoteru Sangyōshi*, 224–27, 230–33.

as a consequence of the other two, the rational privileging of "foreign" or "Western" notions of tourism (bearing in mind that the first and foremost priority was that attraction of foreign currency) and their reproduction within Japan meant that for the rapidly developing Japanese tourist market, the whole idea of tourism, travel, types of service, and types of attractions were, from an early date in the twentieth century, based on a Western norm.

And so, even in the absence of a Japanese Thomas Cook, Japan had developed into a major tourist destination by the early twentieth century, so much so that tourism receipts were in fact of critical importance to its foreign exchange holdings before World War II. And in the process of becoming such a destination—hoping to lure wealthy Americans and Europeans to spend their dollars, pounds sterling, and other currency in Japan—the country embarked on a number of projects that would help to determine how the state would interact with the society over the issue of leisure time into the late twentieth century. It did so in two ways. Led by the Japan Tourist Bureau in the Ministry of Railroads, the prewar predecessor of the Ministry of Transport, the Japanese government first began to determine which tourist sites and facilities were appropriate for international travelers, thus creating the idea of what a "Japan trip" was supposed to be. Second, and relatedly, the Japan Tourist Bureau (JTB) and representatives of private industry worked to establish tourist sites that would appeal specifically to "Western" tastes. This was, needless to say, a strategic decision, as Japan needed to be a suitable spot for Western guests if it was to attract tourism receipts. Japanese policymakers in the Meiji Era surely had no intention of establishing a long-term program that would be used to align Japanese leisure practices with those evidenced in the industrialized West. Yet these innovations paved the way for later and more concerted state efforts to articulate what constitutes the proper use of leisure time.

The Growth of the State Role

A convenient place to mark the origins of a well-defined Japanese state role in tourism might be the 1912 creation of the Japan Tourist Bureau. This would, however, err in assuming that this role was limited to explicit policies to promote inbound tourism. Taking their cue from the private railways that, under fierce competition in the 1890s, had created special theme trains to different entertainment spots (often including them with the *hatsumōde*, or first visit of the year to a shrine or temple), the early managers of Japan's national rail system created a special "skating train" in 1911 that brought urban dwellers out to frozen ponds and lakes during the new year's holidays.[35] Even earlier, the need for an organization to lure more foreign tourists was first mentioned at an 1887 gathering sponsored by Prime Minister Itō Hirobumi; with the prime minister's office's blessing, the *Kihinkai* (Welcome Society) was formally established six years later at a ceremony at the Imperial Hotel.[36] The *Kihinkai's* early leadership included figures who had returned from trips to Europe and North America, including Shibuzawa Eiichi and Ekida Takashi, and it tried to systematize the use of foreign-language guides for visitors as well as coordination between different elements of the tour industry.[37]

In fact, one of the most dramatic steps taken by the Japanese government in trying to attract foreign tourists came with the 1907 passage of the Hotel Development Law, a law that enabled the Railway Bureau (later the Ministry of Railroads) to begin to build an integrated network of publicly owned and operated hotels around the country. Speaking in support of this proposal in 1906, the minister of finance, Sakaya Yoshio, remarked:

> In spite of the sharp increases in the number of foreigners visiting, we still are suffering from imperfect facilities, and we have to make this an important issue for our country. Of course, part of the responsibility to solve this problem lies with the residents of tourist areas, who need to make these areas more satisfactory and convenient for the visitors. But to make sure that there is some profit involved in these local efforts, we need to implement policies that will remove at least some of the obstacles that are impeding flows of incoming visitors.[38]

The passage of the law gave the Railway Bureau the responsibility to build hotels capable of attracting and hosting foreign tourists and also made the attraction of foreign tourists a formal goal for the government. The government created only a few hotels, however, and they were not spectacularly successful.[39] Moreover, the *Kihinkai's* finan-

---

35. Sawa Kazuya, *Nihon no Testudo "Kotohajime"* (The "Origins" of Japan's Railroads) (Tokyo: Tsukiji Shōkan, 1996), 211–16.
36. JTB, *Nihon Kōtsū Kōsha,* 8–9.
37. Ibid., 25–26.
38. Kimura, *Nihon no Hoteru Sangyōshi,* 195.
39. Ibid., 151–54.

cial position was precarious by 1906, since it received much of its funding from private railways that were in the process of being nationalized by the Railway Bureau.

This marked a clear shift in the interest of the Japanese state in attracting foreign tourists and provided an additional impetus to the bureau to become more involved in tourism promotion. Its major response decisively shaped the Japanese tourist industry for decades to come. Following a proposal originally made in 1907 (just after the establishment of national hotels), the Japan Tourist Bureau was created in 1912, later becoming the Nihon Kōtsū Kōsha, or the Japan Travel Bureau, the dominant travel agency in postwar Japan.

To a degree, the JTB was the personal creation of a young Railway Bureau official named Kinoshita Yoshio, who had studied in the United States after his graduation from the University of Tokyo. According to the JTB's official history, Kinoshita is fondly remembered as "the father of the JTB," and his motive for suggesting the establishment of a national tourist organization to the Railway Bureau's head, Hirai Seijirō, was to replace the Russian war reparations that were now expected not to materialize.[40] Another possible motive, however, is suggested by Kinoshita's place within the Railway Bureau as well as by fights between the national railroads, run by the bureau, and private lines. Partly because of his experience overseas, Kinoshita represented a new wave of bureaucrats hoping to make the bureau more "service oriented," in order to allow its lines to compete with the private lines that were taking customers more seriously.[41] If the attraction of foreign tourists was made a national priority, this might help the ministry recoup more money on its railways, a particularly important goal following the nationalization of the private lines in 1906–1907.

Like the *Kihinkai*, the JTB would be plagued with budget problems, though it did receive an annual budget of fifty thousand yen, half of which came directly from discretionary accounts of the Minister of Railroads and half of which was supposed to come from associated rail and shipping lines. To deal with its financial constraints, it established partnerships with existing institutions such as the New York–based Japan Society to set up offices overseas, as it did in 1913, and entrusting a Los Angeles office to an American citizen in 1916. Within Japan,

---

40. JTB, *Nihon Kōtsū Kōsha*, 10.
41. Stephen Ericson, *The Sound of the Whistle: Railroads and the State in Meiji Japan* (Cambridge: Harvard University Council on East Asian Studies, 1996), 89.

it created Japan's first bona fide system of tourist guide offices in cities around the country, armed with pamphlets and basic information for visiting foreigners and even Japanese guests.[42] At first, the JTB for the most part left the creation of comprehensive tours—the precursors to today's package tours—to private industry, cooperating with such industry giants as Thomas Cook & Sons in Europe.

But the budget limitations had an effect on some critical decisions by the JTB, which led it to become more than just a promotional organization; the JTB soon became a travel agency. By 1915, the JTB decided to go a step further toward making travel in Japan easier by selling tour coupons and tickets at their tourism guide offices, especially in their office in Tokyo Station; these tickets allowed for land or sea transport and for lodging within Japan. While this is not tantamount to the activities of today's travel agents, it represented an important new role for the Japanese government, not only in promoting tourism to Japan and providing guidance once in Japan, but also handling the commercial activity of ticket brokering within the country.[43] Its success here was remarkable. In 1915, roughly nineteen thousand foreigners visited Japan, and the JTB was used over eight thousand times by foreign tourists (undoubtedly more than once by many of these, though the percentage of JTB users is difficult to determine). By 1936, the number of foreign visitors had increased to over forty thousand, and the JTB was used by foreigners 154,000 times, a twenty-fold increase in just over twenty years. An average foreign visitor to Japan would use the JTB (for ticket sales and information, evidently) three times or more.[44]

The JTB's success could be felt not only in the expansion of its range of services, but also in the nation's financial coffers. In 1936, visitors to Japan spent approximately 107,688,000 yen. Although this amounted to no more than 4 percent of Japan's overall trade (including both exports and imports), it exceeded Japan's persistent trade deficit (94,000,000 yen) and also was Japan's fourth most important source of foreign exchange revenues (behind cotton, raw silk, and silk products) for the year. The industry had developed a reputation good enough, especially in the painful years after the Great Depression, that the Board of Tourist Industry (the smaller body within the Ministry of Railroads chiefly responsible for foreign tourism; it was directly above

42. JTB, *Nihon Kōtsū Kōsha*, 8–38.
43. Ibid., 31.
44. Kimura, *Nihon no Hoteru Sangyōshi*, 188.

the JTB in the ministry hierarchy) was able to act as an intermediary for a number of investors who borrowed money at preferential interest rates from the Ministry of Finance, to create fifteen hotels around the country, including Tokyo, Nagoya, and various resort locations.[45]

Building a Tourist Experience: Aiding Hotels

By the late 1920s, the benefits of inbound tourism had become more obvious. Building on this trend, in 1923, the Ministry of Railroads had established another body, the *Nihon Bunka Ryokō Kyōkai* (Japan Culture and Tour Association) as a separate body under its control. This office, under its director, Miyoshi Zen'ichi, essentially served as a peak-level organization for consumers interested in tourism by linking together a growing national network of regional tour associations. Among its functions were general advertisement of the tourism industry, the publication of a monthly magazine, *Tabi* (Travel), and research on good tourism spots and facilities. Perhaps sensing that this association threatened JTB's control over the marketing and control of the domestic industry, JTB's chairman, Takahisa Jinnosuke, proposed, in 1930, that the *Kyōkai* be merged with the JTB. Even going so far as to use *Tabi* as a mouthpiece, Miyoshi and other staff members strongly opposed any such move, arguing that their association served the consumers, while the JTB's main business was supporting the service providers. Although they evidently did not go so far as to suggest a conflict of interest, the *Kyōkai* members claimed that the two bodies were better kept separate. The tide started to turn in Takahisa's favor when, in 1932, the JTB took six of the *Kyōkai's* staff members as well as some of its functions (including, notably, the publication of *Tabi*), and two years later the *Kyōkai* as a whole was simply absorbed into the JTB. The JTB at this point achieved the status of special juridical corporation (*shadan hōjin*). As the JTB's official history dryly notes, "It was at this time that Miyoshi took the opportunity to leave the *Kyōkai*."[46]

As important as foreign tourists were to Japan, and as important as the JTB was to the foreign tourists, perhaps its most lasting effect came in its structuring of the domestic tourist industry. As noted, in addition to creating institutional links between lodging and transportation

45. JTB, *Nihon Kōtsū Kōsha*, 48.
46. Ibid., 42–43.

sites, the JTB branched out into ticket and coupon sales, enabling people to make most of their travel arrangements before leaving Tokyo,
or wherever they traveled from. And while the original purpose may
have been to capture foreign exchange earnings from foreign tourists,
the JTB realized the potential financial benefits of selling transportation and lodging tickets to Japanese travelers as well and in 1925 began to sell domestically.[47] This strategy was even more successful
than was the JTB's work vis-à-vis foreigners. In 1926, the JTB's services
(again, information and ticketing, and multiple contacts by one person were counted as separate occasions of use) were used by Japanese
travelers 158,000 times. By 1937, this had increased to over 2,858,000,
almost a 20-fold increase in just over a decade.[48]

The rapid growth in Japanese domestic tourism was important
largely because it coincided with the government's efforts to attract
more foreign tourists by "upgrading" facilities and trying to create
sites that would appeal to specifically foreign tastes. In 1929, for example, the Diet's debate over a bill for national support for the hotel
industry instructively raised some of the major issues involved in
tourism. The House of Peers, for example, focused primarily on the
purportedly beneficial social aspects of bringing in foreigners; indeed,
part of the purpose of international tourism had to be the creation of
"international understanding" and the improvement of Japan's global
image. For the House of Representatives, the primary benefit of tourism was economic. This was, however, not conceptualized in terms of
the putative advantages to the hotel industry, as hotel aid generally
was understood in Europe. Rather, the desired economic outcome
would be badly needed foreign exchange earnings.[49] This cast tourism
as an industrial sector with broader significance for the economy as a
whole.

With the subsequent decision to promote inbound tourism more effectively, the Ministry of Railroads established the previously mentioned Board of Tourist Industry in 1930, charging it with developing
more systematic public assistance to the lodgings industry. Having
successfully pressed the Ministry of Finance for funding, the board determined that hotels were far more expensive to run than were *ryokan*
and therefore more deserving of financial assistance. Furthermore, the
hotels receiving significant funding were "international tourist ho-

---

47. Ibid., 34.
48. Ibid., 188.
49. Kimura, *Nihon no Hoteru Sangyōshi*, 221–33.

tels," which were supposed to meet international standards of size, comfort, responsiveness, and basic management style. Under the somewhat austere financial conditions of the early 1930s, however, components of the plan were ultimately scuttled, and the board focused more on its international promotional activities. But by the 1930s, Japan's lodgings started to meet international standards more effectively than before.[50]

The JTB became the most visible of Japan's prewar tourism organizations, though it fit within a web of government offices responsible for the governance of the industry, generally under the auspices of the Ministry of Railroads.[51] After 1930, the ministry and the JTB received guidance from the *Kokusai Kankō Iinkai* (literally, International Tourism Committee but going by the official English name of Committee of Tourist Industry), which met annually in the office of the prime minister to review tourism policies. Much like the discussion councils that dot Japan's current political landscape, the committee succeeded in making a number of somewhat amorphous proposals regarding the attraction of foreign tourists, which were incorporated into general policies or unceremoniously discarded. Its choice of words was frequently more interesting than its activities. For example, in the first meeting, the tourism experts on the committee tossed around words such as *impureshon* (impression), *confōto* (comfort), and *interesuto* (interest). Each of these words has at least a reasonably accurate Japanese translation (respectively, *inshō, raku,* and *kyōmi*), but the committee's members careful use of these foreign words reflected not only their tendency to equate tourism with Western concepts but also their belief that these foreign words captured the essence of normal tourism practices better than did any Japanese terms.[52]

The JTB began to do more than to simply "improve" services and facilities, even though that was the primary goal. It also began to construct the very idea of a modern tourist experience—mass transit to a

50. Ibid., 268–331.
51. This was not always the case, and the Ministry of Railroads initially struggled with the Ministry of Construction over the governance of tourism (JTB, *Nihon Kōtsū Kōsha,* 42–43). A handy organizational chart showing the structure of the government's role in tourism appears in the final issue of the Board of Tourist Industry's *Kokusai Kwankō* (International Tourism). The magazine appears to have run from 1933 to 1939, and the organizational chart, which lists the various offices (but unfortunately, not the functions except for very general descriptions of the board, the *Kokusai Kwankō Kyōkai,* and the JTB), appears in *Kokusai Kwankō* 7, 4 (fall 1939): inside front cover.
52. Ibid., 245.

tourist site, complete with a standard hotel (front desk, restaurant, lobby, lounge, guest rooms, beds—and therefore reshaped how the Japanese themselves would travel. This was more than a simple response by private entrepreneurs to clear market incentives, because the government itself became part of the shift. And it did not reflect a "natural" shift by Japanese tourists to a Western style of tourist behavior, as if there were a timeline along which tourist preferences would naturally progress. Rather, Japanese public officials pursuing organizational and national goals made short-term decisions that would alter the options available to Japanese travelers and thus transform the entire idea of being a Japanese tourist.

Nationalism, Tourism, and the Collapse of the Prewar Tourism System

The use, however, of Western motifs in travel would become a far more controversial issue. After the assassination of Prime Minister Inukai Tsuyoshi in 1931 by young rightists in the armed forces, the government began a precipitous slide toward out-and-out militarism. Because of the government's increasing reliance on a virulently nationalistic message during the 1930s, the Japanese tourist bureaucracy would begin to make stricter distinctions between what was Japanese and what was not; it would clarify its view that the changes in Japan's tourist industry had been toward "modernization" rather than toward "Westernization." Although there was never an effort to undo the industrial changes that had made Japan's tourist industry more like its European and North American counterparts, the language of the tourism bureaucrats focused increasingly on the Japanese nation and its unique identity.

Of course, as a form of interaction with foreigners, tourism is not necessarily a bad option for rabid nationalists. If one assumes that foreign tourists want to see authenticity and tradition, one might easily justify friendly efforts toward them by referring to their attraction to a country's proud culture and history. And, in fact, this alleviated dilemmas the tourism bureaucrats might have faced. Aside from the occasional criticism from those who opposed Japan's change toward hotels and away from *ryokan*, most people appear to have been not too bothered by the appearance of Western tourists (who still numbered only in the tens of thousands, mostly clustered in a few carefully marked areas). Nationalism, while perhaps mildly troublesome, was not in and of itself the problem. Japan's militarism, on the other hand, ultimately ensured that the JTB and other prewar tourism-related bureaucracies would essentially be forced into increasingly martial roles.

The breakdown of organization in the JTB and its incorporation into a fiercely nationalistic military regime became apparent in symbols as prosaic as the 1930s anthems of the Board of Tourist Industry and the JTB. "Kwankō Nihon no Ka"[53] (Tourism Japan Song), the theme of the Board of Tourist Industry, closed with a rhetorial flourish:

> Made reverent by the rafters and archway of the shrine
> Supported by a 2600-year historical line
> A happy country, as can be seen
> By the fact that the light comes from the East
> Bringing respect to Tourist Japan
> We'll show the world Tourist Japan[54]

If anything, the JTB's official song was an even clearer example of linking Japan's tourist promotion to its putative national character and the needs of the state, its bouncy D-major melody notwithstanding. It also finished with colorful imagery:

> The harmonious heart of justice and peace
> Our proud efforts will never cease
> And we must never start to lag
> In hoisting our fatherland like a flag
> Working together we plant the seeds
> That allow us to enthusiastically proceed[55]

Surviving issues of *Kokusai Kwankō*, the Board of Tourist Industry's quarterly magazine, provide a valuable spot for seeing the shift in the language of tourism policy. The links between the exigencies of tourism policy and a more rabid nationalism in Japan seemed somewhat benign at first. In the autumn 1936 issue of *Kokusai Kwankō*, Takahisa Jinnosuke, the head of the JTB, penned a short article about the need to modify Japan's *ryokan* in order to deal with the anticipated foreign tourists during the scheduled 1940 Tokyo Olympic Games.

---

53. When rendering the older version of the Chinese characters for "tourism" in the Roman alphabet, I use *kwankō* rather than the postwar *kankō*.

54. Board of Tourist Industry, "Kwankō Nihon no Ka" (Tourism Japan Song), *Kokusai Kwankō* 5, 2 (spring 1937): inside front cover. Author's unofficial translation.

55. JTB, *Nihon Kōtsū Kōsha*, 68; "Japan Tsūrisuto Byūrō Ka" (Japan Tourist Bureau Song), words and music Horiuchi Keizō. Author's unofficial translation.

While the article expressed a general desire to present the best face of Japan to foreigners and also to ensure that lodgings fit "community standards and public order and morals," his piece linked *ryokan* to hotels and suggested that with either type of facility, foreign customers could be exposed to the courteous hospitality for which Japan should be known.[56]

These organizational difficulties notwithstanding, authors in *Kokusai Kwankō* became ever more persistent in stressing the uniqueness of Japanese culture and its value to tourism. One important nationalist ideologue, Rōyama Masamichi, stressed that travel was based on a desire to see different cultures and countries and that Japan needed to work out a way to differentiate its national character from that of the other Asian countries, so that there could be a comprehensive travel route in which Japan would stand out effectively from the other countries of the region. He also mentioned the differences between "spiritual" and "materialistic" cultures, ostensibly meaning western Europe and North America with the latter term.[57] The winter 1939 issue carried a remarkable twenty-three-page-long transcript of a roundtable on "Our National Character," featuring participants from the Board of Tourist Industry, the Ministry of Education, and some top universities in Tokyo. The conversation ranged from Japan's historical predilection for peace, the special features of the country's character that made it the rightful representative of Manchuria, the inability of foreigners (particularly Westerners) to understand Japanese culture, and ways of balancing Japan's need to teach foreigners about Japan through tourism with its need to protect its citizens from potential violations of public morality.[58]

By 1938–1939 the articles became remarkably belligerent, especially for the "hospitality" industry. One of the more startling trends was not only the somewhat predictable question of how Japan's "unique national character and culture" could be a useful tourism resource but also how tourism promotion might be useful for the Japanese nation. Koyama Eizō, a professor at Tokyo Imperial University (the precursor to today's Tokyo University), wrote in 1938 of the util-

---

56. Takahisa Junnosuke, "Ryokan ni Tomaru Kyaku e no Kibo" (Our Hopes for Travelers to Stay in Ryokan), *Kokusai Kwankō* 4, 4 (1936): 25–28.

57. Rōyama Masamichi, "Bunka Seisaku to shite no Kwankō Jigyō" (The Tourism Business as Cultural Policy), *Kokusai Kwankō* 6, 1 (1938): 4–7.

58. "'Waga Kokuminsei o Kataru' Zadankai" (Roundtable on "Our National Character"), *Kokusai Kwankō* 7, 1 (1939): 56–78.

ity of tourism in the Japanese national war effort. "Sensō to Kokusai Kwankō Senden" (War and International Tourism Propaganda) criticized Great Britain and China bitterly and argued that they were beginning to lean, in desperation, on the United States for support of their crumbling power in the face of the mighty Japanese Empire. These countries did so largely by spewing anti-Japanese vitriol, when in fact Japan's overseas military activities were merely natural responses to its small land area and large population; in other words, Japan's military activities were an expression of its right to exist. In order to forestall an American entry into the expected war in the Pacific, Japan had to take full advantage of all available forms of propaganda. By promoting more tours from the United States to Japan, Japan would be able to win over the hearts and minds of common people, without whom the democratic government would be unable to fight a winning war. It was also an ideal strategy to use with regard to a neutral country that might yet serve as an intermediary. Koyama concluded that if successful, this strategy would prove a boon to the tourist industry itself, in that Japan would become the heart of the Japan-China-Manchuria travel route, surely the world's most desirable, as well as a culturally and economically powerful one.

In Koyama's analysis, tourism was thus extremely important, not as a form of leisure that was ideal for Westerners and possible for Japanese but rather as a tool for expansionism. His article made a further, somewhat novel contribution by quoting Clausewitz's famous maxim, "War is politics by other means," and concluding that in a time of war, tourism too had to be politically rather than economically driven.[59] In a follow-up article six months later, Koyama claimed that increased tourist routes between Japan, Manchuria, and China would make it easier to understand the Chinese national character and to distinguish Japan from its Asian neighbor.[60] In one of the final issues of *Kokusai Kwankō*, a staff writer followed Koyama's logic on the importance of reaching common American people but adopted a remarkably fatalistic tone about the likelihood that it would work.[61]

Shortly after the attack on Pearl Harbor, the prewar bureaucracy on

---

59. Koyama Eizō, "Sensō to Kokusai Kwankō Senden" (War and International Tourism Propaganda), *Kokusai Kwankō* 6, 2 (1938): 20–23.

60. Koyama Eizō, "Kwankō Seisaku to Minzoku Ninshiki" (Tourism Policy and Racial Awareness), *Kokusai Kwankō* 6, 4 (autumn 1938): 10–13.

61. "Taibei Kwankō Senden Dashin" (Sounding Out the US with Tourism Propaganda), *Kokusai Kwankō* 7, 4 (1939): 20–23.

tourism was essentially wiped out. The Board of Tourist Industry itself was abolished, and in 1943 the Japan Tourist Bureau was formally merged with the *Tōa Ryokōsha* (Greater East Asian Travel Company, the Ministry of Railroads' basic travel representative in the territories conquered by Japan) and renamed the *Tōa Kōtsū Kōsha* (The Greater East Asian Travel Public Corporation). As the name change suggested, and unsurprisingly given the comprehensiveness of the war, its mission was no longer the promotion of tourism but rather the management of some travel facilities and the dissemination of cultural propaganda abroad, a mission foreshadowed by the earlier articles in *Kokusai Kwankō.*[62] To the extent that Japan's tourist industry carried on any activities in this period, they were largely in the form of the confiscation and operation of foreign hotels in the Asian territories dominated by the Japanese armies in the period. Hotel experts from the Imperial Hotel and other spots were sent to the Philippines, Thailand, and Indonesia.[63] Of course, at this late date, tourism policy was completely useless; leisure travel was out of the question for citizens of all parties to the war. The JTB would, however, survive the war in an amended form.

Conclusion

In prewar Japan, was the government role in leisure institutionalized or "taken for granted"? I argue that it was not, in that there was little agreement over what the state ought to be doing. No one doubted that the government could and should encourage tourism and leisure development, but the meaning of leisure and tourism was controversial enough to make Japan's initiatives in these areas highly susceptible to the shift toward militarism. To promote Japan to the outside world was to emphasize particularity rather than to have Japan conform to externally defined standards regarding hospitality and travel style. Even so, the government's effort to turn tourism policy toward a celebration of the national essence confronted and could not fully reconcile itself with the creation of *hoteru* and the shift away from *ryokan*. Tourism was an opportunity to advertise Japaneseness, but its successful marketing relied at least in part on a willingness to make Japan more appealing to European and American tastes, which could not easily be resolved with these countries' vilification.

62. JTB, *Nihon Kōtsū Kōsha*, 84–90.
63. Muraoka, *Nihon no Hoteru Shōshi*, 189–202.

The most important reason for the increasing state role and for the use of European and North American models is simple and obvious. The government needed money, and young officials such as Kinoshita and his colleagues determined that one of the best ways to earn it could be through the attraction of Western tourists. To lure them, they needed, on the one hand, Western-style travel infrastructure and, on the other, something interesting and appealing about Japan. This encouraged the simultaneous transformation of Japanese travel facilities toward an international standard and the lionization of Japanese distinctiveness. Clearly, the prewar era did not display a headlong, perfectly enthusiastic rush to embrace the recreational practices of Americans and Europeans, though to many contemporaries it no doubt appeared as if this were the case. Conservatives probably did not believe that baseball would itself make the Japanese a nation of misshapen alcoholics, but they worried about what effect the invasion of foreign games and recreation might have on their "culturally distinctive" citizens. Travel changed perhaps more dramatically than any other leisure activity, but the goal of attracting Western tourists was simply too important to ignore. And Japan's prewar tourism and leisure bureaucrats would find themselves navigating a tortuous path, veering between the imperatives of attracting foreign cash and promoting Japan's cultural essence.

Consequently, the government role in leisure was not yet fully institutionalized, because it was not yet taken for granted what exactly the state ought to do. That the state ought to have a role, however, was practically unquestioned by the 1930s, as were many of the organizational and program initiatives established by Kinoshita and the JTB. As increasing numbers of Japanese traveled recreationally, using the very facilities, itineraries, travel plans, and routes designed to appeal to the foreigners, they too began to take for granted a standard of leisure behavior that was, however fitfully, acknowledged to be largely of "Western" origin. As new rules for play began to regulate the recreational practices of the Japanese themselves, "the West" was increasingly understood as the model with which an assertive state would be forced to contend.

In the next chapter, we turn to the first thirty-five years of Japan's postwar experience, focusing on the institutionalization and inscription of Japan's leisure policies especially in the 1970s. To be sure, with the country in ruins, the population demoralized, and an occupying army intent on indoctrinating citizens into a belief that American society represented the model to which the Japanese should aspire, the relevance of the United States in the Japanese popular imagination will seem somewhat obvious. But the importance of the American role varied across policy contexts, reshaping the goals of pre-existing government bodies rather than instantaneously creating a Japanese government identical to its American model. That is, without the nascent policy institutions established in the prewar era that articulated both a state role in shaping leisure and a controversial Western model for understanding it, it is highly unlikely that Japan's public policies would have evolved as they did. The rules changed in the early twentieth century in ways that would continue to shape the Japanese political management of play.

A group of Japanese actresses bowling, 1958. Photograph used with permission of the
Mainichi Photobank.

Good and Bad Words in Japanese Leisure Policy in the 1970s

In the years immediately following World War II, leisure policy merited no interest from political leaders trying to rebuild the nation, or from citizens facing the struggles of day-to-day survival. Regardless, the images of a better lifestyle were all around them, and they were rendered largely in English. Desperately poor and occupied by an army of foreign soldiers possessing chocolates, nylons, and enough nutritious food to support a black market in leftovers, Japanese in the early postwar era could hardly have avoided comparing their lot with that of Americans. Defeat and destitution conspired to ensure that—amid debates over political structure, social responsibility, and new moral codes—the lifestyle of wealthy foreign nations, represented by G.I.'s armed with guns and currency, would loom large in the Japanese popular imagination. In his recent overview of occupied Japan, John Dower poignantly describes the "pan-pan girls" who offended conservatives with their willingness to trade sexual favors for the Americans' gifts and money. Children enjoyed dark games in which they pretended to be poor would-be passengers trying to board a first-class train car, such as the special cars for the American army. With Japan's relative position of intense poverty framing much of the political discourse of the Occupation era, "What made America 'great' was that it was so rich; and for many, what made 'democracy' appealing was that it apparently was the way to become prosperous."[1]

With most families struggling just to put food on the table, the very idea of a "leisure policy" would have seemed both grotesque and pointless, and the Japanese government turned in the 1940s and 1950s to far more pressing matters: economic growth, demilitarization, and reintegration into the changed international community. Moreover, the Supreme Command for the Allied Powers (SCAP) sought, in its reforms, to create more distance between the state and the lives of Japanese citizens, fearful of the combined police power and political authority of, for example, the prewar Ministry of Home Affairs (MHA).

But leisure never became a purely "private" phenomenon, and the Japanese government would ultimately think of ways in which leisure development might support other state interests. Aiming first and foremost at national goals such as economic growth, officials would seek to shift recreational opportunities and priorities, whether to attract foreign travelers or to promote domestic consumption of leisure services. In making their plans, however, leisure planners would rely invariably on models drawn from other nations. This made perfect sense: Japan needed to attract foreign visitors, just as it did before the war. And later, when Japan had joined the ranks of rich nations, it seemed obvious to use the examples of the United States and western Europe to show how leisure industries had become important components of national economic development. In making these decisions, however, Japanese officials would become crucial elements of a long process in which they and their citizens would begin to take for granted that the best lifestyles could be seen in these other nations, because they were *ahead*. Leisure too would be understood as another way to determine how a nation was performing on this straightforward timeline of development. In this view, if the lives of citizens were to improve, Japan would have to move closer to standards drawn from the experiences of these other nations.

In this chapter, I trace the changes that resulted in the institutionalization of Japanese leisure policy. In particular, I focus on the interests of political leaders that drew them to leisure, as well as on the language used in policy documents from the era. These documents are crucial because they tell us how officials justified their decisions. Did

1. John W. Dower, *Embracing Defeat: Japan in the Wake of World War II* (New York: Norton, 1999), 121–67, at 136.

they really believe what they were writing? I suspect that they did, or at least mostly. But even if they did not, they chose to write these documents in certain ways because they felt that other Japanese might be persuaded. The words mattered, at least to the authors. If institutions really *are* institutions (that is, taken for granted in people's lives) there is no real way to evaluate them without making an interpretive leap—trying to determine what people believe and accept without questioning. In later chapters, I will argue that my interpretation of these documents illuminates the puzzles in Japan's postwar leisure initiatives.

These initiatives were not immediately important in Japanese politics, and, as this chapter makes clear, economic and social conditions prevented leisure policy from taking the prominent place that its creators aspired for it in the early 1970s. In fact, an early and crucial misfire by policymakers would make tourism, the largest leisure industry of them all, a nearly untouchable topic for nearly a decade. Here too, words—especially the inauspiciously chosen ones—mattered. Leisure thus remained in the background until the 1980s, when Japan had reached a level of affluence that guaranteed it membership in the elite economic powers.[2] But the language of officials and their advisors in the 1970s helps to tell us how they envisioned what that affluence might look like, as well as how Japan was supposed to develop.

Doubling Incomes, Reconsidering the Costs of Development

After his 1948 release from prison as a war crimes suspect, Kishi Nobusuke, a former minister of commerce and industry who had been active in Manchuria during the war, built his political comeback on an affiliation with the Liberal Party. With the linking of the Liberals and Democrats in 1955 as the new Liberal Democratic Party, Kishi's

---

2. For an excellent overview of the development of the postwar Japanese economy, see T. J. Pempel, *Regime Shift: Comparative Dynamics of the Japanese Political Economy* (Ithaca: Cornell University Press, 1998). Another good discussion is Yutaka Kosai's "The Postwar Japanese Economy," in *The Economic Emergence of Modern Japan*, ed. Kozo Yamamura (Cambridge: Cambridge University Press, 1997), 159–202. The impact of the emphasis on general economic growth on the Japanese labor movement is well covered in Tabata Hirokuni's "Industrial Relations and the Union Movement," trans. Charles Weathers, in *The Political Economy of Japanese Society*, vol. 1: *The State or the Market?* ed. Banno Junji (Oxford: Oxford University Press, 1997), 84–108. The theory behind the emphasis on national economic development is well traced in Bai Gao's *Economic Ideology and Japanese Industrial Policy: Developmentalism from 1931 to 1965* (Cambridge: Cambridge University Press, 1997).

right-wing views gained even more currency, particularly in his vehement anticommunism. Becoming prime minister in 1957, Kishi began to work, in general unsuccessfully, on a number of conservative domestic initiatives, including an expansion in the role of the emperor and the curbing of the Diet's powers. His lasting contribution, however, was in the field of foreign relations. In 1959, Kishi successfully renegotiated the security pact with the United States and procured a stronger role for Japan in determining the uses to which U.S. forces would be put.

Japan's leftists were outraged by the treaty, which essentially bound Japan into an anticommunist alliance with the United States, targeted in part against the People's Republic of China. The 1959 protests turned to riots, and in May 1960, violence spilled into the chamber of the Diet as well, where opponents physically wrestled one another. Kishi called in the police and arrested a number of opposition politicians who had tried to prevent the Diet's speaker from taking the chair. With the rest of the socialists boycotting the session, Kishi's faction managed to ratify the treaty but at mortal cost to his own viability as a leader. Within two months, Kishi stepped down, having brought Japanese postwar politics to its most feverish conflict and the government to the brink of disaster.[3]

His replacement, the mild-mannered and temperate Ikeda Hayato, chose to try to reunite the country by shifting public interest toward the goal of national economic growth. In announcing the *Kokumin Shotoku Baizō Keikaku* (Income Doubling Plan), Ikeda put a political label on the growth that would serve as the foundation of the LDP's electoral dominance until the early 1990s. The goal of the plan was to double the income of average Japanese by the end of the decade, a plan predicated on the growth rates that economic policymakers already expected. Because Japan's high-speed growth economy had begun early in the 1950s and the country's economic planners believed that the economy would continue to grow at a steady clip for a decade, the plan probably would have worked even without any additional government action, and the country would have simply pursued an industrial course already charted. The point of the program, however, was to remind the Japanese that the LDP government had their best interests at heart and that the country's national goals focused on the needs of citizens.

3. Mikiso Hane, *Modern Japan: A Historical Survey* (Boulder, Colo.: Westview, 1992).

In retrospect, observers have related the Income Doubling Plan to an increased emphasis on lifestyle and leisure issues in the 1960s. The Leisure Development Center (YKC), for example, cited the plan in its timeline of leisure development as part of the administrative background to rapid changes in leisure and lifestyle in 1960s Japan. By 1962, the national television station NHK was broadcasting some programs in color, the country began to experience the "my car" and golf booms, and by the end of the decade, Japan's economic growth had far outpaced that of other OECD nations, firmly establishing the nation as one of the world's richest.[4] The Income Doubling Plan, however, was not aimed at increasing leisure time per se and dealt with the issue of consumption in the most basic terms. Simply put, most Japanese were still living relatively tough lives in the early days of Japan's economic miracle, and the original plan sought to elevate their living standards so that within a few years per capita consumption might equal that in West Germany.[5] A midterm report published in 1965 by the Economic Advisory Council (*Keizai Shingikai*) focused to some degree on income development but primarily on the industrial expansion (especially in manufacturing sectors) that served as the basis for Japan's growth.[6]

Still, the plan fostered an environment in which people could dream of a more fulfilling life. Not only did the average life span increase by about four years during the decade, but both the GNP per capita and household income more than doubled. And people used their new income; the era witnessed a veritable explosion in the number of leisure and hobby-related items such as televisions, radios, and pianos purchased over the decade. Annual working hours dropped slightly from an average of 2,484 in 1960 to 2,249 in 1970, though the fact remains that at the end of the decade most Japanese had scarcely more time to enjoy their new leisure items than they had had at the beginning.[7]

4. YKC, *Yoka wa Dō Kawatta Ka! Kōdō, Seisaku, Shihyō de Tadoru Wagakuni Yoka no 50 Nen* (How Has Leisure Changed? Fifty Years of Our Country's Leisure, Traced with Activities, Policies, and Indicators) (Tokyo: YKC, 1994), especially 7–8, 35, 40. The YKC does not suggest that the Income Doubling Plan caused the development of leisure, merely places it in the sociopolitical background to leisure change.

5. Keizai Kikakuchō Sōgō Keikakukyoku (Economic Planning Agency, General Program Office), *Shotoku Baizō Keikaku Zasetsu* (Overview of the Income Doubling Plan) (Tokyo, 1960), 56–57.

6. Keizai Shingikai (Economic Discussion Council), ed., *Kokumin Shotoku Baizō Keikaku Chūkan Kentō Hōkoku* (Income Doubling Plan: A Midterm Investigative Report) (Tokyo: Ministry of Finance, 1965).

7. National Institute for Research Advancement (NIRA), *Seikatsu Suijun no Rek-*

Moreover, the rapid development of the Japanese economy, as opposed to some of the enormous income inequalities that have surfaced elsewhere, tended to reinforce a "middle class" identification.[8]

And so what began as an effort to distract an angry nation from massive protests, violence in the Diet, and a somewhat shady ratification of the country's treaty with the United States for national defense, had by the end of the decade come to symbolize in policy terms the country's wide-scale economic advancement. By the late 1960s, however, economic planners and politicians alike began to question the viability of continued massive public investment and rapid industrialization as the foundation for further growth. According to Tessa Morris-Suzuki, in the wake of violent student protests, environmental catastrophes such as the Minamata case (in which the government finally acknowledged mercury poisoning in locally caught fish, years after the region's residents were first plagued with a number of terrible birth defects), and agitation regarding poor working conditions, LDP politicians themselves had begun to stress the need to change Japan's style of development. Similarly, the Economic White Papers published by the Economic Planning Agency shifted in rhetoric from statements about the power of Japan's industrial economy to the need for a more fair and livable society.[9]

Morris-Suzuki notes that in response to the belief that the Japanese economy needed a new direction, LDP politicians and members of the economic bureaucracy evidently had three options available. First was Tanaka Kakuei's vision for more public works, which called "in almost Biblical terms for the leveling of mountains and the raising of valleys" to make Japan's terrain more favorable for further roads, high-

---

ishiteki Bunseki (Historical Analysis of Lifestyle Standards) (Tokyo: NIRA, 1988), 287–357 (statistical materials).

8. I do not make the argument that Japan is a fully egalitarian country but rather that people evidently perceived the benefits of economic growth to be distributed more or less fairly. The percentage of people identifying themselves as "middle class" (including "upper middle," "middle," and "lower middle") grew from just over 70 percent at the beginning of the decade to 90 percent by 1970, and the percentage of those identifying themselves as "lower class" dropped from 17 percent to about 7 percent in the same period. For a somewhat skeptical analysis of the often-cited "middle class" identity, see Ozawa Masako, *Shin 'Kaisō Shōhi' no Jidai* (The New Era of "Class Consumption") (Tokyo: Nihon Keizai Shimbunsha, 1985), statistics on 184.

9. Tessa Morris-Suzuki, *Beyond Computopia: Information, Automation, and Democracy in Japan* (London: Kegan Paul, 1988), 42–69. For a thorough discussion of the Minamata case, see Timothy S. George, *Minamata: Pollution and the Struggle for Democracy in Postwar Japan* (Cambridge: Harvard University Asia Center, 2001).

ways, and cities. This relatively expensive plan fell to the wayside when oil shortages and the end of the Bretton Woods system of fixed exchange rates together rocked the economy. Two other options, for the development of an "information society" (*jōhō shakai*) and for the improvement of lifestyle and welfare, ultimately merged under MITI and EPA programs to make Japan more dependent on knowledge-intensive and service industries.[10] Indeed, under this new conception, Japan would move toward development of "third-wave" or service industries. These would not only provide more stable and safe growth to the country but would also rely in large part on the rationalized development of domestic demand. In short, Japan would have to become, at least to a degree, a consumer society, like the more "advanced" countries of the West.

Learning How to Have Fun: Leisure Policy in the Early 1970s

Searching for ideas of how to create a *yoka shakai* (leisure society), members of the Ministry of International Trade and Industry turned to examples of leisure policy seen in Germany, France, and the United States in the early 1960s. In 1972, the ministry received approval and created the *Yoka Kaihatsu Sangyōshitsu* (Leisure Development Industrial Office) within the Industrial Policy Division, which would "coordinate policy legislation and implementation" in the field of leisure development. The general direction of the policies was made clear in a February 1973 Cabinet statement, the *Keizai Shakai Kihon Keikaku* (Basic Plan for Economy and Society). The plan read:

> We will establish a comprehensive leisure administration [*yoka gyōsei*] that, through national and regional public organizations, will determine the differing needs among our nation's classes [*kokumin kakusō*] and work to establish facilities for a better leisure environment.[11]

Among the more specific recommendations in this report were the need for a two-day weekend, the promotion of community sports, and

---

10. Morris-Suzuki, *Beyond Computopia*, 25–29.
11. "Keizai Shakai Kihon Keikaku"(Basic Plan for Economy and Society), cited in Ministry of International Trade and Industry (MITI), ed., *Tsūshō Sangyō Seisakushi 13: Dai IV ki: Tayōkajidai 2* (History of International Trade and Industry Policy, vol. 13—period 4: The Era of Diversification, part 2) (Tokyo: Tsūshō Sangyō Chōsakai, 1991), 467.

the construction of large-scale recreation facilities, regional public inns, and culture centers and city parks that would become important features of the burgeoning leisure environment.

MITI's Leisure Development Industrial Office then issued, in 1973, its "Wagakuni Yoka no Genjō to Yoka Jidai e no Tenbō" (Our Country's Current Leisure Situation, and Prospects for a Leisure Era), which added more specific recommendations. Among the problems it noted in the leisure environment of 1973 Japan were the lack of leisure facilities, the high cost of land, poor residential conditions, insufficient "leisure communities" (yoka komyuniti) and "technology for fun (play)" (asobi no tekunorojī), lack of leisure information, and the absence of daycare facilities for infants. Consequently, the people most likely to be among the "leisure poor" (yoka jidai kara torinokosareru kanōsei no aru sō) were mothers taking care of young children, senior citizens without physical strength or knowledge of "technology for fun," and people living or working in rural areas far removed from leisure facilities.

MITI argued that there were five categories for government action: the equal distribution of resources, the establishment and maintenance of a minimum level of leisure facilities, assistance to the private sector for leisure development, the removal of obstacles to leisure activities, and creation of additional policies to support the previous four categories. More specifically, MITI's role would be in providing and maintaining information about leisure, development and improvement of equipment and systems for leisure, and, perhaps most importantly, guaranteeing the harmony between industrial activity and society in solving leisure problems.[12] MITI's role would thus include determining what Japanese society would want and providing the information to private firms in order to make sure that investments in leisure development would be tied to probable leisure needs.

The planners of MITI's leisure office had anticipated the need for information on probable leisure development and desirable kinds of leisure industry investment and in 1972 created the YKC. Led initially by one of MITI's most formidable administrative vice-ministers (the highest rank achievable by a Japanese bureaucrat within his ministry career), Sahashi Shigeru, the YKC opened its doors on 26 April 1972. In establishing the YKC, MITI cooperated with the EPA as well as a number of private firms. Although MITI was at the time investing

12. Cited in MITI, ed., Tsūshō Sangyō Seisakushi, 467–68.

huge amounts of time and money in the "leisure society" concept, the YKC was not necessarily a desirable *amakudari* (descent from heaven) post for former bureaucrats. Chalmers Johnson notes that while Sahashi appeared to enjoy his position, he was also somewhat outside the normal chain of industrial policy *amakudari*, in part because of his personality and in part because of his dissatisfaction with the ministry's changes in his last years there.[13]

The YKC's putative function was to serve as a comprehensive think-tank in the support of leisure policy. It would ideally conduct discrete and also comparative research projects aimed at generating a better understanding of leisure, to provide exactly the kind of "harmonization" between social needs and industrial activity that would ensure the smooth establishment of leisure facilities appropriate for a rapidly modernizing Japan. MITI had determined that its three primary functions would be: basic and comprehensive research on leisure development; devising and proposing to the government leisure facility projects with which it would be entrusted; and managing experimental leisure facilities.[14] MITI and EPA members, in cooperation with an advisory board of scholars and a structural board, would produce two reports in the next few years, which together provide an extraordinary glimpse into the way in which leisure policy was conceptualized in 1970s Japan.

The Map for Leisure Policy: Yoka Shakai e no Kōzu

The first of these was a largely unnoticed early research project by MITI, the EPA, and YKC, which not only suggests the extent to which the construction of a leisure society was a policy priority in the 1970s but also illustrates the fundamental assumptions on which this ideal society was to be constructed. Under the Industrial Structure Advisory Council (*Sangyō Kōzō Shingikai*), the leisure division (*yoka bukai*) included 220 academics, journalists, association heads, private industry representatives, and leaders of quasi-public organizations (*kyōkai, zaidan hōjin*, etc.). As MITI's official International Trade and Industry Policy History notes, the researchers together produced a 160-page booklet that outlined leisure conditions in Japan. Published in August 1973 by the Leisure Development Office at the Economic Planning Agency, the *Yoka Shakai e no Kōzu* (Design for the Leisure Society)

---

13. Chalmers Johnson, *MITI and the Japanese Miracle: The Growth of Industrial Policy, 1925–1975* (Stanford: Stanford University Press, 1982), 269–72.
14. MITI, *Tsūshō Sangyō Seisakushi*, 468–69.

hinted at the policy recommendations that MITI would itself make a year later but articulated the reasoning behind them.

In an introduction that now appears startlingly prescient, the report opens with descriptions of how Japan has "caught up to the West" in income and that leisure—which had been ostensibly considered to be subordinate to the needs of work—would have its own independent value. Similarly, the introduction predicts increasing foreign pressure (*gaiatsu*) over Japan's industrial practices (for example, exceptionally long working hours) and that the development of a leisure society would be important in international society. The report thus not only details contemporary leisure practices in Japan but also makes predictions about what will likely happen as well as what the government should do. Among its more specific suggestions are the reduction of working hours and the establishment of a two-day weekend system.

The report goes further, however, in its discussion of why the Japanese government needs a "leisure administration" capable of ensuring the smooth development of leisure facilities and services across the country. At first glance, the report evinces much of the bureaucratic mistrust of a purely open, competitive market that typifies many of Japan's industrial policies.[15] It is worth citing at some length.

> The number-one goal of firms in providing leisure facilities and services is, of course, profit, and so one would expect them to satisfy the needs of consumers to some degree. Even so, there exists a significant gap between the supply of and demand for leisure. For example, with leisure facilities like pachinko parlors, bowling alleys, bar/cabarets, golf courses/driving ranges, resort hotels, *ryokan*, etc., the costs and also the profits involved tend to be quite high, so firms understandably focus on these types of facilities. But demand for these facilities is limited to the upper classes and to certain regions, and a very large number of people are consequently left out of these leisure activities. Additionally, the history of leisure industries is quite short, and firms have no continuous experience with leisure development. As has been seen with bowling alleys, this can lead to an extremely rapid growth in the number of facilities and to excessive competition generated by oversupply. The same kind of rapid growth is now being predicted for "leisure lands" and golfing spots because of the new wave of the leisure boom. In this case too, there is no real contact between leisure land providers, and we now have to worry about the oversupply of these

15. There are many good sources on Japanese industrial policy. For a brief recent overview of the literature, see Hashimoto Jurō, "The Heyday of Industrial Policy Activity," *Social Science Japan* 12 (March 1998): 3–7.

kinds of services. Consumers don't want this, and firms might end up in the same kind of nervous flurry of activity as some did with the bowling alleys. And the problem will be worse than with the bowling alleys, because the scale is larger; they use more land and resources. If too many facilities are built and many end up failing, the costs will be borne not only by the firms but also by society as a whole.[16]

In the same vein, the report cites the need for consumer protection, referring more specifically to issues of price, advertising, and information about facilities and safety. It further mentions, perhaps in part because of a growing sensitivity in the wake of the Minamata catastrophe, the need to protect the general public from the negative externalities of leisure development, such as increased traffic, pollution, garbage from customers, and damage to natural resources.

After discussing these leisure problems, *Yoka Shakai e no Kōzu* describes three basic directions for leisure policy: appropriate guidance and regulation of commercial leisure; the enlightenment of the nation with regard to leisure (*kokumin no rejā ninshiki no keihatsu*); and the use of "community leisure" to foster a greater sense of community and citizenship among residents in given areas.[17] The precise role of government in each of these areas is clearer in the report's final major section of text, *Yoka Gyōsei no Kadai* (Issues for Leisure Administration). These issues include predictable claims that the government needs to regulate leisure markets for the safety and protection of consumers, as well as for the long-term health of the industry. What seems remarkable in the report is its adamant claim that the government has a broader, more important role, largely in the evaluation of leisure resources and the proper development of a "leisure consciousness" in Japan.

The report's statement on the evaluation of leisure resources suggests that there is a trade-off between the development of new leisure spaces and the maintenance of traditional, cultural, or natural resources that people might have enjoyed in ways not easily replaced by bowling alleys or movie theaters:

> The trade-off between development and preservation will become clear with the establishment of an information system (for evaluating

16. Keizai Kikakuchō Yoka Kaihatsu Shitsu (Leisure Development Office, Economic Planning Agency), *Yoka Shakai e no Kōzu* (Design for the Leisure Society) (Tokyo: Ministry of Finance, 1973), 34–35.

17. Ibid., 38–43.

resources), and it will be possible to coordinate this trade-off rationally [*gōriteki ni*]. The evaluation of cultural resources has generally only been undertaken with regard to things thought to have some academic value, but it is also important to grasp the extent to which these resources also have, and will continue to have, a role in the leisure and lifestyle of regional communities. If we are to create a rich lifestyle environment, we will need to evaluate carefully the value of these resources for local environments.[18]

The report is even more pointed with regard to the need to create a better understanding of leisure among Japanese citizens. In discussing this, the EPA authors clearly demonstrate a belief that leisure is not a purely private phenomenon and that a state role is both natural and beneficial:

> Our country has now achieved a level of material wealth sufficient to be considered as the entrance to a new era of leisure. And this means that there will be a rapid expansion of activities for people to engage in freely. Indeed, lifestyle choices are not compulsory, and in the old days this was considered the realm of "freedom" [*jiyū*] for people employed in large organizations, working in some narrowly defined and constraining job; they were released at the end of the day to do as they pleased.
>
> But this situation does not really exist in our country right now. In fact, leisure is now considered to be just the time in one's life left over after work, and people do not sufficiently understand or appreciate the role of leisure.

This ignorance about appropriate or good leisure carries with it serious social risks:

> In the face of expanding leisure and free time, the insufficient formation of a stance toward leisure lifestyle creates a vacuum in people's use of free time and also carries with it the risk of new uncertainty [*fuan*], stress [*kinchō*], and decadence [*taihai*] in modern society. There is a risk that in the midst of this uncertainty, people will turn away from existing forms of entertainment and will turn to dirty or sinful games symbolizing thrills, sex, and speed [Note: *suriru, sekkusu, supīdo*—these are the English words written in the Japanese syllabary katakana, used normally for foreign words], and that there will be a flood of drug-style recreation.[19]

18. Ibid., 46–47.
19. Ibid., 48–49.

In order to prevent this kind of social meltdown as well as to ensure that Japanese people know how to use their free time in an enjoyable, safe, and socially productive manner, the "leisure administration" (*yoka gyōsei*) would have to take a proactive stance. For the most part, this would focus on the need for appropriate education programs (in schools, campaigns, etc.) explaining to people the importance of leisure, as well as appropriate ways of having fun. It would emphasize the "provision of know-how on how to have fun" (*tanoshimu tame no nōhau[20] no teikyō*), the use of leisure advisors, and the development of leisure consultants who could provide valuable advice on worthwhile community leisure. This would ostensibly help people to enjoy themselves while also instilling a civic awareness putatively lacking in some areas. The report pays special attention to the need to coordinate certain kinds of leisure with certain stages in the "life cycle," suggesting in particular the use of volunteers to support the development of "group leisure activities" (*shūdanteki rejā katsudō*) for children and the elderly.

The report's discussion of the state role in the creation of an improved leisure consciousness in Japan concludes with two telling paragraphs:

> In order to come to grips with the coming era of leisure, each of our country's citizens has to learn the ability to make effective use of leisure. To that end, diverse opportunities for people to feel free to enjoy their leisure time all through their lives must be offered. It is also necessary to create educational programs that generate an awareness of protecting the natural environment, the value of lifelong learning, manners and morals [*manā, moraru*] with regard to leisure activities, and the development of a fitting [*fusawashii*] lifestyle stance, which are important for human development [*ningen keisei*]. In Japan, we have typically expected the schools to handle this kind of training, but we should recognize that there are important roles for household education and social education as well, in the field of lifestyle training.
>
> The purposes of leisure policy must include the improvement of people's ability to take advantage of a diverse array of leisure activities; the removal of obstacles to individuals' free choice of leisure-time behavior; and the prevention of leisure's being overly structured [*chitsujōka*] by its relationship to the workplace and one's employment. Within this conception of leisure control, our country tends to think of leisure as being the least important aspect of life, as some sort of

20. *Nōhau* is the katakana, or Japanese syllabary for foreign words, rendering of "know-how."

residual category after work is finished. It will be necessary for us to monitor the development of leisure policy that can help our entire country understand correctly the developing meaning of leisure in human lifestyle [*kokumin zentai ga, ningen seikatsu ni okeru yoka no honrai no igi o tadashiku ninshiki shi*].[21]

Yoka Shakai e no Kōzu thus demonstrates that economic planners in early 1970s Japan felt that the state had an important role in shaping the country into an ideal society and that this ideal society would feature appropriate use of leisure time. Leisure was not merely a private phenomenon, and the state role would have to go far beyond that of mere control over public leisure space (to prevent violence and crime) or of regulation of industry (to protect citizens and firms). It would have to instruct Japanese citizens in how they could enjoy their free time more effectively and to point out that the prevailing emphasis on work over leisure was not a sign of a healthy, mature society. This no doubt represents an effort by MITI and the EPA to assume control over the direction of Japan's leisure development. It remains instructive, however, in how broadly MITI and EPA members sought to demonstrate their interest in leisure; more than merely attempting to regulate the industries, the economic bureaucrats hoped to shape citizens' interests in how they would spend their leisure time.

Modern Leisure and Japanese Identity: Yoka Sōran

Although MITI's official history of overall policy development focuses on the contributions of these 220 researchers to the writing of *Yoka Shakai e no Kōzu*, it unfairly neglects their magnum opus. In 1974, the MITI Leisure Development Office–edited *Yoka Sōran* (Overview of Leisure) was published by Diamond Publishing. This fifteen-hundred-page, two-volume tome shows in remarkable detail the kind of planning and research behind the EPA's guide to the making of a leisure society. In essence, *Yoka Sōran* is the major research project behind *Yoka Shakai e no Kōzu*, and its various sections were penned by large committees of scholars, journalists, and business leaders. What the longer work lacks in terms of concision and clear direction, it makes up for in the complexity of its reasoning and, more important, its illustration of the kinds of tension that the idea of a "leisure society" produced in early 1970s Japan.

This tension becomes evident almost immediately in the work. The

21. Ibid., 50–52.

introductory chapter, apparently authored by the members of the Leisure Committee of the Industrial Policy Discussion Council, starts with a reference to the social insecurity (*fuan*) generated by Japan's rapid economic development, "catching up" as quickly as it did to the industrialized West. Led by Committee Chair Ima Hideumi, then head of the Japan Foundation, the committee announces that in producing a better leisure society, the most important contributions will come from individual citizens. To that end, there is a clear need for policy that will provide guidance for and encourage the kind of social changes necessary for making a better leisure society.[22] Pointedly, the authors remark that by the end of the 1960s, the countries of North America and western Europe had established leisure facilities and equipment that secured a "leisure society" for each of them, but that Japan was lagging in this regard. Although Japan would be laboring from the disadvantage of having poor and underdeveloped leisure facilities, its goal would be to use developmentalist shortcuts to produce affordable and enjoyable leisure opportunities for Japanese citizens. To that end, the country would have to work together to create the necessary "spiritual preparation" (*seishinteki junbi*) for individual and community leisure.[23]

Indeed, it was this very distinction between individual and community leisure that would produce some of the tension generated in the remainder of the book, most notably in the first of its four major sections. "Gendai to Yoka" (Modernity and Leisure) addresses a broad variety of topics and weaves a complex tapestry regarding the proper direction for Japan's leisure development. Describing psychological, social, and even medical features of modern leisure, while also addressing the terminological and philosophical aspects involved, the section includes some impressively sophisticated research. Much of the section is devoted, however, to a marked effort to negotiate the manifold changes in Japanese lifestyles with an enduring national identity. The authors of the "Leisure in Japanese History" subsection, a collection of five professors and one researcher at the Leisure Development Center, trace leisure practices in Japan from the Middle Ages onward and suggest that since the Meiji Restoration, there has been an obvious process of "acculturation," in which appropriate lei-

22. Tsūshō Sangyōsho Yoka Kaihatsutshitsu (MITI Leisure Development Office), ed., *Yoka Sōran: Shakai, Sangyō, Seisaku* (Overview of Leisure: Society, Industry, and Policy) (Tokyo: Dayamondo, 1974), 26.
23. Ibid., 27.

sure practices are increasingly based on those evident in the industrialized West. Much of the problem for Japanese leisure had been a struggle by regimes to extract as much labor as possible from the work force
while also dealing with the fact that the mass media and increasing
knowledge of the West were affecting the way people hoped to spend
their time outside of work. Indeed, the special characteristics of Japanese leisure included the merging of foreign and indigenous leisure
practices. To a large degree, foreign fashions and practices were popular because of the "advanced" status they held for Japan.[24]

If the historians' subsection seemed to welcome foreign leisure practices, even while maintaining that indigenous Japanese leisure still
had a place, the subsection on the "concept of leisure" in part 1 is considerably less sanguine. This larger subcommittee stresses that Japan
is genuinely different from the other advanced industrial countries,
primarily because of its "collectivist" nature (*shūdanshugi*). Unlike
the countries of the industrialized West, where the establishment of a
leisure society focused on the opportunities available to individuals,
in Japan, it would have to address these particular collectivist needs.
The section defends Japan's collectivism against a variety of criticisms
(though never questioning whether *shūdanshugi* is in fact an appropriate way to characterize Japan) and suggests that it in fact places Japan in a position superior to that of the West in the postindustrial
society. The rationalism of the modern world, which radically distinguishes "labor" from "leisure," simultaneously produces a need for
more meaningful leisure and limits enjoyment of leisure time. In the
postindustrial world, leisure and labor would be mixed in a more complex manner, and the *shūdanshugi* of the Japanese—who put a high
social premium on their human networks within the workplace—
would provide an additional "cushion" to smooth over the bumps being felt in early 1970s Europe and North America. This is in part because:

> It is thought that there is no nation on earth that features such ex-
> quisitely introspective leisure practices as the Japanese . . . that is the
> meaning of the *dō* ["the path," as in *budō* (martial arts), *chadō* (tea cer-
> emony), etc.], in that through these practices we are trying to achieve
> human perfection. And that is a big difference with the West.[25]

24. Ibid., 64–69.
25. Ibid., 121–31, quoted section on 130.

Even so, for policy ideas, *Yoka Sōran* emphatically turns to international examples. Indeed, almost four hundred of the book's fifteen-hundred pages are devoted to comparative studies of leisure practices and policies around the world, with examples from every corner of the world. And while the report includes studies of countries as disparate as Spain and Tonga, China and Canada, its emphasis is clear right from the beginning:

> The various subcommittees focused on fifteen countries from North America, western Europe, the communist countries, and four other regions. But if one examines the structure of leisure in these different countries, one sees great diversity from the advanced countries that have already entered an era of a new leisure civilization [*atarashii yoka bunmei no jidai*] to the lesser developed countries that still have no fixed understanding of what "leisure" means.[26]

Although the report's subsequent case studies distinguish between countries, the underlying logic supports the trope developed in the introduction: that the other advanced countries have already moved ahead in leisure, and that Japan's leisure still lags behind.[27] Consequently, the valuable lessons to be gleaned are those generated in the North American and western European cases.

The remainder of *Yoka Sōran* is instructive in terms of the structure of Japan's domestic leisure industries and also demonstrates MITI's concern over the *tatewari gyōsei* (horizontally segmented administration) that essentially divides control over leisure among a number of ministries. As Morris-Suzuki notes, the recession that Japan suffered in the early 1970s as a result of exchange rate changes and the first oil shocks of the decade made some of the grander aspirations of the leisure development policy program somewhat moot. As a consequence, the immediate studies of the structure of Japan's leisure industries may have been less important to the long-term direction of Japan's leisure industry policies than were the international comparisons that helped to encode formally the way that leisure would be understood.

That is, *Yoka Sōran* established clearly that leisure would be understood as a function of economic development and that its place in human society would be conceptualized temporally. More developed

26. Ibid., 315.
27. Ibid., 27–28.

societies would have more advanced leisure, while less developed ones would have less advanced leisure. The ostensibly poor conditions for leisure in Japan of the 1960s were interpreted not as a sui generis phenomenon for the nation but rather as somewhat embarrassing evidence of the nation's backwardness. And just as Japan had had to catch up to the West in its industrial profile, it would have to do so in terms of lifestyle as well.

The wholesale adoption of "Western" leisure practices, however, was not accepted as being unproblematic. Whereas catching up to the West economically, particularly in terms of manufacturing, represented a national goal that did not necessarily suggest Japan was becoming more Western (and less Japanese), the apparent necessity of lifestyle change did. *Yoka Sōran's* defense of indigenous and collectivist practices reflects an effort to define what was foreign and what was Japanese and to negotiate lifestyle change that would protect something inherent about the Japanese character. As leisure policy became more firmly institutionalized, it became an ever trickier issue for national identity: Japan's identity as an advanced country (like any other) and as a unique nation with clear distinguishing characteristics. What prevented this debate from occupying center stage was the economic slowdown that led economic planners to refocus their efforts on manufacturing and trade and on services only insofar as they involved the "information" industries.

None of this should be interpreted to mean that there is objectively a conflict between adoption of Western leisure practices and the putative uniqueness of the Japanese. After all, the paragon of American cultural imperialism—Disneyland—is hardly the unproblematic form of domination in Japan that one might expect. It is not just that some of the features at Tokyo Disneyland, Japan's most popular theme park, have been "Japanized," through coordination between the Disney corporation and representatives of Oriental Land, the company that owns the Tokyo franchise.[28] In fact, Tokyo Disneyland has been viewed by Japanese visitors as a kind of performed "America," in which the same attractions that appear in the American Disney theme parks are given meaning by the very fact that they seem American.[29] Although the meaning of the same activity thus changes across cultures, Japan's leisure policies have tended not to accept this. Their creators have in-

---

28. Interview 28, 27 January 1997.
29. Aviad E. Raz, *Riding the Black Ship: Japan and Tokyo Disneyland* (Cambridge: Harvard University Asia Center, 1999).

stead focused on how to make minor alterations to the adopted be-havior in order to adhere more straightforwardly to a traditional ver-sion of who the Japanese are.

The Risk of Bad Word Choices in Leisure Policy

Leisure policy would soon be confronted by hard economic chal-lenges and further hampered by a critical mistake in policymakers' language. The economic problems that would face Japan in the early 1970s have been widely documented and need no lengthy recapitula-tion here. But with the end of the Bretton Woods system and its effect on the value of the yen, not to mention the first oil crisis, Japan was doubly vulnerable. Dependent on international trade, and therefore highly sensitive to currency shocks, as well as on imported oil to con-tinue its industrial growth, the country struggled during those years to reshift the foundations on which the Japanese economy had pros-pered. With the turn toward defensive measures to protect the nation's growth, MITI, the EPA, and other agencies had far more pressing mis-sions than an adventurous foray into the still largely unknown terri-tory of leisure development.

That said, the YKC and the Leisure Development Desk at MITI con-tinued throughout this period to compile information and reports on the changing leisure environment of Japan, particularly in comparison with those witnessed in the other advanced industrial nations. And al-though the absence of funding available for major leisure initiatives ensured that the research was, for the time being, purely academic rather than tied to any discrete or well-defined policy goals, a role for the state in planning leisure—using clear standards for differentiating good from bad recreation and useful from useless development—was better institutionalized than before. At no time did MITI or any other organization suggest a fundamental rethinking of the role that leisure services ought to play in Japan's economic development. Instead, the YKC continued its research in the expectation that the lessons learned about leisure development overseas would ultimately become rele-vant in planning Japan's development.

In the next chapter, we will investigate the most important such policy—the Resort Law, which would play a part in the rapid over-heating of the Japanese economy in the 1980s. For the moment, it is enough to point out that even if leisure were not the budgetary jug-gernaut it once seemed likely to become, it was now accepted as an important component of a "normal" healthy economy. As a result, other policy organizations began to step gingerly into the field with proposals for meeting some of Japan's public policy goals with the use of leisure development. The best placed of these was, of course, the Ministry of Transport (MOT), which had jurisdiction over the JTB, clearly Japan's most durable public organization in any leisure field. Seeing the opportunity to expand its organizational reach to include massive new tourism development projects, the MOT would undergo a relatively well-publicized policy failure in the 1970s. Although the main long-term consequence of the MOT's initiative would be the virtual prohibition of Japanese government support for overseas tourism projects during the next ten years, it is instructive in its display of the kinds of political conflicts that leisure policymakers could meet.

Outbound Tourism Growth and a New Place on the Policy Agenda

Administrative jurisdiction over the Japanese tourism industry belongs to the MOT, the postwar successor to the Ministry of Railroads, which had been in charge of the JTB, the *Kwankō Kyōkai,* and other tourism-related organs before the war. The country's main travel agency, the *Tōa Kōtsū Kōsha* (The Greater East Asian Travel Public Corporation, otherwise known as the Japan Tourist Bureau), was allowed to remain open, changing its Japanese title to *Nihon Kōtsū Kōsha* (Japan Travel Public Corporation) and its English title to Japan Travel Bureau. Beginning in September 1945, almost immediately after the end of the war, it had changed its name and had become a special public foundation (*zaidan hōjin*) of the new government. The reborn JTB proved both adept and fortunate enough to avoid some of the purges that befell its bosses in the new MOT; in the country's 1947 election, their general director won election to member of the Lower House, where he strongly advised that Japan become a "tourist country" (*kankō rikkoku*). The JTB worked almost immediately to build a national alliance of potential tourist regions and by 1950 had amassed enough capital that it began to advertise overseas once again.[30]

Even had its efforts been quicker, the JTB would have been unlikely to have accomplished much in the way of attracting tourists from

---

30. JTB, *Nihon Kōtsū Kōsha no Nanajunenshi* (The Seventy-Year History of the Japan Travel Bureau) (Tokyo: JTB, 1982), 95–96.

overseas. Virtually all of the nation's functional hotels were being used by the U.S. Occupation forces, and the American leadership also created strict controls on people coming in and out of the country. It was not until 1949 that the government regained something of a free hand in determining how many international visitors would be allowed to come to Japan, and domestic tourism was hardly an issue until later in the 1950s. Still, once the doors for visitors began to open (they had begun to do so symbolically in 1947 with the arrival of the U.S. passenger ship the *President Monroe*), Japan quickly reestablished itself as a major draw for foreign visitors, from six hundred "guests" in 1947 to over one hundred thousand by 1955.[31]

In the wrangling for control over various industries, jurisdiction over tourism was formally invested in the prime minister's office under the Tourism Basic Law on 20 June 1949; six months later, however, control over the various parts of the industry was handed to the Ministry of Transport in a comprehensive law for assisting the international tourism industry. The MOT ultimately would strengthen its role under the Travel Agency Law (1952) and its administrative fiat over Japan Airlines and Japan National Railways, but it was to be limited in terms of tourist facilities, which were governed by laws that referred to the "competent minister" rather than to a specific ministry.[32] Indeed while the ministry still exercised authority over the JTB, the rapid growth of the Japanese economy led the JTB to concentrate more on tour packaging rather than inbound promotion. It would ultimately become a corporation in 1965, beginning its somewhat odd position as a private company with a foundation of the same name still attached to the government. The MOT took the opportunity to create the Japan National Tourist Organization (1959) as a special foundation answerable to the ministry[33] and funded solely by the government with 100,000,000 yen. The JNTO would pursue the standard duty of a national tourist organization: the attraction of foreign tourists, though the government continued to promote purely domestic travel by Japanese as well. To that end, in 1960, the prime minister's office

---

31. Sōrifu Shingishitsu (Prime Minister's Research Office), ed., *Kankō Gyōsei Hyakunen to Kankō Seisaku Shingikai Sanjūnen no Ayumi* (One Hundred Years of Tourism Administration and Thirty Years of the Tourism Policy Discussion Council) (Tokyo: Gyosei, 1980), 41–48.

32. Most of the laws relevant to Japan's tourist industry are available in English as well as Japanese. See JICA, *Tourism Laws and Regulations in Japan* (Tokyo: JICA, 1991).

33. Sōrifu Shingishitsu, *Kankō Gyōsei Hyakunen*, 75–80.

began surveys every five years of Japan's domestic travel market. The Liberal Democratic Party tried half-heartedly to help local spots by calling for "Five-Year Plans" for tourism development but had to settle for limited government support of the domestic industry through low-interest loans and general public relations campaigns.[34]

Japanese postwar outbound tourism was liberalized in 1964, largely because that year's Tokyo Olympics made the country seem a bit backward for not allowing its people to travel abroad, while doing all it could to invite foreigners in. To be sure, the outbound travel market grew fairly slowly at first, in part because the yen remained pegged at ¥360/$1 for years, and in part because of heavy working hours and tight restrictions on vacations by most employers. Still, by the early 1970s the number of outbound travelers began to pick up some speed, topping one million in 1972 and then two million in 1973, the fastest single gain in any year in the postwar period. This reflected the 25 percent increase, between 1970 and 1973, in the value of the yen, from ¥360/$1 to ¥280/$1. The number of outbound travelers stagnated, however, after the 1973 oil shock and would rise only slowly until 1985.[35]

The early trend in outbound travel did not go unnoticed. In particular, MITI and the EPA decided that this was one more element in Japan's rapidly developing leisure society and that outbound travel and facilities for Japanese tourists ought to be built overseas. To that end, the final few pages of the *Yoka Sōran* were devoted to the issue of "international leisure." In particular, the authors noted that it would be necessary for the Japanese government to formulate a policy stance that would enable its people and firms to take advantage of the new "global" leisure environment. The report argued that Japanese tourists had been unprepared for the era of mass international tourism and that a "mental gap" existed, requiring the government not only to provide information to Japanese citizens on how they ought to behave while overseas but also to Japanese firms and foreign countries in order to smooth the development of Japanese-style resorts overseas. The government would have to be involved in designing "international-level" leisure environments and networks both at home and abroad, estab-

34. Koike Yoichi and Ashiba Hiroyasu, eds., *Kankōgaku Gairon* (Introduction to the Study of Tourism) (Kyoto: Minerva, 1988), 49–52. The book notes that chapter 3 ("Kankō Seisaku," or "Tourism Policy"), from which this material is taken, was written primarily by Miyaza Bunji, though chapters are not individually credited.

35. JNTO, *Statistics on Tourism/Japan 1994* (Tokyo: JNTO, 1996).

lishing Japan as a first-class leisure country, and aiding the developing countries to create world-class environments that Japanese might enjoy.[36]

As might have been expected, MITI turned to the Leisure Development Center (YKC) to carry out surveys on the prospects of overseas tourism development by Japanese firms. In 1974, the YKC produced the first of two *Kokugai no Yoka Shigen Chōsa ni Yoru Yoka Fashiriti no Kaihatsu Kenkyū* (Development Research on Leisure Facilities and Overseas Leisure Resources) reports, with the follow-up appearing in 1975. In part working for the *Kikai Shinkō Kyōkai Keizai Kenyūjo* (Machine Promotion Association Economic Institute), the YKC produced a dense report totaling over four hundred pages, arguing that economic development in the Polynesian islands would have to rely at least in part on tourism development. As a tourism development plan, this would not be Japan's finest hour. The report emphasized the importance of constructing an image for the region, deciding on the theme of the "Lost Continent," after dozens of pages of hand-wringing over whether it was or was not appropriate.[37] Furthermore, the report's goals were to provide information to firms and individuals about the region and how it could be marketed. Its suggestions for tourism policy were thus somewhat sketchy: they would have to take account of the needs of the tourists, the leisure facilities available, and the protection of the peoples and environments of the Pacific Islands.[38]

The Cheju Island Tourism Development Incident

Emboldened to some extent by the rising trend of outbound tourism and its increased relevance in policy circles, the MOT, with its mandate over the tourism industry, became involved in the early 1970s in a major development plan for the Republic of Korea. Having normalized relations with the Republic of Korea only in 1965, the Japanese government—particularly under the Ministry of Foreign Affairs (MOFA) and the Ministry of Finance (MOF)—proposed a major Overseas Development Assistance (ODA) plan of financial and technical assis-

36. Tsūshō Sangyōsho Yoka Kaihatsutshitsu, *Yoka Sōran*, 1489–1510.

37. YKC, *Kokugai no Yoka Shigen Chōsa ni Yoru Yoka Fashiriti no Kaihatsu Kenkyū* (Development Research on Leisure Facilities and Overseas Leisure Resources) (Tokyo: YKC, March 1974), section 4, 1–58. The "Lost Continent" debate focused in part on whether Japan, as a non-Western country, shared the West's "romantic" fascination with the idea of the "Lost Continent."

38. Ibid., section 4, 93–108.

tance for Korea. In what would prove to be an ill-advised decision, the ministries decided to include a "tourism development" component, with the MOT proposing a plan for Cheju Island. The plan itself would promote Japanese tourism to Cheju through the development of a ferry service, technical assistance to Korean residents for tourism, and support for Japanese firms that would promote development in the area. Any good tourism development plan must, of course, take advantage of the target region's purported tourism resources; in the case of Cheju, this was taken to be its "nightlife."[39]

To the ministry officials who carried out the research project, there was ostensibly nothing wrong with the word. Cheju is a well-known entertainment town in the Republic of Korea, with bars, casinos, and clubs, and playing up these features of the country in a development report probably seemed to be only natural. The MOT officials faced a rude awakening, and also the most bitter debate over postwar Japanese tourism, when they brought the full package to the Diet. After all, the Diet's powerful left-leaning forces had been marginalized in a number of important policy arenas—such as over industrial policy—but they could still mobilize significant opposition to government initiatives, particularly when these ran afoul of deeply held convictions. Few were closer to the hearts of Socialists and Communists than the sense that the Japanese treatment of its neighbors during World War II had been barbaric because it had been imperialistic. The unity of capital and military force had led the nation to a destructive war with Asian neighbors, and its treatment of the people of Korea and other nations had reflected the callous disregard for life that was logically linked with imperialism. And so a government initiative to build "nightlife" spots, as if the meaning of the word were ambiguous in a region known for its sex markets, in a former colonial territory simply could not have been calibrated any more finely to run into opposition.

In a closed session of the *Kessan Iinkaigi* (Settlements Committee) of the Japanese Lower House on 9 October 1973, with four ministers (of MITI, the Ministry of Agriculture, Forestry and Fisheries [MAFF], the Ministry of Justice [MOJ], and MOF) and over a dozen representatives of other ministries in attendance, Socialist committee member Kobayashi Susumu launched immediately into the "Research Report on the Cheju Island Tourism Development Plan," produced by the MOT. Starting out with a somewhat bitter attack on the proposal to

39. In an interview with a former MOT official, I was told that the word was "night" tourism, though in later Diet debates the word in question is clearly "naituraifu," a Japanese phoneticization of the English word.

use public funds to promote the establishment of more nightclubs and casinos, Kobayashi then moved in for the kill:

> There are special *kisaeng* [Korean word originally similar to *geisha* but now referring more broadly to sex workers] parties and nightclubs for foreign tourists, and these get returned to as the place's tourist resources in the report's evaluation. So are you telling me that with our citizens' money, with our national taxes, our country's administrators [*yakunin*] went to carry out a survey and report on *kisaeng*? You simply have got to be kidding me [*fumajime jya nai desu ka, anata*].

Kobayashi turned his attention to the infamous word nightlife. Mentioning the five basic suggestions from the Ministry of Transport in the report, he referred to the third, which called for an improvement in tourism-related facilities.

> "The country should simplify procedures for admitting foreigners, reduce taxes for foodstuffs" and next, "there is a need in Cheju for better restaurants, nightclubs, and nightlife [*naituraifu*] for foreign tourists." This is the first time I've heard the word "nightlife." . . . Here is a new word [in Japanese] created by the OTCA and the MOT's Tourism Division. And in using this ridiculous [*fumajime*] word in the name of Korean-Japanese relations, they've managed to gravely insult the people of both our countries.

The ministry officials present attempted to sidestep this thorny issue, which completely dominated Kobayashi's lengthy comments on the Cheju Island plan. Aichi Kiichi, the minister of finance, referred to the proper use of tax funds to support this kind of research mission, while Takemura Teruo of the Ministry of Justice's Immigration Bureau attempted to turn the issue of *kisaeng* into one about how they enter Japan as entertainers and occasionally overstay their visas. With other committee members joining Kobayashi's onslaught, the MOT's Tourism Bureau chief Nakamura Daizō sought to back down as quickly as possible:

> Yes, the Tourism Bureau and the Overseas Technical Cooperation Agency [OTCA, predecessor of JICA] dispatched people for this research. And yes, we did the research and the report, so the responsibility for its contents lies with us. The word you're all talking about, "nightlife": it pains me to think that this word might be misunderstood, misconstrued to mean something so abominable. And I think that this recognition will play a role as we put together the final plan.

The damage was done, however. With Kobayashi saying memorably, "Korea is not a sex toilet for the Japanese, and it's not our vomitorium," (*Kankoku wa, nihon kokumin no sekkusu benjo de wa nakute, haku basho de wa nai*) the MOT was shell-shocked, as were other members of the foreign aid community in Japan.[40] The memory of the event, and the bitterness over the consequences, still rankle.[41]

Limits on International Tourism Projects in the 1970s

International tourism development managed to remain something of a topic in Japan's ODA circles in the 1970s but at a much less vaunted level than the authors of the *Yoka Sōran*, the Overseas Resort Facility reports, or the abortive Cheju Island plan had hoped. Before increasing pressure over Japan's trade surpluses would ignite a government passion for supporting Japanese hotel investment overseas, state support for leisure development elsewhere was limited to a few narrow cases. Tourism development was a fairly minor element in development master plans by the Japan International Cooperation Agency (JICA) for Central Java (1973–1974), and West Sumatra (1977–1978) in Indonesia, the Kilimanjaro area in Tanzania (1974–1975), the Pattaya resort area in Thailand (1976–1978), and Southern Egypt (1978–1979). In addition, Bulgaria received a loan from the Overseas Economic Cooperation Fund (OECF) for the construction of a hotel in Sofia (1975), and Bangladesh received another for a Pan-Pacific Hotel in 1977.[42] The Bangladesh project was itself highly criticized in part because of the sense that the project was itself little more than a financial tool to help the Tōkyū group establish one of its flagship Pan-Pacific hotels in South Asia, as well as an ostentatious display of wealth in an exceptionally poor country.[43] Even today, Tōkyū officials

40. The fully twenty-two-page record of this session is available in the records of the 71st session of the Lower House of the Diet (Kokkai Shūgi). See *Kessan Iinkai-giroku* (Records of the Accounts Committee), no. 27, 910–32.

41. I was told, "This was because of the stupid Socialists," in one interview (number 19, 31 August 1995). In an unfortunate but perhaps appropriately tawdry coda to this affair, Hattori Tsuneharu, the former president of New Kansai International Airport and previously a high-ranking bureaucrat at the MOT, was arrested in 1997 for a financial scandal and had been seen spending much of his ill-gotten gains on women and gambling on Cheju Island, by then a well-known nightspot. Some clever observers gave Hattori the nickname "Hattori-kun," a reference to a young ninja in a TV cartoon, for his habit of evading his own bodyguards while sneaking away from the office for his romantic trysts. This was reported in all of the major Japanese scandal sheets, though the best coverage of the Cheju Island aspect was in the *Shūkan Yomiuri*, 9 February 1997, 33–36.

42. ITDIJ, "ITDIJ Overseas Researchers' Manual" (Tokyo: unpublished, 1995).

43. Robert M. Orr mentions this project as one of the OECF's more highly criticized

remain somewhat reluctant to talk about how their firm was able to get a fairly lucrative contract to build a lavish hotel overseas.[44]

With the heyday of leisure promotion in the early 1970s over, outbound tourism was not the hot property it had appeared to be before the slowing Japanese economy and the ill-advised "nightlife" development plan made it a questionable goal. Even when tourism remained in the relatively benign background of development plans overseas, it still came under fire. In the mid-1970s, JICA produced two feasibility studies for the maintenance of the Borobudur Prambanan National Archaeological Park in Indonesia; these ultimately led to two concessionary loans from the OECF to Indonesia in 1980 and 1982.[45] The plan itself should, on the surface, have been considered praiseworthy. A major effort to protect ninth-century remains of ancient temples, the plan was designed originally as a form of international "cultural assistance." But because the plan included a tourism component, including the construction of facilities that could accommodate visitors (who would, the authors reasoned, be contributing financially to its continued protection), it was derided by critics as a sop to wealthy visitors who would almost certainly damage the site. One critic, Murai Yoshitaka wrote of it:

> If they manage to make the park beautiful, the number of tourists is going to increase, and this is the only way that it can be evaluated as being a success. We don't want our tax money, our postal savings going to this project. All it will achieve is to make enemies of the Indonesians."[46]

Nevertheless, the project was completed in 1988 with a fair amount of fanfare and continues to be regarded as one of the success stories of Japanese tourism-related assistance of the era.[47]

Overseas tourism development as an issue in Japan's diplomatic and

---

ones in *The Emergence of Japan's Foreign Aid Power* (New York: Columbia University Press, 1990).

44. Interview 34, 24 February 1997.

45. The ITDIJ mentions this in the brief "ITDIJ Overseas Researchers' Manual."

46. Murai Yoshitaka, *Musekinin Enjo ODA Taikoku Nippon* (Japan: The Irresponsible Foreign Aid Superpower), cited in Watanabe Toshio and Kusano Atsushi, *Nihon no ODA o Dō Suru Ka* (What Should Be Done with Japan's Foreign Aid?) (Tokyo: NHK Books, 1991), 137.

47. Watanabe and Kusano are more supportive than Murai of the project. See Watanabe and Kusano, *Nihon no ODA o Dō Suru Ka,* 132–39. They conclude with the comment that it is difficult to judge whether the project was a success or failure but say that the temple ruins "must be seen" (*mirareru beki*), and that Japan's loans certainly played a large role in increasing the number of visitors.

foreign aid programs remained at best a scattered and haphazard business, at least in comparison with its auspicious beginnings. For the most part, the Ministry of Transport failed conspicuously to make its Tourism Bureau more of a key player in the arena of international development. Outbound tourism, hampered by an artificially weak yen and the relative difficulty of getting out of Japan, was simply not providing enough of a push for policymakers to take a stand with regard to its benefit to the nation, particularly with some of the bitter attacks that the MOT's earlier missteps had provoked.

Like MITI and its role in establishing the YKC, however, the MOT scored one important institutional success in participating in the establishment of the ASEAN Centre. An intergovernmental organization of Japan and the ASEAN (Association of Southeast Asian Nations) member countries, the ASEAN Centre was established in 1981 as a follow-up of sorts to the Fukuda Doctrine. The so-called doctrine, named for Prime Minister Fukuda Takeo, had committed Japan, starting in 1977, to a special relationship in the ASEAN region, based on a rejection of Japanese military presence, equal partnership, and close and friendly ties. ASEAN became an increasingly important target of Japanese ODA funds at precisely the time that ODA was entering its most phenomenal period of growth.[48] As one outcome, the MOFA, MOT, and MITI agreed to establish the ASEAN Centre, which would be 90 percent funded by Japan, and 10 percent by the ASEAN countries. As an ODA project, this intergovernmental organization would be responsible for promoting trade from ASEAN to Japan (Trade Division—guided by MOFA), investment from Japan to ASEAN (Investment Division—guided by MOFA), and tourism from Japan to the ASEAN member nations (Tourism Division—guided by MOT).[49]

Institutions and Limits in Japanese Leisure Policy in the 1970s

The MOT's overall failure with the Cheju Island plan thus slowed its ability to take advantage of the *Yoka Sōran*'s invitation to bring the state back into the realm of international tourism. The imperative for government involvement in leisure development was thus not entirely unproblematic. Even so, the creation of the YKC and the ASEAN Centre—with its role in attempting to shift Japanese outbound tourist

48. On Japanese ODA to the ASEAN region, see Alan Rix, *Japan's Foreign Aid Challenge: Policy Reform and Aid Leadership* (London: Routledge, 1993), 147–52.
49. Interview 22, 12 August 1997.

traffic toward the ASEAN nations—were key shifts that indicated the eagerness of officials to intervene in leisure markets in the service of state goals. And, in part because of the work of the committees behind the *Yoka Sōran* and *Yoka Shakai e no Kōzu,* these developments became genuinely institutionalized.

By institutionalized, of course, I mean that the role of leisure in Japan's economic development, as well as the probable role of the state in leisure, were taken for granted, as was the tension over what leisure meant. With Japan's soaring economy in the 1970s, there could be little doubt that Japanese industries were now internationally competitive and that Japan had entered the ranks of the wealthy nations. Officials believed that to maintain that growth, citizens would need to consume leisure services that could sustain it over the long term; the Japanese would need to behave more like Americans and Europeans. Such behavior ran afoul of the notion, clearly displayed in these policy documents, that the Japanese were and should be culturally unique. By the 1980s, when Japanese nationalism would become even more politically salient, this would become an alarming tension in Japan's leisure policies.

The fiscal and financial challenges facing Japan in the 1970s derailed the major initiatives that government planners might have pushed under more auspicious circumstances, though not the policy organizations and institutions involved in leisure. In chapter 5, I examine the most important leisure policy created in postwar Japan: the "Resort Law," which has been described by critics as one of the key causes of Japan's uncontrolled, spastic growth in the bubble era. One can easily explain the policy by referring to the clear political goals of officials and politicians; they sought to capitulate to some international pressure over Japanese consumption patterns while providing pork barrel benefits to Liberal Democratic Party members. But to fully understand the policy, we must recognize the importance of the institutional context that permitted and defined the state role in leisure. The Resort Law would almost certainly have been absolutely inconceivable in a political environment that did not take for granted that leisure was a public, not purely private, matter. Moreover, it clearly betrayed the expectation that Japanese should, in their leisure time, behave more like Americans and Europeans and that such a shift would be crucial to Japan's continued economic success. It would also place leisure shifts close to the center of the debates of Japan's national identity, over what it means to be Japanese.

Japanese women shopping at Venus Fort, a "women's theme park" in Tokyo, 2000.
Photograph by Merry White.

The Last Resorts of a
Lifestyle Superpower

In 1991, Prime Minister Miyazawa Kiichi announced that Japan, having achieved its status as an economic superpower, would need to become a "lifestyle superpower" (*seikatsu taikoku*). The meaning of the term was vague, though it generally connoted a combination of higher living standards, more space, a better environment for consumers, and a more favorable balance of labor and leisure for Japan's overburdened workforce. Of course, a stance in favor of better lifestyles is about as controversial as vociferous support for one's national team at the World Cup. And if the announcement was not responsible for Miyazawa's rough luck as prime minister—he was vomited on by President George Bush at a state dinner[1] and was also in power when the LDP split, ultimately leading to the end of the party's thirty-eight-year reign—there is little evidence that it provided much help. Even if Miyazawa's pledge was politically motivated, it cannot be dismissed as "mere" propaganda, if only because his statement was designed to *work*. That is, if Miyazawa and his staff believed that a push to make Japan a "lifestyle superpower" would somehow make him a

---

1. An incident that, unfortunately, did not prompt anyone to suggest, paraphrasing Socialist Diet member Kobayashi Susumu from chapter 4, that Japan is not America's vomitorium.

more popular figure, it was only because of a prevailing sense that Japanese had worked too hard for too many years and that they had not had the opportunity to enjoy their position among the world's richest peoples.

This chapter examines why Japanese efforts to improve lifestyles, particularly through leisure development, accelerated during the 1980s, culminating in a massive plan for resort development. The Resort Law, which would ultimately be blamed as one of the main culprits in the rising land values that fueled the unsustainable bubble economy, responded to international criticism of Japan's high savings rate and low consumption but was politically popular because of its jaw-dropping pork barrel value. Its broader ambitions, however, make sense only in the context of the seismic shifts that the Japanese government sought to effect in this era.[2] Governments always pursue social goals to affect the lives of citizens, and Japan's is no exception.[3] But in Japan's case, these social goals reflected intense pressure, particularly from the United States, to open the nation to foreign products, a push that officials would use to mean something broader. Consequently, the dominant word in 1980s politics was "internationalization" (*kokusaika*), which referred to extraordinary efforts to make Japan more open to foreign influences, in politically controlled and determined ways. In practice, this meant that the Japanese government sought—for politically instrumental reasons—to encourage Japanese to behave more like Americans and Europeans.

On one level, it is unsurprising that leisure would be part of this shift. After all, who could object to the idea that Japanese should be allowed to enjoy themselves as Americans and Europeans reportedly did? They had certainly earned it. But the Resort Law begs attention because it provides a compelling example of the problems to which leisure policy could lead. Moreover, in the tsunami of red ink for local governments that followed the law and the end of the bubble economy, fingers pointed wildly over who was to blame. Tellingly, however, even the law's critics would illustrate their arguments with

2. Indeed, two chapters in a recent volume on Japanese leisure refer to the Resort Law in the broader shift toward tourism and resorts in the 1980s and 1990s. See Angelika Hamilton-Oehrl, "Leisure Parks in Japan" (237–50), and Nelson H. H. Graburn, "Work & Play in the Japanese Countryside" (195–212), in *The Culture of Japan as Seen through Its Leisure*, ed. Sepp Linhart and Sabine Frühstück (Albany: State University of New York Press, 1998).

3. For one excellent study, see Sheldon Garon, *Molding Japanese Minds: The State in Everyday Life* (Princeton: Princeton University Press, 1997).

examples drawn from the United States and western Europe. It was now fully taken for granted that leisure could be measured on a universal timeline of development and that the West, or parts of it, was undeniably ahead.

The Transformation of the Meaning of Leisure in Postwar Japan

Lifestyle has been a vexing issue in late-twentieth-century Japan, no doubt because of the enormous personal sacrifices that citizens were called on to make in order to fuel the democratic nation's rise toward its status as a bona fide economic powerhouse. At no time was this demonstrated more effectively (or poignantly) than in the early postwar years when teenagers moved in large numbers from their rural homes to urban areas to work in factories, often under extremely tough conditions.[4] Because the most startling changes in the lives of Japanese citizens were in many ways occasioned by economic development, many Japanese scholars initially sought to theorize lifestyle change as a more or less predictable consequence of economic change.[5] And if the discussion of Japanese lifestyles has opened dramatically in the past few decades, it has largely been because of a diversification of views on what constitutes a good lifestyle.

The debate arises in part because of the opaqueness of the term *seikatsu* (conventionally translated as "lifestyle"). This word remains fundamentally problematic in Japan, and it is generally unclear to what aspect of one's life the term refers. Feminist debates in Japan, for example, have often been divided between *riron-sha* (theorists) and *seikatsu-sha* (pragmatists), who ostensibly deal more with "real-world" issues.[6] Similarly, the Japanese prime minister's office's an-

---

4. For a good discussion of the transportation of child labor from the villages to the cities in the 1950s, see Kase Kazutoshi, *Shūdan Shūshoku no Jidai: Kōdō Seichō no Ninaitetachi* (Juvenile Labor Fueling Japan's High-Speed Growth) (Tokyo: Aoki Shoten, 1997). The shift in lifestyles and self-consciousness is covered on 169–98.

5. For an overview of this research, particularly on the Japanese Marxist scholars who helped to pioneer it, see Watanabe Masuo, *Seikatsu no Kōzōteki Haaku no Riron* (Theories for a Structural Understanding of Lifestyle) (Tokyo: Kawashima, 1996).

6. I am indebted to Beth Katzoff for clarifying this distinction for me. See Amano Masako, *"Seikatsusha" to wa Dare Ka? Jiritsuteki Shiminzō no Keifu* (Who Are the "Seikatsu-sha"? The Genealogy of Images of Autonomous Citizens) (Tokyo: Chūō Shinsho, 1996). Amano does not argue that the *seikatsu-sha* label is appropriate only for women but rather that women's reproductive capacities have made them more alert to lifestyle issues in Japan. Consequently, they have been the leaders of the movement to have lifestyle issues taken seriously in politics. See especially 184–228.

nual survey about *seikatsu* issues has to get first at the question of what *seikatsu* means, giving respondents the choice between such aspects as "leisure lifestyle" (*yoka seikatsu*), residential lifestyle (*jūseikatsu*), and culinary lifestyle (*shokuseikatsu*).[7] There is a historical aspect to this as well. According to Suga Yukiko, under the Occupation, *seikatsu* issues had an explicitly political tone, including universal suffrage, democracy, and equal rights for women. Using the "American model," Japanese lifestyles were supposed to look more open and liberal. Between 1955 and 1970, lifestyle issues became "rationalized" and "modernized," focusing on such immediate markers of improved lifestyles as television sets, automobiles, and other consumer goods. Finally, since the 1970s, the country has begun to inspect the quality of lifestyle, reflecting on the meaning of leisure pursuits within one's life.[8] Some argue that the issue is now one of moving beyond a *yoka shakai* ("leisure society)" and toward a *yutori no aru shakai* (again, using Gavan McCormack's language from chapter 1, "a society that gives me space to do my own thing"). According to one observer, the distinction refers to the difference between enjoying leisure through the purchase of ever increasingly elaborate leisure products and services (the commodification of leisure) and using leisure to enhance one's pure relaxation, of getting to do what one wants to do.[9]

The issue has become one of how a country with obvious material wealth could so conspicuously fail to be a garden of Eden for the pleasure of its citizens. Between long commuting times, long working hours, and crowded living conditions, many Japanese authors have argued that the country, even today, fails to approach the quality of life evident in the other advanced industrial countries. Perhaps the most famous of these authors (her book ran through more than thirty-five printings), Teruoka Itsuko, suggested in 1989 that Japan's rapid expansion of material wealth had not been accompanied by a genuine feeling of wealth, because the mere accumulation of trinkets and

---

7. Sōrifu (Prime Minister's Office), *Kokumin Seikatsu ni Kansuru Yōron Chōsa* (Public Opinion Survey of National Life) (Tokyo: 1992), cited in *Yoka Seikatsuron* (Leisure Lifestyle), ed. Ichibangase Yasuko, Sonoda Sekiya, and Makino Nobuo (Tokyo: Yūhikaku, 1994), 5.

8. Suga Yukiko, "Watashitachi no Jidai no 'Seikatsu Bunka' to Wa" (What "Lifestyle Culture" Means in Our Times), in *Kurashi no Tetsugaku to shite no "Seikatsu Bunka"* ("Lifestyle Culture" as a Philosophy of Living), ed. Matsuda Yoshiyuki (Tokyo: PHP, 1997), 170–201.

9. Ichijō Shin'ya, *Yutori Haiken* (The Discovery of Space) (Tokyo: Tōkyū Agency, 1990).

baubles could not compensate for the lack of free time and space, protection of welfare, and a preserved natural environment that is fundamentally central to a decent human lifestyle. In making her point, Teruoka stressed the example of West Germany, which apparently was something of a utopia. This was a country where old people "do not need to worry," where people put emphasis on their responsibility to society rather than to themselves, and where domiciles are affordable, of high quality, and easily distinguished from one another. The Japanese, in spite of their material wealth, had in Teruoka's eyes failed to create a truly wealthy society, which must focus on better use of free time and an improved environment for its enjoyment.[10]

Much of the rhetoric in the national debate over lifestyle has been fueled by one statement, evidently made by a French delegate, in a European Community (EC) meeting on trade with Japan in 1979. The phrase, that the Japanese were "a nation of workaholics living in rabbit hutches," has been used in practically every Japanese-language work on leisure and lifestyle issues since it was originally uttered.[11] And there is no doubt that the Japanese have in general worked longer hours than have the citizens of most of the other advanced industrial nations since World War II. Although a reduction of overtime since the onset of the postbubble recession has now pushed the registered average number of hours worked per year to below two thousand (and below those worked by Americans),[12] they still fall short of the targeted 1,800 per year that represented the goal of the "Lifestyle Superpower

10. Teruoka Itsuko, *Yutakasa to wa Nani Ka?* (What is Wealth?) (Tokyo: Iwanami Shinsho, 1989), 59, 36, 51 respectively. Ohira Ken makes the argument that the kind of naked materialism decried by Teruoka is actually a reflection of the national priorities of the Japanese, in that as a people they are interested primarily in interpersonal relations. The amassment of material wealth allows them to give better presents and treat friends to better dinners, satisfying a psychological need for closeness. In this sense, to tell the "story" (*monogatari*) of Japan's wealth is really to "talk about material goods" (*mono gatari*). *Yutakasa no Seishin Byōri* (The Psychological Syndrome of Wealth) (Tokyo: Iwanami Shinsho, 1990).

11. The Japanese renderings have been "Usagi kōya ni sundeiru hatarakisugisha" and "Usagi kōya ni sumu hataraki chūdoku." See, for example, Takashima Yoshimi, "'Seikatsu Taikoku' Ron to Tochi/Jūtaku Mondai" (Land and Housing Problems in the Discussions on the "Lifestyle Superpower"), in *Gendai Nihon no Kigyō to Shakai: Jinken Rūru no Kakuritsu o Mezashite* (Society and Firms in Contemporary Japan: Confirming Rules for Human Rights), ed. Morioka Kōji (Tokyo: Hōritsubunkasha, 1994), 168.

12. These numbers are still far higher than they are for French and Germans and still somewhat above those for Britons. For comparative figures, see the Ministry of Labor, *Rōdō Hakusho* (Labor White Paper), annual, and the YKC, *Yoka Hakusho* (Leisure White Paper), annual.

Five-Year Plan" submitted by the Economic Planning Agency in June 1992.[13] Furthermore, anecdotal evidence suggests that the widespread acceptance of *sābisu zangyō* (unpaid overtime) by company employees worried about labor cutbacks makes this figure, if not meaningless, at least somewhat suspect.

Some writers have used the international comparison not simply to point out that Japan is something of an aberration but rather to suggest the likely trajectory of working hours in the future. In other words, normal industrialized countries have shorter working hours, and after Japan had "caught up" to the West, its people would naturally want and receive reductions in working hours. In 1979, one important study, by then director of the Labor Policy Division at the Ministry of Labor, Kuwahara Keiichi, provided lavish comparisons between Japanese working practices and those evidenced in the United States and western Europe (and almost never of the industrializing countries of Asia), remarking with some pride that Japanese have been willing to work hard for the good of their firms and their fellow Japanese. Armed with comparative research polls furnished in part by the prime minister's office, Kuwahara argued that Japanese—while still more fulfilled by their work than were the people of any other advanced country except for Germany—would soon begin to demand more leisure time. The International Labor Organization's stress on the importance of an eight-hour workday would have to be considered valid for Japan as well: "As our society's income grows, so too will the demand for free time. We want leisure time not only to refresh ourselves for more work. Rather, it is definitely natural that we will want to pursue other kinds of living normal for cultured people."[14] Even in the absence of much evidence at the time of increasing demand for leisure time, it was expected to occur, because it was only natural.

The source of the reduction, when it actually happened, would remain controversial. Working hours have dropped in the postwar era in virtually all of the industrialized countries but usually through collective bargaining techniques of national unions, as in Germany and France, or through pressure on political parties by unions, as in the United States. The considerably weaker Japanese unions, now more or less united under the peak organization Rengō, have demonstrated less ability to shape policy, and the reduction in working hours came to some degree out of interministerial bargaining led by the Ministry

13. Takashima, "Seikatsu Taikoku," 168.
14. Kuwahara Keiichi, *Nihonjin no Rōdō Jikan* (Working Hours of the Japanese) (Tokyo: Shiseidō, 1979).

of Labor.[15] In the absence of powerful unions or pressure groups promoting a reduction in working hours and increased access to leisure
opportunities, there have continually been questions in Japan regarding whether the Japanese people know how to have fun, or what has
motivated them to work long hours without demanding better living
conditions. And to be certain, Japan's initial "leisure boom" of the
1970s reflected increases in disposable income and shifts in its use far
more than it did any reduction in hours worked.[16]

That there has been a "leisure boom" of some sort is not, however,
in doubt. The country's overall "leisure market" almost doubled in
the ten years between 1982 and 1993, growing from 39.7 trillion yen
to 76.9 trillion. This growth was particularly rapid in the "travel" and
"entertainment" (*goraku*) categories, reflecting the rising popularity
of resorts, theme parks, and similar kinds of attractions. Household
entertainment items, such as television sets, cameras, stereo systems,
and the like, also boomed during the period, though some forms of entertainment, particularly films and theater, remained stagnant.[17] By
almost any measure, late-1980s Japan had become a country of mass
consumers of recreation items and services, and considerable status
was attached to quality products. Indeed, the ubiquity of consumer elec-
tronics, lavish resorts, and golf courses that required million-dollar
membership fees had become a staple of practically any news item on
changing Japanese society. Someone with experience in Japan only in
the early postwar years would scarcely have recognized Shinjuku, one
of Tokyo's entertainment capitals, by 1988.

An emphasis on work over leisure in Japan is perhaps less mysterious or unusual than it might first appear. Indeed, the neologism
"workaholic" appeared first in reference to U.S. workers, and Juliet B.
Schor scored something of a publishing hit with her 1981 book *The
Overworked American.*[18] The commitment of Japanese labor, how-

---

15. On the weakness of labor in postwar Japan, see John Price, *Japan Works: Power
and Paradox in Postwar Industrial Relations* (Ithaca: Cornell University Press, 1997).
Andrew Gordon's *The Wages of Affluence: Labor and Management in Postwar Japan*
(Cambridge: Harvard University Press, 1998) also covers many of the same issues.

16. Hirota Isao, "Le Concept des Loisirs dans le Japon Moderne" (The Concept of
Leisure in Modern Japan), in *Les Loisirs au Japon* (Japan's Leisure Practices), ed. Chris-
tine Condominas (Paris: Editions L'Harmattan, 1993), 23–47.

17. YKC, *Yoka wa Dō Kawatta Ka! Kōdō, Seisaku, Shihyōde Tadoru Wagakuni
Yoka no 50 Nen* (How Has Leisure Changed? Fifty Years of Our Country's Leisure,
Traced with Activities, Policies, and Indicators") (Tokyo: YKC, 1994).

18. Juliet B. Schor, *The Overworked American: The Unexpected Decline of Leisure*
(New York: Basic Books, 1981).

ever, to the goal of building an economic superpower has remained somewhat startling. More than one observer has argued that the skillful manipulation by firms and the government of questions of nationhood and status in the postwar years—that is, raising Japan's rank to that of the other leading industrialized countries—provided a normative basis for Japan's labor ethos. Until a generational shift, accompanied by an increasingly tight labor market, made new employees more demanding, Japanese workers who remembered the hardship of the immediate postwar period were especially motivated to put the interests of their firms and the nation ahead of their own leisure time,[19] a tendency noted in surveys regarding orientations toward work/play.[20] Watanabe Osamu's widely read Marxist critique *"Yutaka na Shakai" Nihon no Kōzō* (The Structure of the "Wealthy Society" Japan) suggests that Japan's employment and industrial system has encouraged consumption of more and more leisure services while squeezing out additional concessions from labor.[21]

Sorting out the questions of whether the place of leisure in the Japanese lifestyle is anomalous, whether Japanese enjoy their lifestyles,[22] or whether the nation is somehow predisposed to work rather than leisure, is probably impossible. What emerges in discussions of leisure and lifestyle in the postwar era is, however, a strong sense that Japanese lifestyles are not satisfactory and that they can be compared on some scale (and usually unflatteringly) to those evidenced in North America and western Europe. Furthermore, it is now impossible to discuss lifestyle in Japan without taking into account the concept of leisure, since it emerges as the most consistent feature of Japanese works on lifestyle since the 1970s. The prevalence of the debate, a belief that Japanese are somehow unable to make good lives for themselves, and a lingering sense that lifestyles had not "caught up" to those of the West have opened up a space for political action in the field of leisure and lifestyle.

19. Hazama Hiroshi, *Keizai Taikoku o Tsukuriageta Shisō: Kōdō Seichōki no Rōdō Etōsu* (The Ideas That Raised an Economic Superpower: The Labor Ethos in the Period of High-Speed Growth) (Tokyo: Bunshindō, 1996), especially chapter 1.

20. YKC, *Yoka Hakusho*, annual.

21. Watanabe Osamu, *'Yutaka na Shakai' Nihon no Kōzō* (The Structure of the "Wealthy Society" Japan) (Tokyo: Rōdō Junpōsha, 1990).

22. This is actually the subject of a recent work by Gordon Matthews, *What Makes Life Worth Living? How Japanese and Americans Make Sense of their Worlds* (Berkeley: University of California Press, 1996). The narrowness of his research (he interviews a few families in the United States and a few in Japan), however, makes broad conclusions unreliable.

Leisure as a Diplomatic Priority:
The Maekawa Report and Working Hours

New diplomatic pressures would force the issue. Japan was besieged first by the EC (a member of which had given the Japanese the "workaholics in rabbit hutches" label) and then by the Reagan administration. Threatened by an economically problematic (and politically disastrous) trade deficit and even more ominous budget deficits, the Reagan administration decided to devalue the dollar at the 1985 G-5 meeting (leading to the Plaza Accord), symbolizing American concerns about the global economy. Fearing other unilateral decisions that might adversely affect the Japanese economy, Japanese politicians and decision makers went quickly to work to come up with ways to smooth over some of the rough spots that Japan faced. This was the era that generated decisions for import promotion (a series of schemes that would include, in principle at least, the Ten Million Program, which is discussed in chapter 6),[23] the reduction of working hours, and the increased consumption of leisure goods. Because the high-saving Japanese were considered to be producing too much and not consuming enough, the policy proposals to improve Japan's economic relations with other countries focused largely on how to make the Japanese behave more "normally" in their leisure practices.

Sensing the need for some kind of political statement on the subject, Prime Minister Nakasone Yasuhiro formally requested the creation of the Advisory Group on Economic Structural Adjustment for International Harmony on 31 October 1985. Its title was every bit as ungainly in Japanese as in English, so the Advisory Group's final report, submitted on 7 April 1986, was almost immediately dubbed the "Maekawa Report,"[24] after the group's chair, Maekawa Haruo, former governor of the Bank of Japan. Given its fame, the report is surprisingly short: eleven pages in Japanese and seventeen in English. Pointing out that by 1985, Japan's current account surplus had reached the unprecedentedly high level of 3.6 percent of the GNP, the report says bluntly: "The time has thus come for Japan to make a historical transformation in its traditional policies on economic management and the

23. MITI was primarily responsible for the management of import promotion strategies. I thank Theresa Greaney, Masahiro Kawai, and Gerald Curtis for pointing this out.

24. It was actually the first of three Maekawa reports, the latter ones with variations on the name. See David Williams, *Japan: Beyond the End of History* (London: Routledge, 1994), 58.

nation's life-style. There can be no further development for Japan without this transformation."[25]

Throwing down this gauntlet, the report goes on to detail a number of ways in which Japan must be reformed if it is to "attain the goal of steadily reducing the nation's current account imbalance to one consistent with international harmony." The five basic areas that Maekawa and his sixteen colleagues detail for action are: the expansion of domestic demand, the transformation of industrial structure, the improvement of market access for manufactured goods, the stabilization of exchange rates, and an increase in overseas development assistance. Together, these would allow Japan to be in greater harmony with the international community. Of course, on a purely economic level, Japan's prospects for continued economic success were not yet in question; its *political* prospects were. While claiming that Japanese economic management would have to change, the Maekawa Report is not at all critical of Japanese economic bureaucrats. It claims, rather, that the economic bureaucrats would have to shift their focus. Japan would have to be a more open economy like the other advanced industrial countries, and there would be a need for policies that could effect this shift from management to market.[26]

The expansion of domestic demand, particularly through lower taxes and reduced working hours, as well as the creation of a service industry–led economy, figure prominently in the Maekawa Report. And while the ultimate effect of the Maekawa Report remains debatable, there is no denying the impact it had in the Japanese popular imagination. Within a year, well-known economists such as Kanemori Hisao of the Japanese Economic Research Center were already evaluating its impact and success in opinion-leader magazines.[27] The *Nikkan Kōgyō Shimbun* (Industrial Daily), a major economic newspaper, even published two 200-page books on the report and its quasi successor, the 1987 "New Maekawa Report" (which dealt more ex-

25. "The Report of The Advisory Group on Economic Structural Adjustment for International Harmony: Provisional Translation ('Maekawa Report')" (Tokyo: Cabinet Policy Discussion Office, 1986), 1.

26. In some ways, the Maekawa Report's comments foreshadow one of the central points Kyoko Sheridan makes: that a shift to a more classically liberal economy would have to be a managed political decision, and would not simply be a natural shift determined by clear market forces. Sheridan, *Governing the Japanese Economy* (Cambridge: Polity, 1993).

27. Kanemori Hisao, "Maekawa Ripōto Ichinenme no Kenshō" (Evaluating the Maekawa Report after a Year), *Chūō Kōron* (May 1987): 100–107.

plicitly with working hours). The two books focused on the changes that would have to occur to make Japan a more open market but also a country with better living conditions for its citizens.[28] To this day, the Maekawa reports remain emblematic of a sociopolitical shift in Japan: from a country single-mindedly focusing on the expansion of production for overseas markets to one driven by domestic demand more reflective of its advanced status.[29]

In the new focus on demand, one element featured prominently in both the Maekawa and the New Maekawa reports was the emphasis on a reduction of working hours. The issue of international pressure was so strong that it was not merely a generalized statement about working hours but rather, in the Maekawa Report, a clear claim that Japan should "follow in line with the level of working hours in the advanced countries of Europe and North America." The New Maekawa Report made this more specific, arguing that Japan would have to shift, "in the near future, and certainly before the year 2000, to the level of 1800 working hours per year shown in the US and the UK."[30] With the Maekawa Report and New Maekawa Report pointing to Japan's need to reduce working hours—not for economic or purely domestic political reasons but rather to reduce foreign criticism—long-delayed government efforts to reduce working hours received a necessary shot in the arm. This was not an entirely new initiative; the Tanaka cabinet had proposed a five-day workweek in 1973, and a number of large firms had moved in this direction in the 1970s. But Prime Minister Nakasone promised in June 1987 to move Japan to a five-day workweek and even told a foreign press conference that "if Japan has a flaw, it's that working hours are long and vacations are few."[31] With this kind of political capital, it became easier for the Ministry of Labor to work with labor unions and employers to amend Japan's Employment Law, promising a reduction in weekly working hours from forty-eight

28. Nikkan Kōgyō Shimbun Tokubetsu Shuzaihan, ed., *Shin 'Maekawa Ripōto' ga Shimesu Michi* (The Road Indicated by the New Maekawa Report) (Tokyo: Nikkan, 1987); Nikkan Kōgyō Shimbun Tokubetsu Shuzaihan, ed., *'Yutakasa' Nihon no Kōzō* (The Structure of a "Wealthy" Japan) (Tokyo: Nikkan, 1989).

29. Williams, for example, refers to the Maekawa reports as "arguably the most important, and certainly the best known, statement of public policy philosophy to emerge from Japan's corridors of power since the end of the U.S. Occupation in 1952." *Japan: Beyond the End of History,* 158–59.

30. Cited in Morioka Kōji, *Kigyō Chūshin Shakai no Jikan Kōzō* (The Structure of Time in the Enterprise-Centered Society) (Tokyo: Aoki, 1995), 208–9.

31. *Tokyo Shimbun,* 5 June 1987, cited in Frank Schwartz, *Advice & Consent: The Politics of Consultation in Japan* (Cambridge: Cambridge University Press, 1998), 152.

to forty and a shift to a five-day workweek. Throughout these discussions, the necessity of making Japan's national lifestyle more like that evidenced in the industrialized West was used as a major pillar in the demand for change.[32]

The purpose of the Maekawa Report, New Maekawa Report, and subsequent demand promotion schemes was fairly clear: to use the same kind of economic leadership that had ostensibly guided Japan's postwar economic miracle to the new task of aligning Japan's economic behavior with that of the rest of the world.[33] In this sense, under heavy international pressure, the Japanese government attempted to shift, in a somewhat stuttering manner, public understandings of what was in the national interest. But the continuing work of the Leisure Development Center—producing more and more reports and public relations campaigns on the need for shorter working hours, a 5-day workweek, and on appropriate leisure behavior—provided an institutional frame for the supposedly ongoing work to promote leisure. And this emphasis remained into the mid-1990s. MITI continued to promote the development of a "society that gives me space to do my own thing" as one of its major objectives of the 1990s. Even as its reports stressed the importance of this better lifestyle for Japanese, they also pointed to the relevance of this better lifestyle in Japan's foreign relations.[34] And Prime Minister Miyazawa Kiichi's conception of the "lifestyle superpower" evoked many of the same images, especially that of a country with leisure and lifestyle capabilities that would rank favorably with the world's leaders.

The emphasis of leisure policy had thus shifted considerably. Whereas its primary purpose in its limited form in the 1960s had been to build a social consensus around the LDP's developmental schemes, and in the 1970s had been part of an effort to guide Japan's economy into the logical "service sector" phase that normal advanced economies were thought invariably to enter, by the 1980s it was in large part a reaction to international criticism. In each case, but particularly after 1973, economic policymakers mobilized images of normal or proper leisure behavior in the advanced industrial countries and worked to suggest that Japanese should be able to enjoy the same symbols of national

32. Schwartz, *Advice & Consent*, covers the politics behind this revision in great detail.

33. Williams, *Japan: Beyond the End of History*, 57–61, 64.

34. See, for example, the midterm report of the Yutori Shakai Kondankai, "Yutori Shakai no Kihon Kōsō" (Basic Conception of the "Yutori Shakai") (Tokyo: unpublished, 1991).

wealth. The goals of the policies, and the actors, had shifted over time, but the basic direction of policy as well as the legitimate metaphors and claims that actors could make had been much more resistant to change. In some cases this has been as general as a claim that Japanese should work less and enjoy themselves more. In others, it has been as specific as a claim that the country should investigate paragliding and skiing as two increasingly important sports and leisure activities in the era of internationalization.[35] But in each case, there has been a public role in explaining to citizens what normal leisure is—almost invariably based on understandings of a typified industrial West as the norm—and using public relations campaigns or sharing information with producers in order to induce a change in behavior.

Internationalizing Lifestyles and Leisure

That the Maekawa reports collectively pointed to an opening of Japanese markets is unsurprising. After all, Japan's economic emergence had been possible only because of its access to foreign markets, and international criticism of Japanese trade policies had an especially menacing edge. If Japan's behavior were not "harmonized," the consequences could—at least in the minds of economic policymakers—have been catastrophic. Prime Minister Nakasone's appearance on television in a Pierre Cardin necktie, exhorting the Japanese to buy more foreign products, was as gaudy a symbol of the shift as were the "Import Now!" (written in English and probably directed more at the foreign critics than at the average Japanese citizen) bumper stickers paraded around Tokyo.[36] The reports' influence went beyond a straightforward valorization of increased imports; it provided impetus for more wide-ranging campaigns to "internationalize" Japan and the Japanese. In so doing, the social campaigns tied to the Maekawa reports brought issues of Japanese national identity to the foreground of debates over what kind of country Japan ought to be.

The discourses of Japaneseness (*nihonjinron*) discussed in chapter 2 had become only increasingly well defined and clearer throughout the 1970s and 1980s, in part because of the justifiable pride felt primarily

35. YKC, *Kokusaika Katachi Yoka Katsudō no Fukyū ni Kan suru Chōsa Kenkyu* (Research on the Spread of Internationalization-style Leisure Activities) (Tokyo: YKC, 1992).

36. Marilyn Ivy, *Discourses of the Vanishing: Modernity, Phantasm, Japan* (Chicago: University of Chicago Press, 1995).

by social conservatives over the nation's emergence as perhaps the world's preeminent economic power. Aoki Tamotsu notes that much of this change in *nihonjinron* had resulted from Japan's development as an advanced industrial democracy, thus ostensibly de-linking "modernization" from pure "Westernization."[37] In other words, perhaps when Japan was in full "catch-up" mode, it had made sense to talk specifically about modernizing to meet the West, but with Japan's having eclipsed many of the Western powers in its economic status, and with the ostensibly unique virtues of the Japanese (cooperation, teamwork, selflessness, drive), the idea that Japan had to crudely adopt a "Western" stance no longer seemed coherent. With "Westernization" being seen as something of a parochial term for negotiating Japan's relationship with the outside world, *kokusaika* (internationalization) has virtually replaced it and has proved to be just as effective at evading easy definition or explanation as is *nihonjinron*.[38]

It is therefore impossible to capture adequately the campaigns of the era to "internationalize" Japanese lifestyles without addressing the simultaneous and complementary efforts to reconstruct Japanese national identity through an enhanced reliance on *nihonjinron*. That the government placed special emphasis on making Japanese lifestyles more like those of the industrialized West, however, is undeniable. In its 1986 survey on national lifestyles, the EPA wrote:

> In the 1986 survey, we are contributing to an examination of how to deal with *kokusaika* in people's lifestyle. To that end, we are investigating and analyzing structurally the values and consciousness of every stratum of our country with regard to foreigners, foreign things, and foreign information. The contents of our survey include the degree of advancement of internationalization, the countries seen as being the center of Japan's motion toward internationalization [Note: the Western countries, unsurprisingly, would prove to be far and away the most popular choices, far ahead of the Asian countries], social prefer-

---

37. The *kindaika* = *seiyōka* (modernity = Westernization) model began to disintegrate with Japan's more effective rebounding from the oil shocks that plunged most of the Western economies into a depression. By the 1980s, most observers accepted the existence of a "Japanese model" of modernity. Aoki Tamotsu, *"Nihon Bunkaron" no Hen'yō* (The Transformation of Theories of Japanese Culture) (Tokyo: Chūō Kōronsha, 1990), 108–25.

38. Harumi Befu, "Internationalization of Japan and Nihon Bunkaron," in *The Challenge of Japan's Internationalization: Organization and Culture*, ed. Hiroshi Mannari and Harumi Befu (Tokyo: Kodansha, for Kwansei Gakuin University, 1983), 232–65.

ences regarding internationalization, degree of acceptance of internationalization, the comparison of lifestyle standards in our country and those of the industrialized West, our country's social values, and policies to promote Japan's internationalization.[39]

The EPA's report, however, left little doubt that this push was part of an overall drive to open Japan in such a way as to reduce international criticism while also reaping some benefits for the nation. Its three categories of "internationalization" were informational (access to foreign technology and news), human (tourism, international marriage, foreign students), and, significantly, material (consumption of foreign foodstuffs, clothing, and consumer durables).[40]

Within a few short years, few areas of Japan were untouched by the political drive for internationalization, especially as new government offices insisted that the "insular" Japanese were insufficiently aware of what it meant to be part of a globalizing society. This meant that the Japanese would have to be instructed in narrowly defined ways in how to deal with the outside world, or how to deal with foreigners. In 1985, the Ministry of Home Affairs would issue its "Plan for International Exchange Projects," which would propose that local governments become important players in *kokusaika*.[41] To that end, in 1987, the Ministry of Home Affairs (MOHA), in conjunction with other ministries including Education and Foreign Affairs, created the new organization the Council of Local Authorities for International Relations (CLAIR), which would be responsible for coordinating local level programs designed to increase the internationalization of the Japanese. Among the initiatives would be exchange programs for local bureaucrats, the rapidly spreading sister city programs, and, later, local

39. Keizai Kikakufu Kokumin Seikatsukyoku (Economic Planning Agency, National Life Bureau), ed., *Kokusaika to Kokumin Ishiki: Shōwa 61 Nendō Kokumin Seikatsu Senkōdo Chōsa* (Internationalization and National Consciousness: The 1986 Annual Survey on National Life) (Tokyo: Ministry of Finance, 1987), 2. Former UNESCO librarian Matsumoto Shinji echoes this lifestyle emphasis in his 1987 article in the widely read opinion magazine *Chūō Kōron*. Using Paris as his example of an internationalizing city, he focuses much of his article on the difference in golfing styles between advanced golfing nations and lagging golfing nations. "Kokusaikaron Suki no Hikokusaijintachi" (The Non-Internationalized People Who Love Discussing Internationalization), *Chūō Kōron* (July 1987): 150–58.

40. Keizai Kikakufu Kokumin Seikatsukyoku, ed., *Kokusaika to Kokumin Ishiki*, 6.

41. Beverly Ann Ferrell, "Internationalization (Kokusaika) through Education?: A Look at the Japan Exchange and Teaching (JET) Program" (master's thesis, Cornell University, 1993), 11.

level aid projects in the developing countries. By the 1990s, CLAIR would become a more expansive bureaucracy, with program offices in several countries around the world, coordinating human exchange programs for Japan.[42] Local governments too would be prodded into action through national budgeting for *kokusaika* departments in most cities.[43]

CLAIR's most impressive program, and also one of its oddest, has been the Japan Exchange and Teaching (JET) Program. In 1987, combining aspects of two small-scale programs, CLAIR would work with MOHA, MOFA, and the MOE to create this new program, which brought over eight hundred participants from four countries (the United States, the United Kingdom, New Zealand, and Australia), which by the mid-1990s would become three thousand participants from several more countries, including a handful from China, France, and Germany. The JET Program's purpose has notably been not only to teach English in the classrooms—a purpose for which it is ill-suited, since many teachers work at several schools and end up meeting with each class only once or twice in a year—but to "internationalize" the schools, by allowing Japanese schoolchildren to meet foreigners and by altering the pedagogical style to fit the educational experiences of the foreign instructors.[44] The program's emphasis on English and on the industrialized West, a focus that has become slightly blurred since the 1990s, provides further evidence that the EPA's *kokusaika* survey's goals were consistent with the national policy orientation regarding internationalization.

With *kokusaika* initiatives multiplying rapidly at both the national and local levels, Japanese observers throughout the 1980s and 1990s focused on the topic almost obsessively, with no consensus (among the ostensibly consensual Japanese!) on what internationalizaton meant or whether it was good or bad. For some, it was a simple economic phenomenon. Yamaguchi Masayuki, for example, referred to

42. See CLAIR's home page: http://www.clair.nippon-net.or.jp/.

43. See Katherine Tegtmeyer Pak, "Outsiders Moving In: Identity and Institutions in Japanese Responses to International Migration" (Ph.D. diss., University of Chicago, 1998). Tegtmeyer Pak argues that these *kokusaika* departments, though created primarily to manage cultural exchange, would later become the source of innovative policies to deal with foreign residents in some municipalities.

44. See David L. McConnell, *Importing Diversity: Inside Japan's JET Program* (Berkeley: University of California Press, 2000) for an overview of this initiative.

kokusaika as a process allowing international capitalism to force open Japan, as did Commodore Matthew Perry's Black Ships, to foreign influence. Japan's democratization is the most obvious element of change, but continued pressure for Japan to "open" politically (apparently, to become a more liberal nation) and for the Japanese to become "free individuals" demonstrates the extension of the process.[45] Alternatively, "internationalization" might be required by international capitalism; as more low-wage laborers migrated to Japan to take the jobs that Japanese would not, Japan would have to negotiate its national identity with this engagement born of economic necessity.[46] Others assessed it as a cultural phenomenon related, for example, to the diversification of culinary options available in Japan,[47] or to the influence of ostensibly universal (Western) modes of thought and behavior on Japan.[48]

Kokusaika was controversial. As some rushed to embrace the new

45. Yamaguchi Masayuki, "Gendai Nihon Shakai no Kokusaika Katei to Tenbō" (The Process of and Prospects for the Internationalization of Contemporary Japanese Society), in *Gendai Nihon Shakai no Kōzō Henka to Kokusaika* (The Internationalization and Structural Transformation of Contemporary Japanese Society), ed. Yamaguchi Masayuki, Sakui Reiji (Tokyo: Yūhihaku, 1986), 52–91. The other essays in this volume also focus on the immovable economic process of internationalization as driving a trend toward a more Western-style liberal democracy. For some similar arguments, see also the essays in Kisō Keizai Kagaku Kenkyūjo, ed., *Kokusaika no Naka no Nihon* (Japan in the Process of Internationalization) (Tokyo: Aoki, 1987).

46. On this understanding of "international," see Koike Kazuo, "The Internationalization of the Japanese Firm," and Hirowatari Seigo, "Foreign Workers and Immigration Policy," in *The Political Economy of Japanese Society*, ed. Banno Junji, vol. 2: *Internationalization and Domestic Issues* (Oxford: Oxford University Press, 1998), 44–80, 81–106 respectively.

47. See particularly the essays by Ishige Naomichi and Tamura Shimpachirō, the editors of the volume *Kokusaika Jidai no Shoku* (Cuisines in the Era of Internationalization) (Tokyo: Domesu, 1994). Tamura's "Kokusaika to Gendai Nihon no Shoku" (Internationalization and Cuisine in Modern Japan) (15–31) takes a general economic approach to the "inevitability" of *kokusaika* and shifts to a discussion of the difficulty for Japanese farmers of rice—generally considered to be the central element of Japanese cuisine—in an international market that favors economies of scale they cannot sustain. Ishige's "Shoku Bunka Hen'yō no Bunmeiron" (Civilization Aspects of the Transformation in Food Culture) (193–210) is akin to the "glocalization" argument, in that he stresses the appearance of an international food culture based on independently protected national cuisines.

48. Yamazaki Masakazu, "Bunka no Kokusaika to wa Nani Ka?" (What is the Internationalization of Culture?), *Chūō Kōron* (November 1986): 100–121. Yamazaki's point is *not* crudely essentialist, and he emphasizes the importance of continued "cultural construction."

groups of foreign teachers entering the nation, and as others emphasized that Japanese would need to speak forthrightly to foreigners (because brutal honesty is purportedly the Western way), others lamented the looming loss of Japaneseness. Hayashi Chikio, a former Ministry of Education official who was at the time the head of the Japan Public Opinion Poll Association (*Nihon Yoron Chōsa Kyōkai*), would write in 1996 that "today's successors to the 'opening of civilization' in the Meiji Period are such things as 'internationalization' and 'international environmental protection' and the like. These too are about the 'adoption of culture,' but I feel they have a comical, zoo-like feeling to them."[49] Using comparative survey data to demonstrate different orientations by Japanese toward human relationships, toward logic ("fuzzy," as opposed to "linear"), and toward language, Hayashi ended with a rather grim assessment of Japan's internationalization. If more and more students learn English early in order to learn how to communicate with foreigners (more directly than they would in Japanese, to speak without clear status divisions, etc.), there is a chance that Japanese will become like Japanese Americans: looking Japanese but thinking and sounding American. Real international exchange would allow for the protection of national differences.[50]

There has therefore been no shortage of more or less (though, unfortunately, usually less) articulate discussions of the tension between the homogenizing influences of globalization and the need to protect local cultures. In the Japanese case, however, the threat was something other than the cultural sandman known as Global Capitalism. Instead, the Japanese state's efforts to enforce convergence with the world (generally played by the West, or, more specifically, the United States) presented opponents with the claim that the government itself had gone mad, that its internationalization policies were themselves emblematic of a faddish but still threatening fascination with a decidedly un-Japanese cosmopolitanism.

In fact, the Japanese government—particularly under Prime Minister Nakasone's neonationalist tutelage—simultaneously pushed cultural assertiveness along lines that Hayashi would have found laudable. On a scholarly level, this was perhaps best symbolized by

---

49. Hayashi Chikio, *Nihon-rashisa no Kōzō: Kokoro to Bunka o Hakaru* (The Structure of Japaneseness: Linking the Heart and Culture) (Tokyo: Tōyō Keizai Shinpōsha, 1996), 5.

50. Ibid., 217–18.

Nakasone's establishment of the International Research Center for Japanese Studies (which opened in 1987). This gorgeous facility, nestled in the hills outside of Kyoto, has counted among its faculty such famous exponents of *nihonjinron*-esque theories as Hamaguchi Eshun and Nakane Chie, and it continues to produce some of the best research on Japanese history, though often with a decided emphasis on Japanese uniqueness.[51] Moreover, Nakasone's administration pushed local communities to develop *furusato* (old hometown) themes that were designed to boost regional tourist economies while constructing a common, nostalgic past for Japan's mostly urban population. Because most middle-aged Japanese in major cities, however, had little experience with the bucolic life idealized in these campaigns, the effect was to construct an "exotic" vision of Japan, one that would reassert one's national identity while remaining oddly foreign and detached from the average citizen's everyday life.[52]

The *kokusaika* campaigns designed to alter lifestyles—through international education and local programs for foreign residents—thus were accompanied by others that aimed at reconstructing an exclusive national identity premised on persistent *nihonjinron* motifs. None of them, however, would have been likely had not foreign pressure over trade surpluses and increasingly valuable yen pushed the Japanese administrations of the 1980s to adopt their more conciliatory stance toward international harmony. But the proliferation of scholarly treatments of *nihonjinron* and *kokusaika* in the 1980s and 1990s[53] displays that virtually no area of civic life remained untouched by the debate; harmony was far more than simple economics. These would be predictable in, for example, public debates over international exchange programs[54] but would also intrude subtly on some of the core out-

51. Nichibunken (short for Nihon Bunka Kenkyūjo, its Japanese moniker) maintains an informative web page (http://www.nichibun.ac.jp) with English-language descriptions of its research projects.

52. See Ivy's *Discourses of the Vanishing* for a fuller discussion of the "Exotic Japan" campaigns of the 1980s, especially 29–65.

53. In addition to the works already cited, see the essays in Hiroshi Mannari and Harumi Befu, eds., *The Challenge of Japan's Internationalization: Organization and Culture* (Tokyo: Kodansha, for Kwansei Gakuin University, 1983).

54. See, e.g., Advisory Group on International Cultural Exchange, "International Cultural Exchange in a New Era (Unofficial Translation)," report submitted to the prime minister, June 1994. From the prime minister's web page, http://www.kantei.go.jp/.

comes of the Maekawa Report's emphasis on promoting domestic consumption.

As a Last Resort . . .

Nowhere would the new pressure for domestic demand be more clear than in the effort to redevelop Japan as a resort wonderland. It is not necessarily surprising that policymakers, in their efforts to comply with the overall mission of the Maekawa reports, focused on the promise that domestic tourism held. After all, tourism is the largest leisure industry in the world, and even the foundational texts of the leisure initiatives in the 1970s referred specifically to the need to improve Japan's resort environment. *Yoka Sōran* (Overview of Leisure) spoke of the need to consider public support for resort development in order to compensate for the high cost and low quality of leisure resources in major cities.[55] *Yoka Shakai e no Kōzu* (Road to the Leisure Society) stressed that resort development would become increasingly important in Japan and that the government's task would be to ensure that resorts did not negatively affect the environment.[56] The Leisure Development Center (YKC) would produce two reports on resorts in 1973 and two more in 1974, with more appearing sporadically throughout the 1970s and early 1980s.[57] Like many of the other financial plans for national support for leisure development, little came of these references in the 1970s, particularly after the oil shocks convinced policymakers to refocus on manufacturing.

The role of the YKC, a subordinate thinktank of MITI, seems odd here. As noted in chapter 4, tourism policy technically lies under the control of the Ministry of Transport. But the bureaucratic language covering tourism is almost as wracked and fissiparous as is the industry itself, giving other bureaucratic actors an opportunity to intervene in certain aspects of the industry. MITI and the EPA have been particularly engaged, largely because of their responsibility for the nation's overall industrial health. If tourism is not simply an element of the transportation sector but is seen more broadly as a component of the service industries whose growth would have to carry a late-indus-

55. Tsūshō Sangyōsho Yoka Kaihatsutshitsu, ed., *Yoka Sōran: Shakai, Sangyō, Seisaku* (Overview of Leisure: Society, Industry, and Policy) (Tokyo: Dayamondo, 1974), 758–59.
56. Ibid., 46–47, 53–54.
57. YKC, "Shiryō Risuto" (Materials List), unpublished chart, 1991.

trial Japan forward, their interest is far from mysterious. One tool that MITI and the YKC have evidently used to intervene in tourism is a simple discursive one: rather than referring to "tourism" (*kankō*), their reports on domestic tourism facilities call them "resorts" (*rizōto*),[58] thus separating them analytically from the overall tourism sector controlled by the MOT. Despite their efforts and often superior firepower, however, their interventions sometimes meet resistance from other bureaucratic agencies. One member of the MITI Leisure Industry Promotion Office (*Yoka sangyōshitsu*) and a visiting official of the Leisure Development Center said, "It's difficult to run this sort of thing because of *tatewari gyōsei* [horizontally segmented administration]. We're not the only ones with authority over leisure industries."[59]

MITI's and the YKC's roles became only too apparent at the time of the first Maekawa Report and its emphasis on government management of an expansion of domestic demand. In August 1985, MITI announced the "Dai Kihan Fukugō Yoka Shisetsu Seibi Jigyō Kōsō" (Conception of the Creation of Large-Scale Comprehensive Leisure Facilities) and began to work in earnest with six other ministries and agencies (Ministries of Home Affairs; Agriculture, Forestry, and Fisheries; Transport; and Construction; and the Environmental and National Land Agencies) on the issue of resort development. The purpose of this project was much the same as the Maekawa Report: to reduce trade criticism by stimulating domestic demand and aligning Japanese leisure practices with those observed in the other advanced industrial countries. Because of the land-use implications, the National Land Agency took primary control over the project and at the end of 1986 (again, in cooperation with the other six ministries and agencies) made the initial proposal for the implementation of the "Sōgō Hoyō Chiiki Seibi Hō" (Comprehensive Regional Recreation Facilities Law, generally called the "Rizōto-Hō," or Resort Law). With potentially huge pork barrel benefits for politicians, funding proposals for the Resort Law sailed through the Diet and were officially approved on 9 June

---

58. I say "evidently" because this is somewhat speculative. But the difference is both clear and remarkable. When the MOT writes about domestic tours, it almost invariably uses the term "domestic tourism" (*kokunai kankō*), while MITI's reports almost never use the word *kankō* except in a very general sense. No one confirmed for me, however, that this was the main reason. Even so, MITI has attempted to move in on tourism turf by promoting the resort life as well as the construction of resorts in Japan and overseas.

59. Interview 49, 31 October 1997.

1987. The YKC, most likely at MITI's urging, also went back to work on resorts in earnest, producing two reports in 1988 and every year thereafter into the 1990s.

The Resort Law aimed at managed resort development in two possibly conflicting ways. First, it rigged tax and subsidy programs to assist both private firms and public regional development organizations in setting up more ski resorts, golf clubs, marinas, etc. Second, it ostensibly ensured that any major resort project would have to be approved by the government, particularly the Environment Agency, to assure that it would not ultimately prove to be harmful. Coordinating the two was easier said than done. Low-interest (5.3 percent) loans from the Japan Development Bank, the Hokkaido Development Agency, and other government-related organizations to firms and additional assistance to public regional associations made this an attractive venture for a number of communities. Moreover, the plan also called for providing interest-free financing with funds generated by the sale of shares of NTT, the newly privatized telephone company.[60] To seasoned politicians, programs such as this mean one thing: pork. And Japanese politicians are nothing if not seasoned. True to form, the LDP demonstrated interest quickly, announcing an internal committee of LDP Diet members that would work on the promotion of resort construction.[61]

By 1993, the pork had been spread out quite generously. Out of forty-seven prefectures, forty had received approval for some kind of major resort development, attracting governmental assistance and obtaining the right to develop huge tracts of land. Mie Prefecture, the first (in 1988) to receive permission for development under the Resort Law, worked on the construction of golf courses, a marina, hotels, and the like, covering over 150,000 hectares. The approved land area would be

60. Ikeda Toshio, "Yoka Gyōsei no Shinten to Rizōto Kaihatsu" (Expansion of the Public Administration for Promoting Leisure and Holiday Resort Development), in Yoka Seikatsu to Rizōto Kaihatsu: Iwate, Okinawa no Jirei Chōsa o Chūshin Ni (Leisure and Holiday Resort Development in Japan: A Case Study of the Iwate and Okinawa Regions), ed. Kansai University Political Economy Research Institute (Osaka: Kansai University, 1991), 19–51. The initial Resort Law was established in May 1978 but had not been implemented until the 1987 decision.

61. See the helpful timeline in Suzuki Shigeru and Kobuchi Minato, eds., Rizōto no Sōgōteki Kenkyū: Kokumin no "Hoyōken" to Kōkyō Sekinin (A Comprehensive View of Resorts: Joint Responsibility and Citizens' "Recreational Rights") (Tokyo: Kōyō, 1991), 45.

substantially larger in other cases, particularly in Hokkaido (1989; 330,000 ha) and Okinawa (1991; 226,000 ha).[62]

With the availability of national land for development use, government funds for resort development, and the public promise that the Japanese were now a mature society with disposable income and plenty of free time, the issue of resort development took on a new immediacy. Some scholars scrambled to produce articles on the creation of the "resort archipelago" of Japan; another group discussed how to create "Japanese-style" resorts; and still others focused on the new meaning that resorts would have in Japan. The discussions frequently addressed the history of leisure resorts in Japan—most stressing correctly that hot spring resorts (*onsen*) and similar resorts for recuperative purposes were genuinely part of Japanese history—but most scholars agreed that the Japanese people had only recently begun to understand the importance of leisure and relaxation in a modern, industrialized society. With the rapid development of large, high-quality resorts, however, the Japanese were finally beginning to take part in the kind of leisure that was fitting for an economic superpower. In most of these works, it was stressed that this turn toward a resort-powered lifestyle and economy was the natural next step for Japan.[63]

A number of critics, however, began to wonder aloud whether development of a large number of resort sand frenectic competition over the land were either healthy or natural for Japan. With the fierce competition over getting contracts to participate in resort development and what many claim was an overly loose attitude among policymakers toward the environmental implications of resorts, critics had no shortage of targets. In 1991, citing serious and unmistakable harm to the natural environment, the Japan Federation of Bar Associations urged a repeal of the Resort Law. The JFBA also referred to the economic consequences of rapid resort development. With the rapid expansion of marine resorts in Okinawa, it argued, the price of land had increased by

62. Sōmūfu Gyōsei Kansatsukyoku, *Rizōto Kōsō no Chakujitsu na Jitsugen ni Mukete* (Turning toward the Faithful Realization of the Resort Conception) (Tokyo, Ministry of Finance, 1994), 94–96.

63. The works on this are too numerous to cite with any comprehensiveness. See, for example, Maruta Yorikazu, ed., *Rizōto Kaihatsu Keikakuron* (Planning for Resort Development) (Tokyo: Soft Science, 1989); Nihon Kankō Kyōkai (Japan Tourism Association), *Nihongata Rizōto o Kangaeru* (Considering Japanese-Style Resorts) (Tokyo: NKK, 1989); and the more explicit business guide by the Nihon Kankō Kyōkai, *Nihongata Rizōto Keikakuron* (Japanese-Style Resort Planning) (Tokyo: NKK, 1990).

ten or twenty times (though the JBA was unclear as to the time frame on this, or whether it directly resulted from Resort Law implementation), making new development unaffordable for local citizens, as well as driving up the price of utilities such as water and electricity.[64]

The myriad environmental problems associated with resort development were fairly well documented. Japan's golf courses proved to be an especially tempting target for critics. Not only was membership in one of these courses considered to be the ultimate in conspicuous consumption (with foreign reporters commenting frequently on the million-dollar price tag such memberships often included), but the courses themselves were to be blamed for a variety of ecological hazards. Among these were the use and waste of large quantities of water to keep the grounds green in seasons without rain and the rampant dumping of pesticides and herbicides to protect the courses from biological nuisances.[65]

The financial outcomes were for the most part catastrophic. In Mie, the first prefecture to receive approval for a project under the Resort Law, a combination of mismanagement, overly optimistic projections, and bad luck made for a stunning failure. A 1988 "third-sector" (joint public-private) development project under the region's "Coastal Community Zone" (CCZ) plan was scheduled to cost ¥850 billion (approximately $5 billion), with ¥500 billion of that coming from public accounts of one form or another. In one part of the overall development scheme, the town of Ohama relied on a private consulting firm for a plan for the tourist development of its train station area. With a construction and opening cost of ¥3.1 billion, the third-sector developer (which was 49.1 percent owned by the town, with the mayor as president) was stunned to find that it could find virtually no operators willing to pay the exorbitant rent for restaurant, shop, or hotel space. The developer had to rely on ¥2.8 billion worth of long-term loans to bail itself (and the town) out, and the one million tourists never materialized. By 1990, observers concluded that the project was a failure.[66]

64. Nihon Bengoshi Rengōkai (Japan Federation of Bar Associations), "Rizōto-hō no Haishi o Motomeru Ketsugi" (Decision to Demand the Repeal of the Resort Law), 1991, cited fully in Ikeda, "Yoka Gyōsei no Shinten," 49–51.

65. Chiba Kyōzō, "Rizō to Kaihatsu to Kankyō Hakai, Osen" (Environmental Pollution and Destruction Associated with Resort Development), in *Rizōto no Sōgōteki Kenkyū*, ed. Suzuki and Kobuchi, 160–72.

66. Kobuchi Minato, "Rizōto Kaihatsu no Shippai to Zaisei Futan: Mie-ken Ohama-Machi no Baai" (Resort Development Failure and Financial Responsibility: The Case

The timing was thus depressingly representative of the collapse of Japan's "property bubble" in general. In 1990, Tokyo land prices began to tumble for the first time in memory, and they followed suit nationwide in 1991.[67] The precise causes of the collapse of Japan's bubble economy will perhaps never be fully understood, but it is now generally accepted in the real estate press that the Resort Law contributed by rapidly driving up prices, as they did in Mie, and then watching them collapse as many of the development projects went belly-up in the early 1990s. Stories about efforts by golf resorts to stay afloat financially by cutting membership prices have been a staple in the Japanese newspapers for the past few years. In 1992, an external review group organized to evaluate and to defend the Resort Law seemed almost half-hearted in its efforts to find something nice to say about it. The members, including one division leader from Mie, a YKC researcher, and a section head from the JTB Foundation, claimed that resorts were not necessarily bad for the environment (since tourism ostensibly needs to protect an environment to work) and that in a "long-term perspective," some of these projects might still succeed.[68]

The prospects, however, have not looked good, in spite of some strikingly original "theme parks" in Japan. One, Huis ten Bosch, is a reconstruction of a seventeenth-century Dutch city, built in Nagasaki and designed to be an area where people would actually live in a more relaxed, spacious, gracious environment than they might in, for example, Tokyo. Another, Venus Fort, opened in 1999 and is a "women's theme park," meaning that it is an elaborate shopping mall. Built on an area of reclaimed land in Tokyo Harbor, Venus Fort is built to resemble an Italian city, and the "sky" completes a full day's cycle (dawn through dusk, and back to dawn) in the course of a few short hours. Adding to the surreal quality of the mall is the "church," where every few hours, a "service" begins, during which the faux stained glass window (on a television screen) begins to display advertisements.[69] Both

of Mie Prefecture's Ohama), in *Rizōto no Sōgōteki Kenkyū,* ed. Suzuki and Kobuchi, 180–85.

67. National Land Agency, *Kokuchi Tōkei Yōran* (Statistical Overview of National Land) (Osaka, annual).

68. Sōgō Hoyō Chiiki Seibi Kenkyūkai (Resort Law Study Group), *Kongo no Rizōto Seibi no Arikata ni Tsuite: Chūkan Torimatome* (The Way to Deal with Resorts in the Future: A Midterm Evaluation) (Tokyo: unpublished, 1992).

69. I thank Merry White for introducing me to Venus Fort and explaining its rituals.

have attracted visitors, but the recession has made it difficult to tell whether either will survive in the long term. Lessons will undoubtedly be drawn from each. Perhaps Japanese leisure parks of the future will be all-encompassing alternative living environments; perhaps they will be shopping malls.

Japan's resort development schemes of the 1980s thus provide a glimpse into the purposes and tools of leisure policy in its most recent incarnation. Although the Resort Law failed to reshape lifestyle in any fundamental sense (and also contributed to financial catastrophe and environmental degradation), it reflected a conscious effort to turn leisure behavior to some kind of national good. The immediate benefits were, of course, to be in the form of regional economic development, but the broader implication was clear: wealthy Japanese had "recreational rights" (*hoyōken*) as did citizens of other advanced countries. And if the Japanese were seen to be having fun by skiing, going to the beach, playing golf, traveling domestically, and hiking, they were to be considered to be somehow normal. Interestingly, in the somewhat bitter recriminations that were to follow, the issue was not whether resorts were good for the country; it was instead the method used to plan, create, and develop leisure resorts. When the Japanese Communist Party produced a 1991 policy statement on the issue of resort development, it never questioned the necessity or function of resorts. Party officials Ono Takao, Sasaki Katsuyoshi, and Nakayama Ken'ichi argued that large-scale resorts built primarily by major companies with public money ensured that the products would be financially wasteful and unsuited to people's needs. Instead, they suggested smaller-scale holiday spots called "Free Time Towns" (*Jiyū jikan toshi*). Notably, they adopted this concept wholesale from European leisure plans and developments, which were found to provide an appropriate model for Japan's leisure development.[70]

Conclusions and the Turn Overseas

Given Prime Minister Nakasone's strongly nationalist leanings (very much influenced by his admiration for the tough-talking Margaret Thatcher and the almost hypnotically patriotic Ronald Reagan), one might well suspect that he had to swallow hard in 1987 before ac-

70. Ono Takao, Sasaki Katsuyoshi, and Nakayama Ken'ichi, *Rizōto Kaihatsu o Tō* (Questioning Resort Development) (Tokyo: Shin Nihon, 1991).

knowledging that Japan had a problem. But by emphasizing the vexing nature of the nation's merciless labor/leisure balance, he meant to set a popular tone to support government initiatives to expand consumption and to reduce the heavily criticized trade surplus. After all, few Japanese would have argued that the country faced problems that could be overcome through harder work and less leisure, even though some would lament that the more open, cosmopolitan, *kokusaiteki* (internationalized) Japan bore little resemblance to the militantly unique nation that had risen in four decades from desperate poverty to almost unmatched wealth.

Perhaps the emphasis on the government's role in improving Japan's recreation is ultimately what feels so odd. Was leisure supposed to take this much work? Even if the West were the norm, in theory, Japanese could simply have learned from writers, mass culture, and political elites with significant experience abroad about leisure opportunities elsewhere.[71] Yet time and time again, Japanese policy institutions—created specifically to support the programmatic adoption of Western leisure practices in order to serve national goals—would inform policymakers of new opportunities for state action in managing Japan's emergence as a lifestyle superpower. From the Income Doubling Plan announced to build support for the vulnerable Liberal Democratic Party and the initiatives of the EPA and MITI, to the 1997 "Happy Monday" (in Japanese, *Happi Mondei*) Plan designed to convert national holidays into "three-day weekends" to boost domestic tourism,[72] policymakers have taken popular dissatisfaction with lifestyle issues as opportunities to pursue other goals.

To these policymakers, the turn to leisure—and to Western examples thereof—was only natural. After all, leisure had been initially targeted in the 1970s for large-scale government activity and had dropped out of discussion only because more pressing economic concerns had come to the forefront. But it had never been bracketed as *private,* nor had a state role been foresworn. Moreover, the shape of the state role was hardly ever in doubt. If Japan were to be "harmonized" with its global partners, its people would have to behave like Americans and Europeans—even though there had been no direct demands by any

71. This is very much the point made by Tamura Tamio's *Shōraku no Keifu: Toshi to Yoka Bunka* (The Geneaology of Fun: The City and Leisure Culture) (Tokyo: Dō-bunkan, 1996), especially 252–80.
72. *Japan Times,* 21 October 1997, 1.

Western leaders that Japanese leisure behavior start to approximate that found in Europe or North America. Policymakers could have interpreted the foreign pressure over Japan's workaholism and consumption patterns in a variety of ways, without taking the extraordinary steps involved in studying and promoting "Western" types of leisure. Instead, policymakers took it for granted that citizens in advanced industrial nations engage in broadly similar practices and that Japanese deviation from this mold was unacceptable. As noted in chapter 1, when I asked one Leisure Development Center official in 1997 why his organization sent representatives to western Europe and North America—as opposed to South Korea or Zimbabwe, for example—to study leisure practices for use at home, he looked at me quizzically, probably assuming that I had simply made a mistake in my Japanese rendering of the question. "Because," he said slowly, "those are the advanced nations."[73]

In chapters 4 and 5, I examined some of these motives and initiatives, which are sufficiently broad to undermine any argument for a single cause that can explain all of Japan's leisure policies. Even so, the pattern of policy and the tension involved is strikingly ubiquitous. Regardless of the goals of policymakers, they have turned relentlessly to examples from western Europe and the United States to determine how Japanese lifestyles ought to change. So too in some cases have their opponents—as with Ono, Sasaki, and Nakayama in their assault on the Resort Law. By reaching for the norms of other advanced industrial nations, however, their programs were among the broad collection of "internationalizing" policies that convinced some critics that the government itself played a role in threatening the uniqueness of Japan's culture. But even a cursory glance at state efforts to promote an essentialist understanding of Japaneseness shows that *nihonjinron* were well institutionalized and that the Japanese government continued emphasize cultural uniqueness alongside international harmonization. In the next chapter we focus on perhaps the most remarkable of Japan's major postwar leisure initiatives: the Ten Million Program,

---

73. I have been forced reluctantly to accept that one of the costs of doing research aimed at teasing out what people "take for granted" is the momentary tinge of embarrassment I feel whenever an interviewee responds to one of my questions with a disbelieving stare and suddenly slowed-down speech.

designed ostensibly to double the number of Japanese tourists traveling abroad each year. This extraordinary effort would provide a clever way to synthesize these two conflicting institutional strands: it would allow the Japanese to behave more like Americans and Europeans by recognizing and appealing to their "uniquely" Japanese nature.

A Japanese tour group in Florence's Piazza della Signoria, Italy, 1999. Photograph by
Merry White.

It Takes Ten Million to Meet a Norm

At a reception in Tokyo in June 1995 for Malaysian tourism trainees in one of the "Look East" initiatives arranged between the two governments, attendees need not have been diplomats, hospitality professionals, or, in my case, tourism policy researchers to have been glad to be there. At the height of the rainy season, the banquet hall of a pleasant Tokyo hotel served as welcome shelter from the windy deluge that had nearly knocked one of the event's planners into an especially deep and oily puddle. We were there to honor young Malaysians from the hotel and tourism sectors who had come to Tokyo for three months to work in the hospitality sector as trainees of major Japanese firms. The "Look East" policy has received a fair amount of scholarly and journalistic attention in Japan in recent years, as it has demonstrated Malaysian prime minister Mahathir Mohammad's staunchly pro-Asian, anti-Western political orientation in the 1980s and 1990s.[1] In "Look East" programs, dozens of special training missions were set

---

1. Mahathir is famous in part for having proposed the creation of the East Asia Economic Caucus, designed as an "Asians Only" alternative to Asia-Pacific Economic Cooperation (APEC), which would include "Western" nations such as the United States, Canada, New Zealand, and Australia. See Yong Deng, "Japan in APEC: The Problematic Leadership Role," *Asian Survey* 37, 4 (April 1997): 353–67.

up between Malaysia and Japan, for technical transfers in sector-spe-
cific programs. This one, organized by the International Tourism Development Institute of Japan (ITDIJ), a special foundation created by
the Ministry of Transport (MOT) in 1987, had found positions for the
ten Malaysians in Japanese hotels and restaurants.

With the rain tapping at the windows, this party represented the final formal gathering for the group and included speeches from the
trainees' bosses at the recipient firms. In front of an audience made up
of ITDIJ figures, representatives of the Ministry of Transport and the
Japan International Cooperation Agency (JICA—the main body for
technical transfers in Japan's development assistance policies), each
company president, division director, or liaison summed up the
trainee's work experiences and praised him or her for their efforts. The
young Malaysians had been asked to dress in traditional Malaysian
outfits, which contrasted effectively (and rather brilliantly) with the
drab business suits the rest of us wore. One hotel manager had been
fortunate enough to have two trainees at his firm and called them up
to stand with him while he spoke. Finally, he said that they had
learned traditional Japanese manners and hospitality; on cue, the two
young men, decked out in colorful Malaysian dress, bowed slowly and
said together, "Irasshaimase," a ritualized Japanese greeting that essentially combines "May I help you?" with "Welcome."

Scenes such as this occur at tourism training centers and hotel
schools practically every day around the world and are therefore as
ubiquitous as they usually are dispiriting. The idea of adopting the appearance of a "native" while demonstrating the skills necessary for
catering to foreign guests is neither new in Japan nor unique to Japan.
What is unusual, however, is the fact that this was part of a government program, a policy effort to promote Japanese outbound tourism
in part by helping people in developing countries to learn the skills
necessary to deal adequately with Japanese visitors. This meant, in the
case of the Malaysian program, looking identifiably Malaysian
(through dress) but being obviously accustomed to Japanese practices
(in the form of traditional greetings and polite body language).

Compared with the Ministry of Transport's (MOT) other policy areas (the ministry—which was combined with two others in 2001—
had jurisdiction over Japan's rail, aviation, and shipping sectors, among
others), the effort to promote tourism overseas clearly occupied only
a tiny fraction of the MOT's overall activities. Since 1987, however,
the government has been directly and consistently involved in pro-

moting Japanese tourism overseas, as well as in creating overseas tourist sites and environments in which Japanese can feel safe, comfortable, and relaxed. The training of Malaysian tourist industry representatives in the correct way of receiving Japanese visitors was one manifestation of the MOT's policy of facilitating Japanese outbound tours. Indeed, the implementing agency, the ITDIJ, was established in 1987 alongside the Ten Million Program, an MOT policy designed to double the number of tourists traveling overseas annually within five years (from five million in 1987 to ten million in 1992). These programs therefore aimed at conveying two messages: to Japanese, you should get out more; and to other countries, you need to adapt to make yourselves more attractive to Japanese visitors.

Nearly all governments try to do the opposite: to convince outsiders to visit and possibly to convince citizens to visit domestic tourism spots before venturing overseas. On one level, the policy seems easy to explain: by encouraging outbound tourism, the government could reduce the country's heavily criticized trade surplus. This relatively straightforward account sees tourism as a purely economic issue, in which the state's interest is directly and purely mandated by the red and black ink showing up each month on the balance of payments figures. Yet even a cursory glance at these efforts—to get Japanese people to go have fun overseas and to encourage foreign countries to become more Japanese-friendly—recognizes that the government's policy choices seem odder than simple efforts to share the wealth. After all, if the United States had a trade surplus, it would be odd to consider the president's throwing his weight behind a campaign to get Americans to visit France, Japan, Costa Rica, or Cameroon. It is not the black ink in the trade balance book, unimaginable though that might seem to an American born in the last few decades, that is so striking; it is the apparently accepted role of the state in telling citizens that they ought to travel overseas.

The Ten Million Program is the most remarkable of Japan's leisure initiatives. Although the Resort Law undoubtedly had more disastrous effects for the nation, its overall thrust—as a regional development scheme larded with pork barrel opportunities for politicians—seems comparatively easy to grasp. In contrast, the Ten Million Program (which was ostensibly designed to double the number of annual Japanese outbound tourists) has no real analogue. Although many governments have highly liberal rules regarding outbound travel—the German government has supported targeted tours for Germans to visit

European sites of Nazi atrocities—only the Japanese government has established a clear policy advocating more trip overseas. None of Japan's leisure policies displays a more perfect solution for the tension between the pressure to be an advanced industrial nation like any other and the domestic militancy of Japan's exclusive national identity. By combining the perceived requirement that Japanese citizens travel abroad in numbers more similar to those of the standard reference points in the West, with an emphasis on the uniqueness of the Japanese national character, the policy and its related foreign aid programs made a simple but powerful link: Japanese would behave "normally" when their "special" needs were recognized and catered to by the global environment. If the world were to recognize and to cater to Japan's uniqueness, Japanese would be like any other advanced industrial nation.

No one, however, designs a complex public policy only to solve a thorny metaphysical question of who a nation is supposed to be. The Ten Million Program's creation was a complicated process, and this chapter examines it by paying attention first to the instrumental motives behind the plan: the MOT's efforts to gain control of foreign aid funds to increase its mission and to provide important postretirement spots to its bureaucrats. But by focusing only on the instrumental motives, we risk missing the institutional environment that gave purchase to these motives.

Although unusual, the policy counted as more than a simple novelty or curiosity. It signaled to Japanese investors a government commitment to promote outbound tourism, and it designated resources, particularly to Thailand, that would shift development priorities and strategies. Although perhaps less noticeable than those associated with the disastrous Resort Law, the Ten Million Program's effects merit attention.

Economic Power and the International Travel

The story of Japan's startling economic rise in the mid- to late 1980s is well known in the United States. A slumping American economy, combined with a huge surge in Japan's economy, led a number of observers to press the idea of a "Japan Model" ever more forcefully. Japan became something of a bogeyman in the U.S. media, with a rising trade surplus, the symbolically powerful purchases of such icons as Columbia Pictures and Rockefeller Center, and a new assertiveness on the part of Japanese commercial leaders. Property values rose dramatically as did stock prices, and the paper wealth in Japan virtually doubled within the space of a few short years. Japanese citizens began to take advantage of the country's rising economic fortunes, spending more on leisure and tourism than in the past and particularly on outbound tourism. Indeed, with the value of the yen practically doubling overnight, an increase in outbound tourism was one of the more predictable consequences of Japan's new economic circumstances.[2]

By any standard, the increase in Japanese outbound tourism was astonishing. In 1980, approximately 3.9 million Japanese traveled abroad; by 1985, this figure had increased by approximately one million, to 4.95 million. For over a decade, the number then increased by approximately one million each year, approaching ten million (9.66 million) in 1989, almost eleven million in 1990, and around sixteen million by 1997 (see figure 1). With the rapid increase in outbound tourists beginning between 1986 and 1987, a 1987 plan to double the number of outbound tourists by 1991 (from the five million of 1986 to 1991) was, perhaps, less than bold. Indeed, with the rising value of the yen and the international strength of the economy, few doubted that Japanese outbound tourism would grow by leaps and bounds, and no other nations demanded that the government actually do something to increase these numbers. With massive pressure on Japan to open its markets and to import more heavily, tourism remained one of the few major areas of trade to stay off the negotiating table, at least as far as Japan's most fervent critics in North America and Europe were concerned. The Maekawa Report and the various consumption promotion schemes of the 1980s can easily be viewed as rather direct responses to international criticism, but at no point had any of Japan's international partners suggested that the nation needed to put more of its citizens abroad, whether to solve the balance-of-payments surplus or to promote global understanding.

Japanese policymakers, however, seized on the possibilities that a radically altered international monetary environment presented. With Japan's exports likely to suffer from the increased value of the yen, and with assets overseas suddenly cheap, MITI and other policy

2. For a good overview of the economic change in this period, see Edward J. Lincoln, *Japan's New Global Role* (Washington, D.C.: Brookings Institution, 1993). He deals specifically with the issue of overseas tourism on 98–103. Lincoln's earlier work *Japan: Facing Economic Maturity* (Washington, D.C.: Brookings Institution, 1988) takes up some of these issues at the time of Japan's rapid economic ascent.

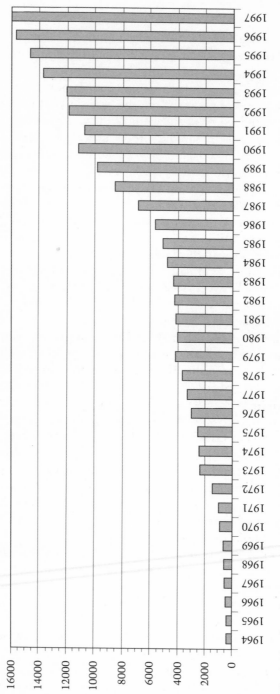

Fig. 1. Number of Japanese overseas tourists, 1964–1997 (in thousands). *Source:* JNTO, *Tourism in Japan* (Tokyo, annual).

organizations sought to capitalize on the opportunities provided.[3] Although perhaps most noticeable in the rapid expansion of Japan's foreign direct investment, particularly around the Pacific Rim, Japan's place in international human exchange also provoked some concerned glances. After all, an open international environment invited the possibility that the Japanese state could try to use the movement of people as well as products for national benefit.

By way of illustration, we can look at the Ministry of International Trade and Industry's "Silver Columbia Plan," which is often mentioned in the same breath in policy circles as the Ten Million Program. For years, elderly British and Germans have taken up full-time or seasonal residence abroad, most notably in southern European and Mediterranean countries. Noticing this trend and concerned about rising costs of health care for Japan's aging population, in 1986 MITI proposed the ultimately doomed Silver Columbia Plan, which aimed at relocating many of Japan's elderly to warmer countries with lower costs for health care, including Spain, Greece, Australia, and the Philippines. Surely elderly Japanese were entitled to the same pleasant change of pace, especially in their "Silver" years, though no one seems to know precisely what the "Columbia" in the title meant.

Sadly, these nations that would likely have been directly affected by an influx of elderly Japanese appear to have treated the plan with hostility even greater than the bewilderment and curiosity it aroused elsewhere. In fact, the subsequent proposal of the Ten Million Program came at an unfortunate moment, as some MOT representatives overseas on tourism-promotion missions were accused of trying to pawn off Japan's elderly on unsuspecting people. In other words, were these Japanese to settle overseas of their own accord (and very few people ever took MITI up on this plan), there probably would have been little trouble, but the fact that the state itself was involved suggested that Japan was trying to take advantage of other countries; the involvement of the state made what otherwise would have been construed to be purely private into a political dispute.[4]

---

3. For one examination of MITI's role in the massive growth in foreign direct investment following the Plaza Accord, see Walter Hatch and Kozo Yamamura, *Asia in Japan's Embrace: Building a Regional Production Alliance* (Cambridge: Cambridge University Press, 1996).

4. For a good discussion of Silver Columbia and the international reaction, see Sasaki Takeshi, *Ima no Seiji ni Nani ga Kanō Ka* (What's Possible for Government These Days?) (Tokyo: Chūō Shinshō, 1987), 17–20.

Tellingly, however, the Silver Columbia Plan—though reviled as a bad idea—was not seen as fundamentally odd in Japan. In fact, the plan failed not so much because it was considered an inappropriate goal for the state, but because no one really wanted to go. After a lifetime of hearing ambivalent messages about the outside world, few of Japan's elderly demonstrated a real willingness to pack up their bags and settle down overseas. After all, where could one buy Japanese food, or watch Japanese television, or visit one's family? And wasn't it dangerous in the other countries?[5] The problem was that no one really wanted to leave Japan, not that it was weird to think that the government would ask anyone to.

The Silver Columbia Plan—notwithstanding the embarrassment it caused—provides an important comparative case for assessing the environment in which the Ten Million Program was conceived and realized. With a radically altered political economic environment, Japanese policymakers began to investigate how a strong yen and a more open economy might be turned to national advantage. With responsibility for ensuring Japan's continued industrial development in spite of the challenges posed by the Plaza Accord and the Maekawa reports, MITI unsurprisingly moved quickly to think broadly about the problem. Other ministries, however, also recognized genuine incentives for thinking about internationalization. Among the most important was the rapid growth of Japan's Official Development Assistance (ODA) programs, which provided ministries and agencies the chance to expand control over budgets and use them to meet their own goals.

The Budgetary Lure of ODA

The reputation of Japan as an economic rather than political giant has some truth to it. Hampered by a domestic reluctance to engage questions of war responsibility, Japan's diplomatic links with its closest neighbors, China and Korea, have been strained. It has yet to sign a peace treaty with Russia, waiting for a solution to the question of four islands off the northern coast of Hokkaido, which were seized

---

5. Tamai Katsumi provides an amusingly sarcastic discussion of the plan in "Shiruba Coramubia Keikaku no Gu" (The Foolishness of the Silver Columbia Program), *Bungei Shunju* (April 1987): 324–29. She focuses on the sorts of social difficulties Japan's elderly would be likely to face, making their final years a disturbing experiment in cultural interaction.

by the Soviet Union in the closing days of World War II. And even in Southeast Asia, where Japanese ODA and prime ministerial links have been exceptionally strong, there is lingering mistrust, particularly in Singapore and Indonesia.[6] Furthermore, with Japan's ability to export seen as a crucial linchpin of its success, the Japanese government has traditionally been reluctant to undermine this source of support through dramatic liberalization of the domestic market for foreign suppliers.[7] Finally, the rapid growth of Japan's trade surplus has provoked criticism regarding the country's alleged predatory behavior, making ODA a good choice for visibly recycling Japan's gross income.[8] Throughout much of the 1980s, increases in ODA allocations outpaced other developments in the Japanese budget.

Through most of the postwar era, Japan's principal aid arms were the Overseas Economic Cooperation Fund (OECF), which answered to the Ministry of Finance and administered concessional loans, and the Japan International Cooperation Agency (JICA), responsible for technical assistance and run primarily by the Ministry of Foreign Affairs.[9] Because of the size of Japan's aid programs and its otherwise limited international profile, ODA has long been one of the main topics for research on the nation's international relations. Some scholars have defended Japan's aid programs against the frequent charge that they are selfish, mercanitilistic, and overly tied to the export needs of Japanese firms.[10] Others have emphasized that foreign aid functions as part of a regional development strategy that uses Japanese aid to

6. On the differing responses to Japan among the ASEAN countries, see Paul H. Midford, "Making the Best of a Bad Reputation: Reassurance Strategies in Japan's Security Policies," *Social Science Japan* 11 (November 1997): 23–25.

7. There are a number of books on the question of Japan's trade behavior. The most widely cited of these remains Chalmers Johnson, *MITI and the Japanese Miracle: The Growth of Industrial Policy, 1925–1975* (Stanford: Stanford University Press, 1982). On the philosophical underpinnings of the "developmental state" model, see also Bai Gao, *Economic Ideology and Japanese Industrial Policy: Developmentalism from 1931 to 1965* (Stanford: Stanford University Press, 1997).

8. For an economic analysis, see Terutomo Ozawa, *Recyling Japan's Surpluses for Developing Countries* (Paris: OECD Development Centre Studies, 1989).

9. The most complete history of Japan's ODA policies can be found in Alan Rix, *Japan's Economic Aid: Policy-Making and Politics* (London: Croom Helm, 1980).

10. For positive assessments, see in particular Robert M. Orr Jr., *The Emergence of Japan's Foreign Aid Power* (New York: Columbia University Press, 1990); Robert M. Orr Jr., "Collaboration or Conflict? Foreign Aid and U.S.-Japan Cooperation," *Pacific Affairs* 62, 4 (winter 1990): 476–89; David Halloran Lumsdaine, *Moral Vision in International Politics : The Foreign Aid Regime, 1949–1989* (Princeton: Princeton University Press, 1993), which argues that Japanese behavior has changed to meet international norms.

support private investment initiatives of Japanese firms. Whether one believes that this practice is part of a strategy for embedding Japan in the international political order,[11] helping Japanese firms create production networks giving them control over the Asian region,[12] or for using a combination of public and private finance to do as much as possible for regional development,[13] there is little doubt that Japanese ODA is often linked tightly to patterns of Japanese foreign direct investment. The government's role appears to be the construction of infrastructure that will be useful for private economic development, often led by Japanese firms. Particularly during the 1980s, this role offered special opportunities to those administrative organs that could link their efforts to private plans for overseas investment, because the possibility of creating genuine "economic cooperation" for development gave a boost to those requesting ODA resources. The Ministry of Transport would have a clear winner in real estate mogul Tsutsumi Yoshiaki.

The Bubble Economy and Tsutsumi Yoshiaki's Suggestion

Most of the investment of interest to MITI and to other Japanese administrative offices interested in *keizai kyōryoku* (economic cooperation) has traditionally been the foreign direct investment of Japanese manufacturers. And yet when we think of the rapid expansion of Japanese investment in the 1980s that best typified the bubble economy, we tend to think of the odder status symbols purchased by Japanese investors at the time: Rockefeller Center, hotel chains, and the like. In addition to frightening Americans who started to believe that the "American Century" had come to an end (roughly sixty years short of a full century, it should be noted), the expansion of Japan's real estate and services investment would eclipse manufacturing and ultimately become the source of many of Japan's economic problems in the 1990s. Because Japanese banks were willing to accept land—which was of practically astronomical value in Tokyo—as collateral for loans, they were willing to lend handsomely to a wide variety of borrowers with-

11. Kozo Kato, "Helping Others, Helping Oneself" (Ph.D. diss., Cornell University, 1996).

12. Hatch and Yamamura, *Asia in Japan's Embrace*, 43–61.

13. This is the argument that Japanese aid officials give to defend what they call *keizai kyōryoku* (economic cooperation). David Arase describes the logic in *Buying Power: The Political Economy of Japan's Foreign Aid* (Boulder, Colo.: Lynne Rienner, 1995), though his analysis is highly skeptical of the magnanimity suggested by such an argument.

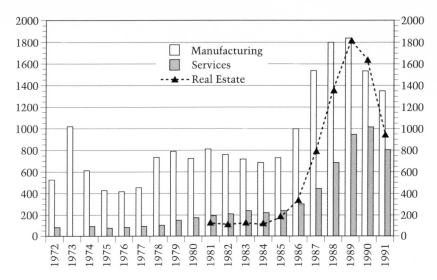

Fig. 2. Instances of Japanese overseas investment, global, by year. *Source:* MITI Policy Bureau, International Planning Division, *Waga Kuni Kigyō no Kaigai Jigyō Katsudō* (Japanese Firms' Overseas Activities) (Tokyo, annual).

out adequately testing whether the investments would be fruitful or not. And the urge to invest, particularly abroad, where assets had suddenly become cheap, proved to be too tempting for many businesses and private individuals to resist.[14] One of the main outcomes of the flurry of speculative energy in the Japanese economy came in the area of foreign real estate. Although manufacturing investment grew handsomely, as did investment in services, in real estate the change over the course of just a few years was nothing short of explosive. In 1982, there were eighty-six instances of overseas investment in real estate by Japanese firms. At the peak in 1989, there were 1,808, an increase of almost 2000 percent in seven years (see figure 2).

The behavior among some firms and individuals was so frantic as to be practically nonsensical. Indeed, Christopher Wood cites the belief that real estate values only rise and not fall as being important in many of the ill-advised investment decisions; interviews in Tokyo suggested

14. Although a bit extreme at times in its depiction of the "outrageous speculation" in mid- to late-1980s Japan, Christopher Wood's *The Bubble Economy: The Japanese Economic Collapse* (Tokyo: Tuttle, 1992) is a lively and well-written account of the era. Wood, a journalist with *The Economist,* clearly evinces both the magazine's persuasiveness on banking issues and its inflexible stand on the benefits of the free market.

that he is correct to have cited this faith.[15] In some cases, American property brokers were able to get lists of property owners in Tokyo (whose land would be useful as collateral), invite them to a sales pitch at a hotel conference room in Tokyo, and sell vastly overpriced office buildings or hotels in Los Angeles or Hawaii to collections of individual investors. Hotels became favored parts of investment portfolios and took on a value beyond their expected rental benefits. Indeed, management revenues were considered less important than their value as equity, meaning that owners and builders planned to buy and sell the hotels for a profit, not necessarily to operate them in the long term. In the short term, they evidently counted on the boom of Japanese outbound tourists to make them profitable ventures.[16]

Although not a neophyte (and vastly more skilled as a business professional than many "karaoke bar" owners who lost millions on bad property investments at the height of the bubble economy), one of the most famous symbols of Japanese bubble-era property speculation was Tsutsumi. One of two half brothers in charge of the Seibu Group, a major industrial conglomerate, Tsutsumi Yoshiaki was the favored illegitimate son who inherited the better part of the family's industrial holdings. His half brother Seiji (the family's legitimate son) inherited the Seibu department store chain.[17] Tsutsumi Yoshiaki would be listed by the end of the decade as the richest man in the world, until the collapse in property values and Bill Gates together toppled him.[18] With a personal fortune in the billions of dollars, he was the foremost Japanese tycoon of the decade. Tsutsumi had evidently determined by 1986[19] that Japanese outbound tourism was going to be the wave of

15. In early 1997, I completed a consulting report for the ASEAN Centre on the nature of Japanese investment in the ASEAN region in the field of tourism. Several of the interviewees at hotel firms, construction companies, and real estate firms cited this as being one of the main factors in the bubble. In the oddest interview, one senior representative of a large firm told me that he had come to have tremendous respect for "overseas Chinese" investors. I asked him why, and he told me, "They have a different way of thinking about it than we do. They buy stuff when it's cheap, then they sell it when it's more expensive." This was one of the few moments in any interview in which I was glad that I was not a native speaker of Japanese, because I was able to use the expectation of incomprehension to cover my utter speechlessness.

16. Wood, *Bubble Economy*, makes this point, seconded in interview 31, 28 January 1997.

17. Lesley Downer, *The Brothers: The Hidden World of Japan's Richest Family* (New York: Random House, 1994).

18. More recently, falling property values drove him from number seven to number twenty-two on the list in *Forbes* magazine. "Gates' Wallet Doubles in Size Atop *Forbes'* Billionaires," *Associated Press*, 14 July 1997.

19. My information here is based on interviews at the ITDIJ, where I spent a year as a translator once or twice a week. There is no written record of this process, and I

the future in leisure and tourism businesses, in which his own group was heavily invested. Interested in figuring out ways to rationalize and to systematize public and private cooperation in the field of overseas tourism development, Tsutsumi approached acquaintances in the MOT and proposed the creation of a quasi-public foundation that would be in charge of tourism development projects. This foundation ideally would use ODA funds to promote the development of tourist sites overseas, thus allowing the Japanese government to provide some of the "public goods" (regional development plans, possibly financing for infrastructure such as roads, and water and sewage systems) that would enable firms, like Tsutsumi's, to invest overseas more confidently. The 1987 result of the proposition, the International Tourism Development Institute of Japan (ITDIJ), would be a key player in the arena of Japan's outbound tourism development programs, though in the long run its effects were probably somewhat less positive than had originally been hoped. In any event, the MOT was ostensibly only too happy to apply for governmental funds to match Tsutsumi's offer, as well as to request them of related firms in the tourism and travel industry. Organizations such as the ITDIJ provide valuable benefits to ministries, primarily in the form of *amakudari* ("descent from heaven," or postretirement) positions for Japanese bureaucrats.

Amakudari *and Bureaucratic Politics in Japan*

The vaunted role of the bureaucrats in Japan is not, as one might believe, particularly well-rewarded, at least in the short term. Salaries in the ministries are generally lower than similarly skilled professionals might make in private business, the road to advancement is fraught with peril and competition, and the working hours are considered to be almost absurdly rigorous. Even so, there is still intense competition to become a member of the Japanese civil service, particularly the ministries, and most members are recruited from the top schools, with an especially heavy percentage coming from the elite Faculty of Law at the University of Tokyo. Because of the salary limits and early retirement norm, one of the most important incentives for young people entering the ministries is the promise of lucrative postretirement

---

can only speculate as to dates and the actual flow of events. What is clear from the interviews is that the ITDIJ was, as an organization, originally conceptualized by Tsutsumi, and that the MOT was eager to cooperate with him to create this organization, which he nominally chaired. When I asked my bosses at the ITDIJ if I would be able to interview Tsutsumi, they laughed and said, "Maybe if you got an introduction from the Prime Minister or someone like that."

employment at a private firm or quasi-public foundation. Although there are legal restrictions on immediately parachuting into firms over which one's ministry has direct jurisdiction, bureaucrats have proved adept at finding employment spots that generally yield better working conditions and significantly greater remuneration than do the ministries themselves. Although determining specific norms regarding *amakudari* is difficult (and increasingly so, now that it has become a widely criticized and more secretive practice), one apparent rule is that the higher ranking the bureaucrat, the more handsome the post-retirement position.[20]

Although some analysts find that *amakudari* is a beneficial practice for firms and bureaucracies alike, in that it provides the foundation for a network allowing easier monitoring, communication, and compliance, there is in general constant pressure to increase the number and quality of the positions, even by establishing new positions. One of the motives for ministries in creating quasi-public foundations (*zaidan hōjin*, for example) under the purview of a given ministry, is thus to provide postretirement employment for exiting members.[21] With quasi-public actors dotting the Japanese political landscape and employing retired bureaucrats who had served twenty-five to thirty years in ministries, the competition for funds to create new agencies takes on an almost personal significance for members of the Japanese ministries.

Indeed, insiders and outsiders alike suggested to me that the ITDIJ had been created as an *amakudari* spot.[22] Its general director in the 1990s, Arai Koichi, had been a longtime member of the Ministry of Transport, and several of its other senior members had been employed by JICA, which was partly responsible for the ITDIJ. And there is no

20. Ulrike Schaede, "The 'Old-Boy' Network and Government-Business Relationships in Japan," *Journal of Japanese Studies* 21, 2 (1995): 293–317; Ulrike Schaede, "The Ministry of Finance, Change, and Sherlock Holmes," *Social Science Japan* 7 (August 1996): 6–8.

21. Chalmers Johnson covers this aspect of *amakudari* to some degree in *Japan's Public Policy Companies* (Washington, D.C.: American Enterprise Institute, 1978). He evaluates *amakudari* into the private sector (with a somewhat positive appraisal, at least compared to the tone of 1990s debates) in "The Reemployment of Retired Government Bureaucrats in Japanese Big Business," *Asian Survey* 14 (November 1974): 953–65, and in *MITI and the Japanese Miracle*, 63–73.

22. This was mentioned to me on a few occasions by people at the ITDIJ. For reasons of confidentiality, however, I decline to call these interviews (although the respondents knew the nature of my research and understood what they were doing in describing this to me), and I will not use their names.

reason to doubt that the MOT and JICA would have wanted to create more organizations to provide lucrative postcareer opportunities for ministry members. It bears mentioning here, however, that there is no written record of the MOT having had this motive, and the comments I received from ITDIJ employees may have reflected their dissatisfaction with having been seconded there from Japanese private firms and other tourism-related organizations. I cannot test the veracity of these statements except to suggest that they make sense as descriptions of a coherent strategy, and that they jibe well with a commonly noted inclination in the Japanese civil service. Even so, bureaucrats are to some degree limited in what kinds of organizations they can create, as well as where they can obtain the funds necessary to maintain them. Fortunately for the MOT, the increasing emphases on leisure and internationalization in post–Maekawa Report Japan provided an auspicious environment for the articulation of a new course for Japanese outbound tourism.

Tourism—Good for the Nation?

Ever since the 1973 Cheju Island debacle described in chapter 4, the Ministry of Transport had been attempting to consolidate a genuine policy position with regard to outbound tourism and had slowly but surely clawed back some amount of respectability for the industry. In 1978, with the help of the MOFA, the MOT was able to win Japan's ratification of an agreement to join the World Tourism Organization, an international organization dealing with tourism under the auspices (until fairly recently) of the United Nations. Pressing the advantages of putting Japan's growing outbound market to work for international development, MOFA and MOT representatives spoke in a preliminary session to the Lower House's Foreign Affairs Committee within the Diet on 28 February 1978. The ministry representatives faced mostly friendly questions, as they argued that international tourism ought to be a higher policy priority. Sugiura Kyōya, the head of the MOT Secretariat Tourism Policy Division, stressed that the MOT maintained programs to handle incoming tourists and to make them comfortable while in Japan, and also that it was trying to cope with problems of outbound travel.

No doubt remembering the rough treatment the MOT had faced earlier, he was well prepared to handle a question by Lower House member Tanaka Emiko, who spoke about the "exceedingly bad manners" of Japanese tourists overseas, particularly in the Republic of Korea and the Philippines. There was little doubt as to what particular problem she was describing. Sugiura responded:

> I regret to have to say it, but what the Honorable Member has suggested about the terrible conduct of Japanese tourists, particularly in Southeast Asia, Korea, Taiwan, etc., appears to have some truth to it. . . . [When a few people behave like this] it leaves a mistaken image abroad with regard to all of Japan. And I firmly believe we have to do something about this. What the MOT is doing is comprehensive PR, public relations campaigns, trying to inform all Japanese about proper behavior on overseas trips. In particular, we're focusing efforts on the travel agents and tour conductors, especially those tour conductors who have caused problems, and we're providing strong guidance on how they have to run their tours. We take this very seriously. And we are making sure that the travel agents themselves keep Japanese tourists informed of how they're supposed to behave overseas. I am very much hoping that these efforts will show some success.

Tanaka responded, "Go ahead and join the World Tourism Organization, but don't do anything that will get Japan's privileges revoked (*Nihon ga kenri teishi o ukenai yō ni, WTO ni sanka shite*)."[23]

The later debate in the foreign relations committee, on 14 April 1978, within the Lower House was similar, with a few questions raised about the sex tourism issue. The MOT and MOFA, however, managed to win entry into the WTO by playing up two aspects of the move: first, it would bind Japan into a multilateral organization with regard to tourism aid and would thus reflect a cooperative international stance; second, because of the rapidly increasing number of Japanese tourists (this comment was made several times by committee members and respondents alike), it could be seen as Japan's contribution to the world economy.[24] The Diet passed the resolution later that year.

The Ten Million Program

In highlighting the contribution that Japan could make to international development through international tourism assistance, the MOT in the late 1970s foreshadowed the justification for the creation

---

23. For the full text of the debate, see the records of the 84th Session of the Diet (*Kokkai*), *Sangi Gaimu Iinkai Kaigiroku Dai 4 Kaigo* (Lower House Foreign Affairs Committee Records, no. 4), 28 February 1978, 66–73.

24. 84th Session of the Lower House of the Diet (*Kokkai Shūgi*), *Gaimu Iinkaigiroku Dai 14 Go* (Foreign Affairs Committee Records, no. 14), 14 April 1978, especially 341 passim.

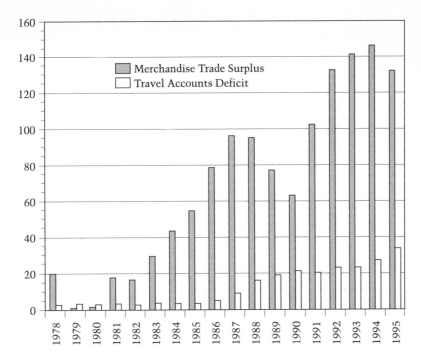

Fig. 3. Japan's merchandise trade surplus versus travel accounts deficit (in billions of U.S. dollars). *Source:* International Monetary Fund, *Balance of Payments Statistics Yearbook* (Washington, D.C.: IMF, 1996).

of the Ten Million Program in 1987. Japan's international travel accounts had been in deficit for years, and that deficit began to grow remarkably both in absolute terms and relative to Japan's swelling trade surplus (see figure 3). This meant that tourism represented one of the ways in which Japan's wealth might be redistributed in the international community and that outbound tourism—especially if it led to increasing deficits in the travel accounts—would be good for Japan's public relations.

And so, with Tsutsumi pushing for the creation of a quasi-public organization that would serve as a linchpin for Japan's overseas tourism assistance programs, and the MOT looking for a way of justifying a more assertive stance vis-à-vis international tourism, the MOT's Tourism Section held a planning meeting sometime in 1986 or 1987 to outline the ministry's position. Two versions of the story, neither of them available on paper, have been reported to me. One former MOT insider, apparently present at the meeting, told me that a senior section member came up with the idea of promoting Japanese tourism to Asia; this would justify Japan's tourism development schemes in the area and would also help to redistribute the trade surplus on a regional basis. The idea was rejected because it too closely resembled a neocolonialist policy that would have Asian critics talking of a second Great East Asian Co-Prosperity Sphere. As a result, another ministry member suggested that it be created as a general outbound tourism promotion program.[25] Another Tokyo tourism professional, with contacts inside the ministry, told me that she had heard that the idea of promoting general outbound tourism actually came from a female staff member but that it was quickly appropriated by men in the ministry and she received no credit for it.[26] I have no way of confirming or disproving either story. The MOT thus announced in September 1987 the *Kaigai Ryokō Baizō Keikaku*, or *Ten Mirion Keikaku* (Overseas Trip Doubling Program, or Ten Million Program for short), the purpose of which was to double the number of tourists leaving the country each year from the five million of 1986 to ten million by 1991. Significantly, everyone expected the plan to "succeed," in that reasonable projections had Japan clearly topping ten million by 1991.[27]

Of course, what is striking about this is that the MOT was not and is not responsible for reducing Japan's trade surplus. That burden fell almost exclusively to MITI, which responded after the Maekawa Report with a series of import promotion schemes designed to reduce the surplus without endangering key sectors of the Japanese economy. But the outcome of the Maekawa Report—which stated clearly that Japan somehow had to change, to become a country of consumption as well as production, to become a normal country like others—provided one normative foundation for the claim that outbound tourism was beneficial: that it would be a way for Japan to contribute economically to the world, by redistributing its gains from trade through spending on overseas leisure. The Ten Million Program's overall purpose would be displayed in the MOT's own assessment of the plan:

> With improvements in income levels and the growth of free time, the spread of the package tour, etc., the number of Japanese outbound

25. Interview 19, 31 August 1995.
26. Interview 18, 28 August 1995.
27. The formal name, *Kaigai Ryokō Baizō Keikaku*, was itself an obvious reference to the *Shotoku Baizō Keikaku*, the Income Doubling Plan. Like the Income Doubling Plan, the Ten Million Program was designed to put a policy name on a projected development. .

tourists is definitely growing. Especially with the appreciation of the yen [*endaka*] and the relatively cheap prices [ostensibly in comparison with domestic tours], there was a big jump, to 5.52 million travelers in 1986, the first time this number has exceeded 5 million.

Even so, if examined as a percentage of the population, by 1986 only 4% of Japanese traveled abroad annually, compared with the other advanced countries [*senshinkoku*]: 39% of UK citizens, 34% of the West Germans, 16% of French, and 12% of Americans, meaning that it is definitely a low level for us. Even when compared with another Pacific country, Australia, we travel abroad less than half their rate of 10%.

Drawing up the promotion of outbound travel would increase international mutual understanding [*kokusaiteki na sōgō rikai*] and would mean the cultivation of our people's sense of the international [*kokumin no kokusai kankaku no kan'yō*]. It would furthermore promote the economies of other countries, result in an improved balance of payments between our country and others, and will definitely help our country secure a stable existence in an international society with greater interdependence [*sōgō izon kankei no fukumaru kokusai shakai ni oite wagakuni no anteiteki na sonritsu o kakuhō suru*].

For this reason, the Ministry of Transport, in cooperation with other relevant ministries and agencies, has created the Overseas Trip Doubling Program and aims within five years to bring the number of Japanese outbound travelers to the level of at least ten million per year. This would bring us, as a percentage of the population, to about the level in Australia.[28]

This excerpt, taken from the *Keikaku no Igi* (Meaning of the Plan) section of the report, suggests quite clearly that the program's strategic motive was to contribute to an improved balance of payments and that it was expected to succeed. Its value to the nation would be not only in terms of its improvement of Japan's international relations but its doing so through making Japanese enjoy themselves in a manner befitting an advanced industrial nation. After all, even the *Australians* were traveling abroad.

In terms of concrete achievements, the MOT's efforts yielded some obvious successes over time. It managed, after a few years, to convince the Ministry of Education to allow school trips to include overseas travel, a longtime ban that had frozen foreign countries out of one of Japan's more stable and lucrative tourism markets. More pointedly, it convinced the Ministry of Finance (MOF) to raise the limits on un-

28. *Ten Mirion Keikou no Seika* (Result of the Ten Million Program), from the Ministry of Transport Policy Bureau, Tourism Section, Planning Divison, in cooperation with the Transport Promotion Association (Tokyo: MOT, 1994), 1.

taxed goods purchased overseas to an almost unbelievably lavish ¥200,000 (at 1998 exchange rates, which are similar to those of 1988–1989, this is about three times the amount allowed Americans), though this is not listed in the Ten Million Program results report as a consequence of the plan.[29]

For the most part, however, the MOT's efforts in the Ten Million Program were in the field of public relations. It worked with the Japan Association of Travel Agents (JATA), the Japan Travel Promotion Association, the Japan National Tourist Organization (JNTO), and other organizations to create ad campaigns that "upgraded" the image of outbound tourism. One longtime JNTO staffer claimed that these campaigns were effective. The government did not use any kind of coercion to promote outbound tourism but rather used its position of moral authority to encourage outbound tours. It ostensibly created an environment in which people felt better about taking overseas trips, that doing so was not a sign of slothful indulgence, as it had been in the workaholic 1960s and 1970s, but rather the just desert for a job well done. When I asked how many Japanese knew of the existence of the Ten Million Program, he replied, "Everyone knew about it."[30] I heard the same comment from MOT members and colleagues, but I was told in virtually all of my casual conversations with Japanese unconnected to the MOT—politically savvy and knowledgeable individuals, as well as friends who avoided newspapers and are not well-informed in current events—that they had not heard of the program. Indeed, a search of indexes for the major national newspapers uncovered only one contemporary article directly about the creation of the Ten Million Program, a short piece in the evening edition of the *Asahi Shimbun*.

The apparent failure of the MOT to inform people that there was, in fact, a Ten Million Program does not necessarily mean that it had no public relations impact. Indeed, most Japanese visiting travel agencies at the time would have seen a number of pamphlets from organizations such as the JNTO[31] regarding how to enjoy an overseas trip,

29. I heard this comment from a former MOT member, and it is consistent with other information I have, but it curiously remains outside of the MOT's report.

30. Interview 1, 6 February 1995.

31. The role of the JNTO in helping to promote outbound tourism is actually quite remarkable. The United States Travel and Tourism Agency (USTTA) was in fact prohibited from engaging in any promotion of overseas sites; although this may have been an extreme case, national tourist organizations are designed clearly to attract inbound tourists. In recent years, "outbound" activities, frequently involving an "international cooperation" aspect, have become among the JNTO's defining missions.

what kind of trip might be especially enjoyable (particularly through the *Betā Hōmustē Tsuā Kyanpēn* (Better Homestay Tour Campaign), and a proliferation of guides regarding proper "manners and morals" during overseas trips, in part a reference to the concerns over sex tourism earning the Japanese tourists a bad name. The emphasis, starting at around this time, was not only on promoting tourism but also encouraging a proper, more "normal" tourism. That is to say, travelers were not supposed to go abroad in the short-term group trips, the "collectivist virtues" of which had been extolled fifteen years earlier in the *Yoka Sōran* (*Overview of Leisure*, discussed in chapter 4), but rather on longer, more individualized trips, like people in other countries.

The emphasis on a certain style of travel came up specifically in a report that appeared more or less alongside the Ten Million Program. As noted in chapter 4, policy coordination in Japan's leisure industries suffers to a degree from the fact that jurisdiction is divided across ministries, a condition lamented at least by members of MITI. Noting the growth in outbound tourism and its potential benefits for redistributing Japan's trade surplus (for which it was held politically responsible), it produced in 1988 a report entitled *Kaigai Taizaigata Yoka* (Overseas Stay-Style Leisure). This referred primarily to the idea that instead of short, multi-destination trips, Japanese outbound travelers should take longer breaks, as did Europeans and, to a somewhat lesser extent, Americans. This kind of travel was thought to be of better value to the nation in terms of both *kokusaika* and "normal" leisure development and would have the added benefit of providing opportunities for Japanese firms to invest abroad. Japanese firms, the report argued, had a special understanding of the Japanese market in terms of the needs of Japanese spending time overseas.[32]

The emphasis on *kokusaika* reflects an important element of the overseas travel program. When MITI referred to the utility of overseas travel in Japan's internationalization, echoing the cultural goals of the Ten Million Program, it explicitly appealed to the normative foundations of Japan's shifting foreign relations programs. Citing not only outbound travel but also the recent Silver Columbia Plan, *Kaigai Taizaigata Yoka* argued that this kind of travel would open Japan to foreign cultures and countries, making Japan more accepting of the world, and vice versa. This did not, however, obviate the need for the

---

32. MITI Industrial Policy Bureau, *Kaigai Taizaigata Yoka: Kunizakai o Koeru Yoka no Shōrai Tenbō* (Overseas Stay-Style Leisure: The Future Prospects of Leisure that Crosses National Borders) (Tokyo: Tsūshō Sangyō Chōsakai, 1988).

creation of infrastructure that would make Japanese feel at home overseas; indeed, the goal was not to make them somehow less Japanese but rather to mediate a sense of Japanese identity with a broader world that demanded some form of cosmopolitanism on the part of its leading citizens. The outbound travel schemes of the era thus relied on the mobilization and use of a widespread belief that Japan's insularity was somehow troublesome and aberrant but that its uniqueness and homogeneity were beneficial and worthy of mediation and protection. Resulting efforts to promote Japanese-style tourism infrastructure overseas thus reflected the overall trend toward promoting internationalization in spatially and temporally delimited ways.

The apparent contradiction here—that Japanese should travel more like everyone else but that they had special needs—reflects the longstanding dilemma for Japanese leisure development policy: how to make Japan more "normal" while maintaining something essentially Japanese. And it would be this emphasis, on representing the special needs of the Japanese, that would provide the basis for what was perhaps the most important aspect of the Ten Million Program: an expanded role for Japanese aid in helping to develop tourism sites overseas, by explaining to developing countries what Japanese tourists ought to be doing and experiencing there. The purpose of the Ten Million Program to the Ministry of Transport is perhaps most recognizable here.

The Institutionalization of Japanese Tourism-Related ODA

The ITDIJ in Comparative Perspective

When the MOT announced the creation of the Ten Million Program in September 1987, it established, in the very same month, the ITDIJ with Tsutsumi as its titular president. With tourism-related assistance getting an added shot in the arm from the apparent benefits of Japanese outbound tourism in terms of economic redistribution, internationalization, and the enjoyment of "normal" leisure practices, the ITDIJ's mission was at first fairly easy. Designed to create master plans and feasibility studies for tourism development around the world and provide technical guidance on attracting foreign tourists (in particular, Japanese tourists), the ITDIJ would work as an agency to carry out tourism subsections of JICA's overall development surveys. It would also work in Tokyo, training visitors from the developing world in the art of tourism development. Correspondingly, the number of tourism-related aid projects rose dramatically.

Between 1973 and 1986, Indonesia, Tanzania, Thailand, and Egypt received technical assistance from Japan in the field of tourism. Only Bulgaria, Bangladesh, and Indonesia received loans, though Fiji, Mexico, and China also received some direct assistance in hotel construction. Between 1987 and 1995 (the most recent year for which I have complete data), however, additional development surveys and tourism feasibility studies were carried out in Indonesia, Thailand, Malaysia, Greece, the Philippines, Panama, Kenya, Jordan, Mexico, Sri Lanka, and Vietnam. Others were proposed for a number of other countries as well, including Zimbabwe, the Czech Republic, and Bulgaria (which did receive a preliminary report). Thailand, India, and Jamaica have also received generous loan packages for tourism development since 1987.[33]

Based on my understanding of the Japanese aid process, as well as interviews with members of private industry and the ITDIJ, I speculate that in the late 1980s and early 1990s, there were a number of ways in which tourism-related aid projects were created. On occasion, JICA—striving toward a more global approach to ODA, in part because of criticism of Japan for focusing too heavily on Asia—would promote tourism development schemes in aid-recipient countries because of a sense that tourism was a viable development option there. In these cases, if such an overall master plan was requested by the developing country (Japanese aid is on a request basis), it could ask the ITDIJ to organize and dispatch a research team to the country to do preliminary reports and then an overall development master plan for tourism for a given region. In other cases, firms connected to the ITDIJ could determine their own investment priorities, contact the ITDIJ and JICA, and then convince the recipient government to request a certain kind of development master plan that would be favorable to their project. This way, they might be able to link their own project to a wider development scheme that would generate some of the infrastructure (roads, sewage, etc.) that would facilitate travel.[34] This is, however, somewhat speculative, as no one was to make clear to me precisely why certain tourism development projects were implemented and other potential projects were avoided.

What is clear, however, is that with the end of the bubble era, the bloom is off the rose. To some degree, the ITDIJ and tourism aid pro-

33. *ITDIJ Overseas Researchers' Manual* (Tokyo: unpublished, revised 1995).
34. This is consistent with Arase's description of the aid process in *Buying Power.* No one ever told me this directly, but several members of private industry alluded to it in describing their own investment procedures.

grams function at high capacity if Japanese private firms demonstrate an interest in investing overseas. As noted above, the investment environment in the late 1980s was accepted in almost absurd ways to be favorable, leading to drastic overinvestment; with the collapse of Tokyo property values and the resulting disappearance of the value of collateral, an astonishing number of Japanese investors pulled out of their overseas hotel projects in order to cover interest payments back in Japan. With the sudden rush, property values in many of these overseas markets also plummeted, forcing most of the remaining Japanese investors to pull out at enormous losses. Japanese banking rules make it virtually impossible to determine how much money was lost, though the extraordinary level of debt in Japanese banks indicates the severity of the problem, much of which is clearly related to falling property values in Japan and overseas. Almost every professional I spoke with in Tokyo in the field told me that they had no plans to invest in tourism projects overseas any time in the middle term, with most even laughing at the suggestion.[35] Moreover, the MOT's ambitious Holiday Village Plan, introduced in May 1989, stressed that "private investment would be encouraged to improve superstructures [*sic*]," and that this would be one of the fundamental building blocks for Japan's promotion of global tourism development. The absence of private industry support, however, drove a stake through the heart of the Holiday Village Plan; though never formally abandoned (it still comes up from time to time in development studies, particularly for Asian countries), it has clearly fallen far short of expectations.[36]

The ITDIJ, however, has become an accepted institution. It still undertakes the mission of promoting tourism development around the world, emphasizing a Japanese style of travel, and it does so with a trained staff mostly on loan from travel-related firms and governmental organizations such as the JNTO. Even without any direct interest in making new tourism-related investments, firms still lend employees and contribute financially to the ITDIJ for a variety of reasons. One well-informed respondent informed me that firms probably

35. The results in my 1997 report on Japanese investment in tourism-related facilities in Asia for the ASEAN Centre were unambiguously negative. David Leheny, "Survey on Japanese Investor Interest in Tourism-Related Projects in the ASEAN Countries" (Tokyo: unpublished, 1997).

36. From the English translation of MOT's *Horidei Bireji Kōsō: Kokusai Kankō Kaihatsu Sōgō Shien Kōsō* (Holiday Village Plan: Comprehensive Plan to Support International Tourism Development) (Tokyo: MOT pamphlet, 1989).

worried that if they did not cooperate, the MOT would informally punish them by refusing their requests (for licenses, etc.) in the future.[37] In other cases, firms could contribute a smaller amount of money than a senior employee's expected salary, and farm senior workers with little chance of promotion out to the ITDIJ, thus reducing payrolls while maintaining something of the "lifetime employment system" that has been ballyhooed in Japan.[38] In either case, the ITDIJ has become a relatively stable feature of the tourism development environment, even as the prospects for Japanese investment have waxed and waned.

And the ITDIJ's position is, without question, an unusual one. Although other governments and international organizations engage in tourism-related ODA programs, these are in general quite limited, poorly institutionalized, and focus on such features as protection of the natural environment rather than on proactive efforts to generate more tourism to a given country. The comparative politics of tourism-related ODA has only recently begun to attract more attention, and we still lack any broad-based study. The only such research I have seen was in fact carried out by the ITDIJ in the form of two internal reports, roughly one hundred pages apiece: the 1994 *Kokusai Enjo Kikan no Kankō Kaihatsu Kyōryoku Jittai Chōsa* (Report on the Current Status of Tourism Development Cooperation Programs of International Aid Organization) and *Kokusai Kikan Oyobi Ei-Fu-Do Kankō Kaihatsu Kyōryoku Jittai Chōsa Hōkokusho* (Report on the Current Status of Tourism Cooperation Programs for International Organizations, the UK, France, and Germany), produced in 1995. The United States was almost certainly left out of the research because of its well-known public stance toward tourism: that it is better left to private industry and is inappropriate for aid efforts.[39]

37. When I asked, "Is that legal?" the informant gave me a disbelieving glance, as if only a child would ask such a naive question, and said, "Of course it's not legal."

38. In fact, I was told that employing skilled senior workers late in their careers was one of the benefits the ITDIJ provided to the country. Interview 19, 31 August 1995. The "lifetime employment system" is currently under strain from Japan's economic problems in the 1990s, though debates remain as to whether the system was ever quite as complete as observers have generally given it credit for being. For a positive view, see Sato Hiroshi, "Still Going! Continuity and Change in Japan's Long-Term Employment System," *Social Science Japan* 10 (August 1997): 16–18. John Price offers a more skeptical view in *Japan Works: Power and Paradox in Postwar Industrial Relations* (Ithaca: Cornell University Press, 1996).

39. This is the official line, which, it should be noted, differs in some respects from actual practice. The above-mentioned Japanese financial assistance to Jamaica, for ex-

The reports demonstrate that tourism-related aid programs from France and the United Kingdom tend to focus on former colonies and similarly related states. For example, the United Kingdom, which does not consider tourism to be a particularly high priority, distributes some marginally concessionary loans to former colonies through the Commonwealth Development Corporation (CDC). For France, tourism development represents no more than 0.5 percent of overall aid disbursements, again concentrated in its former African colonies, largely through the financial assistance organs Proparco and the Caisse Française de Développement. Germany, which is perhaps second only to Japan in the public support for outbound tours (largely through bilateral agreements for tourism promotion with victims of German aggression in World War II), takes a more proactive stance vis-à-vis tourism assistance, but this is to a degree motivated by a strong public concern with environmental protection. With tourism promotion programs around the world (including more than ten in Africa, several in Africa and Asia, and a large number in Latin America and the Caribbean region), Germany's overall aid apparatus does address tourism development but largely as an issue of harmonizing tourism development with environmental protection.[40]

The limited American stance toward tourism-related aid has been notable for its durability. The United States Department of Commerce evidently considered the possibility of using American development assistance funds to work on tourism development overseas briefly in the late 1950s, but the plan went nowhere. Even so, a consulting report, published by Commerce in 1961, illuminates some of the thinking behind U.S. policy. Noting that tourism, with overall revenues of $6 billion per year (a third of that spent by Americans) was becoming a major industry, the report emphasized the possible benefits to Asia of tourism development. In particular, the report recommended top-level government support for tourism development (which it never received) and said that American tourists "bring wealth in the form of good will and understanding."[41]

---

ample, has been disbursed and used in cooperation with USAID (which administers it but does not contribute its own finance). Interview 5, 16 May 1995.

40. ITIDIJ, "Kokusai Kikan Oyobi Ei-Fu-Do Kankō Kaihatsu Kyōryoku Jittai Chōsa Hōkokusho" (Report on the Current Status of Tourism Cooperation Programs for International Organizations, the U.K., France, and Germany) (Tokyo: unpublished, 1995).

41. This quotation is actually from the opening statement by Luther H. Hodges, the secretary of commerce. What is most notable here is the difference between this un-

For the most part, international organizations have also treated tourism development as something of a neglected member of the aid family. Although the International Bank for Reconstruction and Development (IBRD), the International Finance Corporation (IFC), and the International Development Association have each, from time to time, provided loans and grants for hotel, resort, and tourism development, the projects themselves tend to be small, with most assistance limited in amount unless linked to broader environmental concerns (e.g., an $850 million package to Mexico in 1978 that focused on ecological issues). The International Labour Organisation (ILO) has focused on tourism industry training, because tourism is taken to be a labor-intensive industry that, if developed, can help labor markets in developing countries. Under the general rubric of the United Nations, the World Tourism Organization[42] has engaged in literally dozens of tourism-related projects since the late 1970s, but these have been limited purely to technical cooperation, training, and the occasional master plan.[43]

These limits notwithstanding, the World Tourism Organization represents perhaps the most similar organization in the world to the ITDIJ. The ITDIJ, however, is emphatically part of the Japanese aid apparatus, not a multilateral organization, and its broad-based tourism promotion schemes, master plans, and training seminars reflect a distinctly national orientation toward how the world's tourist destinations ought to deal with Japanese visitors. And in the ITDIJ's programs, as well as those of related organizations in Tokyo, the emphasis has squarely been on tourism development that would allow Japanese visitors to enjoy themselves abroad as do Americans and Europeans, by embedding Japanese-friendly infrastructure within the overall travel patterns emulated in the policy texts noted above. As noted in chapter 2, tourism in general relies on a mixture of the friendly and foreign.

derstanding of how Americans can help the world versus the Japanese understanding of *kokusaika* as transforming Japan. The bulk of the report is written by Harry G. Clement of Checchi & Company, a consultancy, *The Future of Tourism in the Pacific and the Far East* (Washington, D.C.: U.S. Department of Commerce), 1961.

42. The acronym has been WTO, but the organization has historically been so limited in size and scope that no one bothered to worry about adopting the WTO acronym for the World Trade Organization in 1994. On the World Tourism Organization's programs, see *World Tourism Organization Technical Cooperation: Objectives, Missions, Projects* (Madrid: World Tourism Organization, 1995).

43. ITDIJ, "Kokusai Enjo Kikan no Kankō Kaihatsu Kyōryoku Jittai Chōsa" (Report on the Current Status of Tourism Development Cooperation Programs of International Aid Organizations) (Tokyo: unpublished, 1994).

Visitors travel to see the strange and the exotic, but most tourists aim to stay in familiar, comfortable accommodations, to eat and drink familiar cuisine, and to keep the foreign at arm's length. Tourist destinations thus respond by producing a simulacrum of what they are supposed to be, "staged authenticity" as kind of performed exoticism for the visitors.[44] The ITDIJ's contribution has been to educate developing countries in what kinds of exotic features Japanese tourists want to see, and what kinds of elements need to be familiar to make them comfortable.

Instruction in Exoticism and Familiarity

The ITDIJ's programs are not, it should be noted, designed solely to promote Japanese tourism. Many of the technical training materials and development plan recommendations represent "generic" tourism advice, in the sense that it is difficult to distinguish them from the recommendations of the World Tourism Organization, the ILO, or programs by individual European states. Even so, the ITDIJ's emphasis on training in how to deal with Japanese tourists is unmistakable and is in fact one of its attractive features for developing countries. Some of its efforts are entirely new in type, begun only since the organization's 1987 inception. The majority—the development master plans, tourism training seminars, the dispatch of experts to developing countries, outbound tourism promotion forums, and the like—are, however, preexisting policies that have now been largely entrusted to the ITDIJ. The ITDIJ, in turn, has done its best to institutionalize these programs, in the sense of remaking them as annual events with thoroughly systematized policies for Japan's tourism cooperation efforts.

Among these is the somewhat quiet "Kaigai Ryokō Sokushin Foramu" (Overseas Travel Promotion Forum), an annual forum for which the ITDIJ serves as organizer of the investment section. Inviting in members of private industry, the ITDIJ extols the virtues of overseas investment in tourism and highlights some of its recent findings with regard to the tourism potential of destinations. In 1994, for example,[45] the ITDIJ's materials summarized its recent findings with regard to ten countries, including some in Southeast Asia (the Philip-

---

44. "Staged authenticity" is one of the most important themes in the sociological and anthropological literature on tourism and is the creation of Dean MacCannell, in *The Tourist: A New Theory of the Leisure Class,* 2d ed. (New York: Schocken, 1991).
45. These reports are not publicly available, and this was the most recent year for which I was able to get data.

pines, Vietnam, Laos) and others farther from Japan (the Dominican Republic, Turkey). Most of the information contained in the report differed little from any other tourism study of the countries; it provided details on numbers of tourists, length of stay, accommodations, travel infrastructure, etc. In most cases, however, the ITDIJ ultimately focused on the marketability of the destination for Japanese tourists and emphasized solutions that would make it easier and more comfortable for Japanese to travel there. In Turkey, for example, the problem was the lack of Japanese-language guides; the Czech Republic would need assistance from Japan, particularly in the form of teams of experts who could explain requirements for hotels for Japanese, as well as their special dietary and culinary needs. This was not ubiquitous, however: the comments for the distant Dominican Republic did not deal specifically with the needs of Japanese tourists.[46]

The emphasis on how to make Japanese tourists comfortable also permeates JICA's annual "Comprehensive Tourism Seminar," held for roughly one month each year for roughly fifteen to twenty invited representatives of the national tourist organizations of developing countries. The program consists of daily lectures and workshops. Participants are asked to prepare somewhat lengthy profiles of the tourism projects in their own countries (in English) and to work in groups on small problem-solving exercises. The seminar's lectures— given by members of Japan's tourism industry, scholars working on tourism and conservation issues, and occasionally by civil servants from the MOT—veer between general comments on the nature of tourism promotion, marketing, planning, and conservation, and the special needs of the Japanese travel market. These are often fairly mundane considerations about language and food but sometimes more nuanced ones regarding hotel room preferences and organizational needs.[47]

The matter is not simply one of comfort and familiarity, however. Comprehensive Tourism Seminar participants, like those in the smaller tourism-training program as part of the Japan/Malaysia "Look East Program," have also relied on something of a performed authen-

46. ITDIJ, "Kaigai Ryokō Sokushin Fōramu Dai 10 Kai Kankō Toshi Iinkai" (10th Meeting of the Tourism Investment Committee for the Overseas Travel Promotion Forum) (Tokyo: unpublished, June 1994).

47. I served as translator/coordinator for the Comprehensive Tourism Seminar in 1995. There were no overall proceedings of the seminar, and these comments are based on my daily observation.

ticity for the benefit of members of Japan's private industry. The 1995 Look East visitors, for example, were asked on several occasions to wear "traditional" clothing to formal receptions with industry and government representatives, though the men generally wore Western suits and neckties during lectures and other, less ceremonial segments of the program. This yielded the somewhat perplexing moment in which Malaysians—in their traditional clothing—were asked to say "welcome" while managing a perfect Japanese bow for the final reception's guests.

The 1995 Comprehensive Tourism Training Seminar participants were far less sanguine than were the "Look East" members. It had been expected that they would bring traditional garb to Tokyo, though many participants had been unaware of this request. As a result, when they took a trip to western Japan and were asked to attend a regional international tourism promotion meeting, many were stunned to be asked to wear authentic local clothing.[48] A man and a woman from Latin American nations were also asked to perform a salsa dance together for the crowd. The traditional garb continued to be a sticking point for the seminar's remaining days, and all were asked once again to wear authentic local clothing for the final reception at JICA's training headquarters.[49]

The seminar itself provided an opportunity for the ITDIJ to suggest to participants that their governments formally request tourism development master plans from Japan. Because, as noted above, Japanese aid is granted on a request basis, this suggestion provides one of the tools the ITDIJ has to keep itself busy, by generating interest from abroad in the probable utility of Japanese tourism assistance.

The master plans ultimately created by the ITDIJ almost always focus, at least in part, on the special needs of Japanese travelers, or sometimes Asian travelers (for whom the Japanese apparently provide a useful proxy). In some cases, the main issues involved have been the comfort and ease of travel for visiting Japanese. A 1995 report for

48. Over lunch that day in JICA's cafeteria, a Caribbean delegate wryly noted, "I forgot my grass skirt."

49. I should add here that the highly skilled Japanese interpreter (my translating work was mostly limited to written texts) wore her kimono to this particular reception. The other representatives of JICA and the ITDIJ, men and women alike, wore Western suits. As an American, I was told that I would be expected to wear a Western suit as well.

Tunisia, for example, emphasized that the country's cuisine was unsuitable for Japanese (since it specialized in local and French food), that there should be more Japanese-language guides, more promotional efforts in Japan, that the country needed more 5-star hotels (since Japanese tourists had, during the bubble's peak, been famously lavish with accommodations budgets,) and that "characteristic souvenirs as well as goods made from leather or pelts should be sold." Interestingly, the solution to linguistic problems in hotels was considered to be better English-language training for the staff, since Japanese visitors would most likely be unable to communicate in French (and since Japanese-language instruction was practically out of the question for logistical reasons).[50]

Comfort has not been the only arena in which the ITDIJ's plans become important for describing what Japanese tourists want to experience, however. As with the traditional clothes requested of the JICA seminar participants, much of the tourism trade relies on the construction of an "authentic" and "exotic" (yet familiarly so) image for foreign visitors. The ITDIJ has also provided advice on how to make an image suitably exotic for the Japanese or Asian travelers (who are discussed when there are some apparent similarities between Taiwanese or Korean tourists and Japanese tourists). In a 1995 report for Sabah State in Malaysia, the ITDIJ's researchers argued that demand for the region was shifting away from its previous base of European visitors and toward Asian travelers. To engage their special needs, the state would have to improve the quality and diversity of traditional handicrafts and souvenirs and also to emphasize the MICE (Meeting, Incentive, Conference, and Event) packages that are a cornerstone of Asian travel.[51] Another report for Bulgaria stressed that the country should increase the variety of its folk dance performances, hinting that new celebrations and festivals ought to be created to give them a more traditional feel.[52] These recommendations only became problematic when they might have affected the recipient government's ability to attract more familiar markets of Americans or Europeans.

---

50. ITDIJ, "International Tourism Development Study for Tunisia: Summary Report" (Tokyo: unpublished, 1995).

51. ITDIJ, "International Tourism Development Study for Malaysia: Summary Report" (Tokyo: unpublished, 1995).

52. ITDIJ, "International Tourism Development Study for Bulgaria: Summary Report" (Tokyo: unpublished, 1995).

The ITDIJ is not alone in its efforts to make the world comfortable and exotic for Japanese tourists, even though it has been the key player since its 1987 inception. The ASEAN Centre conducts annual seminars each year in each of the ASEAN countries on how to attract Japanese tourists. It had traditionally been led by a tourism expert flown in from Japan for a few days to the capital of each country, but budget constraints in recent years had evidently led the ASEAN Centre to ask members of the Japanese business community living within the relevant city to explain Japanese tourist needs based apparently on materials given to them and their own understanding of the market. Additionally, the ASEAN Centre has, for years, run a special "Japanese-for-tourism" training course in each country, to provide some Japanese-language training to members of the local tourist industry in the different ASEAN countries.[53] And JICA has dispatched tourism experts, many of whom are late-career professionals much like those in the ITDIJ, to a number of countries as a part of their overall mission. A JICA representative was on staff at the Tourism Authority of Thailand office in Bangkok for several years.[54]

Additionally, a potential competitor with the ITDIJ has been created in Osaka. In 1995, the Japanese government evidently out-flanked Indonesia (which had lobbied for the honor) in its effort to host the new Asian headquarters of the World Tourism Organization. Derided in some circles as part of an urban development effort for the Osaka shore across from the New Kansai International Airport (built offshore on an artificial island), the Asian headquarters opened in 1995 but was initially hamstrung by an apparent lack of mission, since the staff were Japanese tourism experts and former bureaucrats who were trying to understand what the World Tourism Organization expected of them.[55] Within two years, however, the MOT had created a sister organization—which shares the office space—called the Ajia Taiheiyō Kankō Kōryū Sentā (The Asia-Pacific Tourism Exchange Center). Funded in part with public funds and in part from private contributions (largely from regionally based firms in the Kansai area), this organization works with the World Tourism Organization to carry out quasi-Japanese, quasi-multilateral tourism assistance mis-

53. Interview 55, 11 November 1997.
54. Interview 54, 11 November 1997.
55. Interview 12, 25 July 1997.

sions to countries in the Asian region. Its mission is similar to that of the ITDIJ.[56]

These programs are perhaps not what was originally envisioned by the Ten Million Program's creators, or by those of the Holiday Village Plan or even the ITDIJ in 1987, but in an era of diminished investment by Japanese firms in tourism and real estate overseas, they represent a continuous, institutionalized pattern of attempting to facilitate Japanese outbound tourism. With outbound tourism considered to be beneficial to the nation—both in terms of the naked strategic motive of visibly redistributing gains from trade and from the more normative goals of "leisure development" and *kokusaika* (internationalization)—Japan's efforts to explain to the world how it should be both exotic and familiar, how it can appeal to Japanese tourists' curiosity while keeping them comfortable, have become a relatively stable, if small, part of Japan's overall ODA policies. The MOT has clearly been delighted to report that Japan's numbers of outbound tourists have risen to "normal" levels befitting an advanced industrial country and has been willing to continue to encourage more as well. Suggesting that in order to make Japan more like the rest of the world, it will be necessary to make the world more suitable for the Japanese, its programs have encouraged developing countries to consider how the "different" Japanese might be coaxed into becoming increasingly "normal" visitors.

Evaluating Japan's Tourism-Related Aid

The list of foregoing projects and programs includes, to be sure, its distasteful elements. The idea that Malaysia needed more attractive traditional handicrafts, or that the participants in an international seminar had somehow violated the spirit of the event by not bringing colorful local garb, grates on some of the recipients of Japanese aid. But by the same token, Japan's aid efforts—far more proactive than are any other country's in the field of tourism—have not been without their supporters, particularly within the tourism industry in the Asian region.

Ideas among tourism professionals, scholars, and bureaucrats in other countries with regard to the motives of Japan's tourism-related

56. Interview 47, 28 March 1997.

aid remain mixed. A senior official at the Australian Tourist Commission informed me that he feels that the Japanese government has no real role in Japan's outbound tourism;[57] indeed, the tourism "summits" between the two countries have been attended only by members of private industry in Japan but by Australian civil servants and tourism professionals alike.[58] Another respected professional in Australia's tourism industry, particularly with regard to inbound tours for Japanese, argued that the Ten Million Program was effective and that the government needed to do something to encourage Japanese to travel abroad more.[59]

A member of the Tourist Authority of Thailand (TAT) related a more Machiavellian view: "We wanted Japan to open its trade markets to us, but it was only willing to open up tourism. That's why we have the Ten Million Program." Most TAT officials, however, in general praised Japan's tourism-related aid efforts. Even where they felt things could be improved, the durability of these institutionalized programs made them far superior to anything evidently offered by other countries.[60] And if nothing else, the role of the Japanese government in shaping outbound tourism has also led it to be enormously cooperative with other countries regarding information on the market. Even one of the skeptical Australian officials told me that this made Japan an easier country to deal with than, for example, the United States, which was "useless" in its tourism-related documentation.[61] The overall receptiveness, particularly in the Pacific region, to Japan's tourism aid programs, including the Ten Million Program, probably reflects a gratitude that Japan is doing *something*—for whatever reasons and with whatever degree of success—at a time that tourism remains a low development priority for other countries and multilateral organizations.[62]

57. Interview 57, 13 November 1997.

58. Austrian Tourist Commission, *The 2nd Australia-Japan Tourism Summit* (Sydney: unpublished, 1997).

59. Interview 61, 14 November 1997.

60. Interview 54, 11 November 1997.

61. Interview 59, 13 November 1997.

62. For example, see Habibullah Khan, "Foreign Investment in the Tourism Sector in Selected Asian Developing Countries," paper for the "Investment and Economic Cooperation in the Tourism Sector in Developing Asian Countries," seminar run by the United Nation's Economic and Social Commission for Asia and the Pacific (ESCAP) (Bangkok: ESCAP, 1991).

Development schemes for tourism invariably stress the importance of both "image" (exoticism) and "comfort" (familiarity), and they do this whether they are created by international organizations or by individual aid donor states. The fact that "comfort" is generally treated ubiquitously suggests the extent to which there has been an established model for the international tourists: usually white, English speaking (if not necessarily as a native), and European or American. Japan's tourism-related aid seems startling in part because of its programmatic underscoring of the needs of Japanese tourists (or, sometimes, Asian tourists, if the Japanese organizations can identity some similarities in traveling style). To point at this as being uniquely troubling in the midst of the cultural constructions and staged simulacra that dominate the field of tourism as a whole would be to suggest that there is something "normal" about European or American understandings of tourism, and that the Japanese emphasis is somewhat aberrant. Indeed, this kind of belief produces a sense that Asian tourism generates faulty or demeaning touristic attitudes on the parts of visitors, who ought to be more open to their environment.[63]

The Japanese policies are distinctive, however, in their programmatic and systematic effort to reshape tourist images and facilities to suit what is perceived to be a distinctly national need. Governments make tourism development and marketing recommendations virtually all the time with regard to their own territory, and American and European travel firms and airlines have been doing the same for decades with regard to tourist destinations abroad. Moreover, the effort to construct and unify a "national" culture of colonies motivated a number of more specific programs during the era of colonialism. What distinguishes the Japanese case, however, is the extent to which one government has developed an institutionalized role—one with clear rules and parameters, one that is "taken for granted" by partici-

---

63. A 1998 front-page story in the *New York Times* included the following passage:

> Many Chinese visitors are arrogant about the superiority of their own cuisine and culture, especially compared with that of their Asian neighbors.
> "I hate Thai food," said Chen Jing, 32, a factory manager. "I think China has many more places worth visiting than Thailand."

Seth Faison, "In Thailand, the Chinese are Coming, as Tourists," *New York Times*, 5 April 1998, 1. Faison did not mention the arrogance of American or European tourists who complain about the English-speaking skills of their hosts, deplore the lack of safe drinking water, or take part in Bangkok's nocturnal markets.

pants and outsiders alike—in telling other countries how they ought to appear in order to appeal to Japanese visitors. And whether this is effective or ineffective, functional or dysfunctional, good or bad, it is not something that we have witnessed elsewhere.

Conclusions

This leads us to the tricky question of whether the Japanese truly do have different needs than do visitors from other countries. Obviously, for decades—at least since the era of the *Yoka Sōran*—elements of the Japanese government have argued that there are differences, whether because of the Japanese desire to be in group tours, the desire for Japanese food, or more prosaic concerns such as the inability to communicate in languages other than Japanese. The popularity of group tours has dropped appreciably, however, and as Japanese tourists travel abroad with greater frequency, many of them are choosing "skeleton packages" that essentially place them within a comfortable format (a good hotel, possibly one with Japanese-speaking staff) but a loose daily itinerary that allows them to travel individually. Increasingly, Japanese travelers are going abroad individually or in small groups, much like Americans or Europeans; most sources cite this as a result of the increase in "repeat travelers." Japan, in this logic, has become a "mature market."[64]

Some experts deny that there is anything special about Japanese tourists, or rather, that there is anything unusually special about Japanese tourists. All tourist markets are different, one Australian analyst told me, and Japan's tourists, while peculiar in some respects, are really no more so than visitors from any other country.[65] One frequently cited difference, however, appears to be in the nature of the stay. Unlike Americans and Europeans, who reportedly would pick a beach location or somewhere they can spend a long trip (between ten days and three weeks) relaxing, Japanese tourists tend to be "multi-

64. I am somewhat resistant to this notion, since it implies that there is something ubiquitous about a desirable way to travel. If people travel in large groups, the logic goes, they are doing so because of insecurity and they would naturally prefer to be in smaller groups. As a nation becomes more accustomed to travel, the logic goes, it "matures," and people travel on individualized, Special Interest Tours (SIT) more frequently.

65. Interview 60, 13 November 1995.

destination travelers." Simply put, this refers to their tendency to travel to one location, experience as many features as possible within two or three days, before flying to another city or country nearby: the four-cities-in-one-week tour (a travel style that once made Americans infamous in Europe).[66]

This particular characterization of the Japanese market seems to be accepted both by Japanese policymakers and by tourist analysts abroad, and it underscores some of the tensions in Japan's tourism development projects. On the one hand, MITI's protourism report *Kaigai Taizaigata Yoka* clearly reflected an effort to break this tendency by encouraging Japanese travelers to go to a balmy beach location, stay on the beach, and relax, as do people in the West. To be sure, their needs would have to be met by Japanese firms with a specific understanding of the Japanese market, but the style of the tour would have to be more generic. The ITDIJ's efforts, in contrast, appear to deal with this inclination by encouraging tourist developments overseas to create as many kinds of tourist attractions within a small geographic area as possible, in order to ensure that there are so many kinds of things to do that Japanese can choose to stay in one resort area for a while, or at least for a few days to experience everything available before moving on.[67]

The extent of difference between Japanese travelers and overseas travelers is perhaps impossible to determine (and the consumption of experience is ultimately so individualized a phenomenon that any such comparisons would be questionable in merit). But there appears to be agreement between Japanese policymakers that some difference exists; this has led to genuine policy outcomes. The MOT thus built the Ten Million Program in part from a general expectation—one that was basically untested because no one really felt that they needed to check—that Japanese really are different from "Westerners," and that their essential cultural differences explained their comparable reluctance to travel abroad. Moreover, it would have to be the government's

66. Interview 59, 13 November 1997. In one study, Japanese tourists spent an average of 3.5 nights in Bali, compared to twelve for European visitors, though this difference was almost certainly inflated by the differences in distance involved. Imai Yoshinobu, "Bari-to" (Bali), in *Tōnan Ajia-Ōsutoraria no Rizōto no Genjō to Kadai* (Topics in Resort Development in Southeast Asia and Australia), ed. Nihon Shisutemu Kaihatsu Kenkyūjo (Tokyo: Nihon Shisutemu Kaihatsu Kenkyūjo, 1989), 67.

67. Interview 19, 31 August 1995.

responsibility to correct the problem. Although the MOT's goal was almost certainly to establish greater links to ODA budget resources that would help the ministry in other ways, its best opportunity for doing so appears to have been to capitalize on the institutionalized pattern of Japanese state intervention in leisure. It would help the Japanese be more "normal" by recognizing the constraints placed on them by their uniqueness, and it would help to alter tourist sites overseas accordingly.

Are there other explanations for the policy other than the primary one offered? An obvious one would be support for travel-related businesses. One economist in Tokyo suggested to me that the purpose of the Ten Million Program was to support Japan's air carriers. Indeed, with the 1984 privatization of Japan Air Lines (JAL) and the opening of scheduled international service for All Nippon Airways (ANA) in 1988, along with the scheduled opening of New Kansai International Airport in 1994,[68] Japan had invested considerably in international travel. As civil aviation expert Kawaguchi Mitsuru notes, however, the Ten Million Program came too late to give much of a boost to JAL, and even if it were designed to help ANA, it should have been established in 1984 or 1985.[69] This does not mean, of course, that the MOT never considered the connection, but no one from private industry or the ministry ever suggested that this was a principal motive, in spite of the eagerness of some to convey fairly cynical interpretations of policy decisions.

In fact, those who stood to gain handsomely from overseas travel were not necessarily the airlines (who would be forced to compete with lower-priced airlines from other countries) but rather the large travel firms and hotel or construction companies involved in overseas resort development. The role of travel agencies is a bit easier to dismiss. Japan's major travel agencies are unusually large by American standards, with JTB and Kinki Nippon Tourist, among a few others, controlling an extremely large share of the outbound package market.

---

68. Satō Bunsei provides an overview of these initiatives in *Nihon no Kōkū Senryaku: 21 Seiki no Eapōto* (A Civil Aviation Strategy for Japan: 21st-Century Airports) (Tokyo: Simul, 1985). Satō, a former high-ranking MOT official, defends privatization and explains why Japan needs new international airports in Kansai and Chubu, to take some of the increasing load off the overburdened Narita International Airport.

69. Kawaguchi Mitsuru, *21 Seiki no Kōkū Seisakuron* (Civil Aviation Policy in the 21st Century) (Tokyo: Seizando, 1993), 156–57.

These firms, working together under an industrial peak organization known as the Japan Association of Travel Agents (JATA), have proved themselves successful in lobbying for policy change in their interests, as the more recent change in the Tourism Agency Law (1995) suggests; they raised capital requirements for firms packaging outbound tours, in order to discourage upstart competition.[70] Interviews with JATA officials, however, suggested that they treated the Ten Million Program with a kind of disdain: recognizing that outbound travel was good for the country, MOT was attempting to steal JATA's thunder by creating the program to take credit for something that JATA itself was accomplishing. In the view of the officials I spoke with, the Ten Million Program was an unnecessary public relations scheme that merely deflected attention from JATA's obvious successes in creating better, cheaper tours, with more information and guidance.[71]

The role of private industry cannot be discounted entirely, however, especially because of the role of Tsutsumi in pressing for the establishment of the ITDIJ. By teaming up with the MOT to provide a basis for private support for the creation of this new organization, Tsutsumi appears to have played his hand exceptionally well, something for which he has been justly famed. Tsutsumi wanted joint public-private work for tourism development, probably to make outbound tourism development more secure and cheap, facilitated by the use of ODA funds. By proposing the creation of this organization, he managed to take advantage of the MOT's clear hopes for accessing the ODA budget and for creating more potential *amakudari* positions for its members. The effort received a normative boost from the pressure to reduce the trade surplus, in that it fit within a general orientation toward reducing the trade surplus without undermining the manufacturing base of the economy. The MOT was not in and of itself responsible for the trade balance but certainly proved itself adept at claiming this to be the primary goal of the program.

And indeed, it was almost certainly these two motivations—access

---

70. On the changes in regulations and the development of tourism, see Lonny E. Carlile, "Economic Development and the Evolution of Japanese Overseas Tourism, 1964–1994," *Tourism Recreation Research* 2 (1996): 11–18. In Japanese, see Sasaki Masato, *Ryokō no Hōritsugaku* (Travel Laws) (Tokyo: Nihon Hyōronsha, 1996). Sasaki, a former member of the legal affairs team at JTB, covers the 1995 revisions on 145 passim.

71. Interview 17, 17 August 1995. One JATA member blurted out (in English) that the Ten Million Program was "bullshit."

to the aid budget and *amakudari* positions—that led the MOT to engage in a full-out offensive to promote outbound tourism in 1987. Hoping for the benefits provided by the creation of new organizations, it emphasized the value to the country of outbound tourism and stated baldly that this was to be a new initiative for its tourism policy division. In so doing, it managed to overcome some of the lingering mistrust for tourism-related aid generated by the catastrophic Cheju Island debacle in the early 1970s. The connection between the Ten Million Program and the imperatives of Japan's ODA policies has not been discussed on much by observers of the policies,[72] but the timing of the Ten Million Program's creation and the ITDIJ's establishment, both in September 1987, indicates that the two were linked. MOT and ITDIJ officials in general spoke of the two as being part of the same broad initiative.

Had MOT officials not been eager for more bureaucratic resources (particularly in the aftermath of administrative reform movements that had led to the privatization of JAL and of Japan National Railways) from ODA, presumably there would have been no Ten Million Program. And had Tsutsumi not been clever enough to approach the ministry with his idea, no one would have considered establishing the ITDIJ. The clarity of the strategic motives is, however, somewhat misleading. By focusing only on these goals, we risk missing the institutionalized expectations that enabled MOT policymakers to believe that they could gain access over contested ODA funds by claiming that they would help the Japanese to have leisure lives like their counterparts in other advanced nations. By their logic, the tourists' world had not been created with Japanese in mind. In order to ensure that Japanese tourists feel comfortable enough to do their duty to themselves (the Japanese, after all, should enjoy "normal" leisure) and the country (Japan, after all, needed to catch up with Australia, at least), other countries would need to come to grips with the special needs of the Japanese, to embrace them as they would any honored guest from Europe or North America. Without the intervention of the Japanese

---

72. The only other broad examination I have seen of this topic is Matsui Yayori's highly critical work *Ajia no Kankō Kaihatsu to Nihon* (Japan and Tourism Development in Asia) (Tokyo: Shinkansha, 1993). Matsui is a feminist journalist whose work has focused largely on sex tourism in the past, and her research examines many of the negative outcomes of tourism. She touches on both the Ten Million Program and ODA policies in tourism, but does not connect them; her concern is more with the problems that Japanese tourists cause the residents of tourist destinations overseas.

government, what Japanese tourists would find overseas might be unpredictably foreign, far from comfortable, and strange enough to be unappealing as a holiday. For owners of tourist facilities around Asia, and for those representatives of developing countries who learn to say "Irasshaimase" while wearing traditional clothes, the effort still matters.

The beginning of Golden Week, when many of Japan's national holidays are strung together to create each year's most popular time for vacation travel. A train platform at Tokyo Station, April 2002. Photograph by Hayawaka Miyako.

Failures of the Imagination

In a published collection of travel-related conversations with the poet Osada Hiroshi, the philosopher and cultural historian Tsurumi Shunsuke recounts two stories that suggest that Japan has lost a battle with foreign culture, especially as embodied by Disney. In the first, the renowned silent film narrator, arts scholar, and essayist Tokugawa Musei has traveled to visit the Japanese Imperial Army in Singapore in 1943 and surprisingly finds that they have some access to American films. A screening of Disney's *Fantasia* astonishes Tokugawa with its simple but universal charm; it is at that moment, he would later argue, that he realizes that Japan is going to lose the war. In the second story, one of Tsurumi's own students has just returned from a trip to Tokyo Disneyland and is captivated by the "Main Street Electric Parade," in which the various Disney characters hop on brightly lit vehicles and move slowly through the Main Street part of the park to the hallucinatory accompaniment of calliope versions of famous Disney songs. She tells Tsurumi, "Now I understand why we lost the war to America." In spite of his fascination with and even appreciation for the appeal of Disney, Tsurumi argues that the Disney formula for a happy, better life is disturbingly reminiscent of Aldous Huxley's *Brave New World*.[1]

1. Cited by Tsurumi Shunsuke, in Tsurumi Shunsuke and Osada Hiroshi, *Tabi no Hanashi* (Travelers' Tales) (Tokyo: Bunmeiron, 1993), 379–80.

Two features of the comment merit attention. The first is the sense that Disney's charm is non-Japanese: it comes from abroad. Presumably, Japan on its own is incapable of generating anything this universally appealing. More important, however, is the idea that the charm preceded the American victory, and the universal appeal of this distinctively American way of viewing the world was in part responsible for the war's outcome. This cultural transmission occurs not because America wins and forces its brightly colored dystopia of anthropomorphic rodents on the world but rather because there is something about it that fundamentally plays well. This culture travels, because this is what people want, or will ultimately want.

The State, Norms, and Globalization

Tsurumi's comments are sophisticated; he himself graduated from Harvard and is no simple America-basher. *Fantasia* is a charming movie, and the Main Street Electric Parade is almost charming enough to overcome its creepiness. Even so, they signal the loss of something in Japan's struggle to maintain its identity in a world it did not create. Tsurumi's recounting of Tokugawa's comment on *Fantasia* reminds us that concerns about the homogenizing effect specifically of American culture around the world actually preceded the recent spate of literature on globalization. These books, even at their most hopeful, tend to suggest that American symbols (such as the golden arches of McDonald's, perhaps the closest thing the world has to a universal iconography of the bogeyman) are everywhere, but perhaps they can be appropriated by local cultures. McDonald's means something different in Singapore than in Cincinnati.[2] Between domination and resistance, there is an ambiguous netherworld of cultural appropriation, in which flotsam and jetsam are mixed and matched. I have no doubt that this middle ground captures the truth more adequately than do simplistic views of American cultural hegemony or, on the other hand, of the brave, unyielding responses of globalization's opponents, from Seattle to Lagos to Jakarta.

The middle ground, however, is usually the murkiest terrain. It would be far easier if we could simply predict the inexorable homogenization of cultures through the processes of economic globalization,

2. James L. Watson, ed., *Golden Arches East: McDonald's in East Asia* (Stanford: Stanford University Press, 1998).

or, on the other hand, that defiance will be a unifying rallying cry among those fighting to defend "authentic" cultures. A mixture demands that we look at the mechanisms through which cultural symbols are transmitted and connect them more thoughtfully to power. The state has become the preeminent expression of modern political power, but it has been nearly absent in discussions of globalization, except as the thing most likely to be displaced as the world becomes increasingly integrated. I have tried to argue that the state is both more important and differently implicated in processes of cultural change than globalization theorists of all stripes would have it.

To make this point, I have relied on theories of international norms, though I have used them in ways that diverge from their original purpose. Most research on norms has found that states might adhere to norms that constrain bad behavior (such as the manufacture of land mines or the use of chemical weapons)[3] and thus come to put human interests in front of state interests.[4] But Japanese leisure policy is different. No international organizations, no formal pressure, and no transnational movement forced the Japanese government to rethink the way its citizens enjoy their leisure. Instead, Japan's leaders, in working to determine the kind of society they want to lead and how best to achieve it, have looked to examples from abroad to determine what is right, proper, and "normal" for an advanced, modern state. At least for Japan—and I suspect for other states as well—history is understood to be a national phenomenon, in which similar processes of "advancement" occur within national boundaries. In this view, the future of one country can be meaningfully predicted by looking at the current conditions of a more developed state.[5] And in Japan's case, this has meant that the government has interpreted citizens' recreational practices to be one more way in which the government can assess whether it is lagging or is caught up.

Why leisure? For reasons detailed in chapters 3 and 4, the Japanese government already had accepted that leisure could be another area

3. This literature is discussed in greater detail in chapter 1, but two useful and wildly divergent examples are Saskia Sassen, *Globalization and its Discontents: Essays on the New Mobility of People and Money* (New York: The New Press, 1998); and Thomas Friedman, *The Lexus and the Olive Tree* (New York: Farrar, Straus & Giroux, 1999).

4. This is how Emanuel Adler, Beverly Crawford, and Jack Donnelly define "progress." See their chapter "Defining and Conceptualizing Progress in International Relations," in *Progress in Postwar International Relations*, ed. Adler and Crawford (New York: Columbia University Press, 1991), 1–42, at 2.

for state intervention in citizens' lives, in order to promote the national interest, broadly understood. Leisure thus stood as something that was partly public, not entirely private, and therefore something that the government could and should be examining. Given that political decisions about leisure invariably involve concerns over what is good or bad in people's leisure choices, it is not surprising that the Japanese government would make such evaluations on its own. And to a government obsessed with economic development, placing economic growth as its postwar raison d'être, there were few options for judging the right way for people to enjoy their leisure time other than to look at what the more advanced countries—the more developed people—were up to.

The "middle ground" theorists on globalization are therefore right: choices are more complex than a resist-or-submit dichotomy. If my judgment of Japan's leisure policies is correct, however, the state lies at the center of these decisions, with ramifications for studies of globalization and of politics. This is not simply because the state is still important, a point I would defend in the face of claims that the state's role is in decline.[6] Instead, Japan's experience with leisure policy displays the way that the institutional nature of the state—the way people take it and what it represents for granted—affects leaders' ability to conceive of proper behavior and the appropriate trajectory of change: forward, into a future that can be inferred from the experience of the "advanced" nations. Nations and states are thus subject to norms interpreted from those places that are "ahead." Globalization might best be understood as something other than the spread of McDonald's, Hollywood films, or the like. Instead, it might appear to be nothing so much as a failure of the public imagination, of the ability to conceive of a future different from that discovered in the more "developed" nations.[7]

5. On this point, see Benedict Anderson, *Imagined Communities: Reflections on the Origin and Spread of Nationalism* (New York: Verso, 1991), especially chapter 5. He argues that nations come to imagine their histories in ways that refer to other "established" national narratives. So it becomes important for Thailand and Jamaica to have "their" French Revolutions, because the French-style revolution (which was in reality a group of only tangentially related riots, rebellions, beheadings, and usurpations of authority, which we have labeled in retrospective a singular revolutionary event) has become a ubiquitous element in a broad national narrative. He expands on this point in his more recent book, *The Spectre of Comparisons: Nationalism, Southeast Asia, and the World* (London: Verso, 1998).

6. See Susan Strange, *Retreat of the State: The Diffusion of Power in the World Economy* (Cambridge: Cambridge University Press, 1996).

7. This is my reading of the claim that "there has often been a tendency to adopt

The Politics of the Main Street Electric Parade

These failures of the imagination will likely outlast Japanese leisure policy, because they are more deeply institutionalized. Japan's leisure initiatives have responded to clear political and economic incentives, such as the demand to reduce the nation's highly criticized trade surpluses or the pressure for pork barrel projects such as those enabled by the Resort Law. With Japan facing its most prolonged recession of the postwar period, policymakers have been pushed to cut corners wherever possible and to ensure that any economic initiatives they put forth are clearly targeted to restore growth. In 2001, the Japanese government adopted the most far-reaching administrative reforms of the postwar era, with many ministries and agencies combined in new ways. The Ministry of International Trade and Industry (MITI) was joined to the Economic Planning Agency (EPA) in the new Ministry for the Economy, Trade, and Industry (METI). The Ministry of Transport (MOT) was linked to two other pork barrel behemoths, the Ministry of Construction (MOC) and the National Land Agency, becoming the new Ministry for Land, Infrastructure, and Transport (MLIT). To reduce budget burdens, they were also encouraged to consolidate or abolish some of the many foundations and special organizations they sponsored. The Japan National Tourist Organization escaped complete eradication because it presumably contributed to the economy by attracting foreign tourists. The Leisure Development Center (YKC) was "abolished," though a new foundation—the "Institute for Free Time Design" (Jiyū Jikan Dezain Kyōkai)—adopted the same headquarters, the same functions (such as publishing the annual "Leisure White Paper"), and even the same website.[8]

Government-run leisure organizations can no longer justify their activities and budgets by explaining that Japanese people work too hard or that the government's main interest should be in lifestyle. Instead, with the recession looming as the dominant problem in Japanese politics since the early 1990s, these institutions emphasize that leisure improvement is critical to Japan's economic revitalization.[9] If

---

a teleological view . . . describing Western history as some kind of necessary unfolding of these features." See John W. Meyer, John Boli, and George M. Thomas, "Ontology and Rationalization in the Western Cultural Account," in *Institutional Structure: Constituting State, Society, and the Individual,* ed. George M. Thomas, John W. Meyer, Francisco O. Ramirez, and John Boli (Newbury Park, Calif.: Sage, 1987), 12–37, at 31.

8. For a summary, see the Jiyū Jikan Dezain Kyōkai's website at http://www.yoka.or.jp. Accessed 20 April 2002.

9. A colorful recent pamphlet on "Yutori Yoka" (Leisure with More Time and

these organizations and institutions are to survive, they will likely have to make a convincing case that their initiatives will be indispensable to Japan's reemergence as an economic powerhouse. There would be nothing new, of course, about the claim that leisure industries help to anchor a "normal" advanced industrial nation, but it remains to be seen whether these organizations will be successful in shifting their goals to fit a political climate radically different from that of the 1970s and 1980s. Further budget cuts might result in the eradication of national leisure policy functions in the Japanese government. Of what consequence will my argument be then?

I wish to claim neither too much nor too little for the importance of the approach outlined in this book. After all, I have focused on Japanese leisure policy to the exclusion of other policy arenas, and I would not wish to export my argument to account for health care initiatives (to name one example) without making significant revisions. But my research on the use of Western models has already drawn on the experience of other issue areas, as has my interest in the "theories of Japaneseness" (*nihonjinron*) that informed Japanese concerns over virtually everything from national cuisine to immigration policy. In spite of the changes in Japan's political economy since the 1980s, I have seen little that suggests either the diminution of Western models or the weakening of *nihonjinron*, even as they subtly respond to new waves of immigration and international travel. The precise content of theories of Japaneseness and of Western models will change, as they have many times already, but they will still be relevant to Japanese public debates over development, progress, and legitimacy.

My sense, then, is that the motifs I have identified as crucial to understanding Japanese leisure policy will continue to be important in discussions over what kind of nation Japan is supposed to be. Because political actors in Japan will still focus on how Japan should best "develop," and how it can best achieve "progress," they will continue to learn lessons from those countries that somehow arrived at progress first. But because the ability to distinguish between what is Japanese and what is not will still shape conceptions of political and social legitimacy, these lessons will require negotiation over how Japan can develop yet

---

Space) from the MLIT emphasizes that if people take longer vacations and spend more during their trips, they can have a dramatic effect in stimulating the economy. It finishes, almost as an afterthought, with the slogan "Yutori yoka no genjitsu de 'Seikatsu kōzō kaikaku' wo!" (With the realization of leisure with more time and space, we'll revolutionize the structure of lifestyles!).

still remain Japanese. And before Japanese leisure policy initiatives shuffle off this mortal coil, they will still rely heavily on an understanding of what "normal" people in the West do for their leisure time.

The precise causal chains illuminated in this book combine particular elements of Japanese political history, including *nihonjinron* and the institutional legacies of prewar railroad development; they cannot easily be transplanted to explain developments outside of Japan. But Japan is not alone in its long struggle toward "development," and Western examples (especially that of the United States) now loom large in every part of the globe. I would submit that policy decisions made elsewhere may reflect the same kind of limits and constraints evident in Japan's leisure policies. By engaging in the kind of interpretive research methods used here, scholars might be able to find instances or patterns of policymaking in policy alternatives that were never considered because they had not appeared in more "advanced nations" first.

I do not wish to undermine the claim that these decisions are "rational," a theoretical cornerstone of much research in political science, especially with the turn toward rational choice approaches in the discipline. Simple assumptions about interests and predicted utility have enabled scholars to use rational choice theories to elucidate important aspects of even "cultural" problems such as ethnic conflict.[10] Indeed, none of Japan's leisure policies can be understood without considering the incentives facing policymakers, as well as their assessment of how best to achieve easily understood goals. These goals—e.g., the expansion of bureaucratic territory and budget, or the use of leisure industries to stimulate economic growth—seem clear because we understand the institutional environments that create them. Bureaucracies and markets are so common that we can assume from the outset what some of the basic interests of participants will be: bureaucrats want more control, governments want reasonable economic growth.

My suggestion is not that we do away with links between interests, strategic interactions, and outcomes but rather that we recognize that other "taken for granted" factors can affect how these links will be constructed and understood by the actors involved. By embedding rationality in this way, and by paying attention to the options that simply never occur to policymakers, I suspect that we can make the

10. For one excellent example, see David Laitin, *Identity in Formation: The Russian-Speaking Populations in the Near Abroad* (Ithaca: Cornell University Press, 1998).

concept of rational choice more, in a word, interesting—not to mention relevant to topics that political scientists have generally not addressed.

Japan is part of a system of states, in which ideas of development, progress, and modernity are largely taken for granted by policymakers around the world. Their institutionalization makes it extraordinarily difficult for leaders to take a radical step outside of these ideas—to look at the broad experience of the advanced industrial nations and to simply say no. Even as the basic interests driving leisure policy fall away, I suspect that these broader institutional factors will not. The importance of the Western experience in Japan is not that it is considered self-evidently good or morally right; it is instead accepted as "ahead," as a symbol of "progress." It would be *inconceivable* to leisure policymakers that Japan could have learned anything useful about leisure from nations in Latin America, Southeast Asia, or Africa, because leisure ostensibly develops along the same path as economies and political systems. My own sense is that this is not just about leisure, and not just in Japan.

Moreover, by opening up new issue areas such as leisure for analysis, political scientists grasp something more about the relationships between international relations and comparative politics, and between the public and the private. As Joel Migdal notes, the links between state and society are peculiar to each government, and the state is a cultural construct that cannot be understood solely with conventional political science tools. Instead, political scientists—especially American political scientists—must break down their own institutional walls: the ones that make us take for granted what is public and what is private.[11]

My hope, therefore, is that this approach can "de-institutionalize" some of the key assumptions in political science, about the reasons for the astonishingly limited range of options that most policymakers seem to face on a daily basis. In another world, one in which a political form other than the state had developed, or in which low-tech performance rituals dominated people's free time, the Electric Main Street Parade might be seen as a freakish aberration, one doomed right from the start. The rules of play might have been written differently. As they are now, people simply try to find the best way to follow them.

11. Joel S. Migdal, "Studying the State," in *Comparative Politics: Rationality, Culture, and Structure,* ed. Mark Irving Luchbach and Alan S. Zuckerman (Cambridge: Cambridge University Press, 1997), 208–35, especially 221–30.

INDEX

Note: Italic page numbers refer to illustrations.

Cornell Studies in Political Economy

A series edited by Peter J. Katzenstein